The Early Mod...

LONGMAN SECONDARY HISTORIES

R. J. Cootes and L. E. Snellgrove

1 The Ancient World
2 The Middle Ages
3 The Early Modern Age
4 Britain since 1700
5 The Modern World since 1870

The Early Modern Age

L. E. SNELLGROVE

LONGMAN

LONGMAN GROUP LIMITED
London

Associated companies, branches and representatives
throughout the world

First published 1972
Fifth impression 1976

ISBN 0 582 20511 5

Filmset by V. Siviter Smith & Co Ltd
and printed in Great Britain by
Hazell Watson & Viney Ltd, Aylesbury, Bucks

Contents

Preface

This book has been designed chiefly for pupils aged about thirteen or fourteen, that is, those in their third year at secondary school. Great care has been taken to keep the language clear and simple. As an aid to clarity, and in the hope of stimulating genuine interest and understanding, some topics are given a more generous allocation of space than is customary in a book of this kind. It is felt that most pupils derive little benefit from a brief and superficial coverage of history, however necessary an overall picture of the period may be.

As far as possible social and economic topics have been fitted into the chronological framework. In this way the flow of events— their causes and effects—may be better understood. At the same time some reference has been made to world and, in particular, European events in order to avoid a narrowly based 'British' view of the subject.

At best, general textbooks are a springboard for more thorough study. Consequently this book is offered not as a course in itself but as a focus for a course, giving shape and direction to pupils' studies. It is assumed that teachers will want to use all kinds of additional material with their classes, and to this end it is hoped that the 'More about . . .' sections following each chapter will prove helpful. In this connection it should be noted that most of the books recommended are for pupils; only in certain cases did the scarcity of such material force the author to suggest a more advanced work. Most of the suggestions for follow up work have been tried and tested by the author in the classroom but it is not claimed that they are either ideal or comprehensive in their coverage of the topic.

I would like to thank Roger Lockyer and Richard Cootes for their advice in the final preparation of this manuscript and Jean Snellgrove for help and hard work beyond the call of wifely duty.

L. E. SNELLGROVE 1972

Acknowledgements

The author and publisher are grateful to the following for permission to reproduce photographs:

Aerofilms, pages 49, 59 and 218–219; Ampliaciones y Reproducciones Mas, page 35; Ashmolean Museum, pages 67 (Heberden coin room), 165 below (dept. of Antiquities) and 167 (dept. of Western Art); Associated Press, page 125; The Trustees of the British Museum, pages 14–15, 63, 83, 86–87, 98, 104–105 and 210–211; Lord Clifford, Ugbrooke Park, page 200–201; The College of Arms, page 39; The Courtauld Institute of Art, page 62; The Department of the Environment, Crown ©, pages 164 and 204–205 (below); Fox Photos, page 212–213 (above); John R. Freeman, pages 144–145 and 148–149; Giraudon, pages 61 (above), 134–135, 220–221 and 226; Glasgow University Library, Hunterian Collection, page 102; Guildhall Library, page 106–107 and 108–109; The Dean and Chapter of Hereford Cathedral, page 11; John Hillelson Agency photo by Erich Lessing, page 194; A. F. Kersting, pages 36–37, 73, 130, 188, 189, 190 and 243; The London Museum, page 184 (below); The Mansell Collection, pages 16, 32–33, 46, 70–71, 100–101 (above), 100–101 (below), 102–103, 106, 118–119, 120–121, 146–147, 152–153, 162–163, 168, 184–185 (above), 186, 204–205 (above), 206, 215, 225 and 229; Mary Evans Picture Library, pages 92–93 and 100–101 (centre); Ministry of Public Building and Works, pages 38 (below), 57 and 161; National Galleries of Scotland, page 84; National Maritime Museum, pages 12, 80–81, 90, 174, 175 and 179; Nationalmuseum Stockholm, page 51; National Portrait Gallery, pages 24, 27, 42 (above), 44–45, 56, 58, 66, 68–69, 72, 78, 95, 98–99, 114–115, 142, 156, 180–181, 181, 195, 196–197, 201, 203, 207, 234–235 and 236; Sidney J. Newberry, page 25; Marquis of Northampton, page 143; Pepysian Library, page 42–43 (centre); Picturepoint, page 230; Public Record Office, Crown ©, pages 38 (above), 79 and 108–109; Radio Times Hulton Picture Library, pages 20–21, 22, 42–43 (below), 64–65, 91, 96, 110 (above), 112–113, 116–117, 118, 133, 138–139, 158–159, 176, 182, 183, 210, 212–13 (below) and 242; Rainbird Ltd. photo by Werkstatte Meyer, pages 222–223 and cover; Royal Windsor Library, page 60; Scala, pages 4–5, 6–7 and 8–9; Science Museum London, pages 13 and 16–17; Staatsbibliothek Berlin, pages 52–53 and 139; Edwin Smith, page 178; The Swedish Institute, pages 136 and 233; Collection Thyssen-Bornemisza, page 43; The Victoria and Albert Museum, page 128–129; Walker Art Gallery, Liverpool, page 40; The Wellcome Trustees, page 198. The photographs on pages 54–55, 61 (below), 154 and 232 are reproduced by gracious permission of Her Majesty the Queen.

1 Constantinople and Florence
The Renaissance

Early in 1453 a vast Turkish army gathered before Constantinople. For a thousand years the city had been the centre of a Christian empire known as Byzantium. Before that it was the eastern capital of the great Roman empire. By the fifteenth century much of its power and glory had gone. Muslim Turks ruled most of its old territories. Many Byzantine scholars and artists had left the city itself and gone to Europe. The population had been reduced by disease. Now a few thousand soldiers prepared to resist the young Sultan Mehmet's troops.

The siege of Constantinople

The Sultan did not expect an easy victory. Many armies had besieged Constantinople—few had captured it. Standing on a peninsula it was well placed for defence. To the north was a narrow strip of water called the Golden Horn. To the east and south lay the Sea of Marmora. Although the Turks had blocked the Golden Horn with a wooden barrier hung with chains, the sea was patrolled by warships sent from Genoa and Venice to fight for the Christian emperor. On its landward side Constantinople was encircled by three walls, the longest eight miles in circumference and strengthened at intervals by towers sixty feet high. Its soldiers were well equipped compared with the Turks and their commander, John Justiniani, was an experienced officer. Finally, there was always a chance that reinforcements would come from Europe.

When the first large-scale assault failed, Mehmet ordered his cannon to break down the defences. Some of these primitive weapons were surprisingly effective. One could throw a heavy ball nearly a mile. After weeks of continuous bombardment even Constantinople's great walls began to crumble. Meanwhile wonderful rewards were promised to the first Turk to set foot on them; dreadful punishments were given to those who showed fear. On the Christian side the Emperor Constantine could not believe that God would allow 'His own' city to fall. Monks prayed daily for help.

Each day hundreds of Turks were killed or wounded. The Christians, on the other hand, suffered few casualities because of their superior armour. For a month the desperate struggle continued. Time and again the defenders threw back those Turks who attempted to enter the city. Yet each attack left them more tired; each day that passed saw more gaps appear in their ranks. Once three supply warships from Italy broke through the Turkish fleet. The Sultan replied by having some of his own warships dragged overland and launched into the Golden Horn behind the city. Fixed on wheels, the ships rolled along with sails set as if at sea! Across the harbour

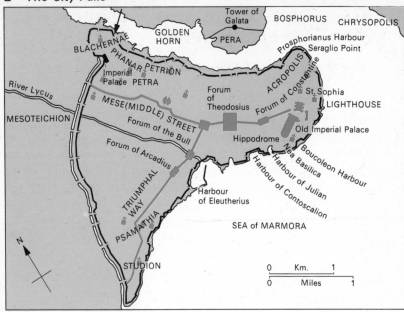

'Christian dam holding back the Muslim flood.' Constantinople in 1453

his engineers laid a bridge of barrels fixed in pairs. Reinforcements could now be brought from Pera (see map) and the defences alongside the Golden Horn threatened. The net was closing around the city.

On 28 May a procession of priests moved slowly through the streets of Constantinople, blessing damaged parts of the wall. That evening Constantine rode to the cathedral and prayed for divine assistance. About an hour after midnight the noise of drums, trumpets and war cries signalled a fresh assault. Soon church bells were clanging a warning. Men grabbed weapons and rushed to their posts, women ran to help with repairs and first aid, old people and children hurried to the churches for shelter. A first wave of lightly armed Turks was driven off after two hours. As they fell back, the Sultan's finest troops were seen to be advancing by the light of torches. They threw ladders against the walls or climbed upon each other's shoulders. The exhausted Christians slashed and hacked them down until dawn broke.

Suddenly a band of Turks noticed that a gate had been left open in the wall. They rushed through and climbed a stairway leading to the top of a tower. At this vital moment a cannon shot struck John Justiniani in the chest. The dying general was carried away just as the news began to spread that the enemy had broken in. The confusion caused by this news was noticed by the Sultan himself. 'The city is ours,' he shouted to the warriors who ran past him. A giant called Hasan was first on the walls. He was killed but thousands followed him. Giving up hope, Constantine tore off his imperial badges and threw himself into the fight. He was never seen again. By midday on Tuesday 29 May 1453 the streets were running with blood. Constantinople had fallen.

The Renaissance

The capture of Constantinople shocked the Christian world. To the mainly Greek population who lived there it meant the end of a civilisation. Tuesday, the day of the disaster, became an unlucky day for all Greeks. In fact, the city's fall did not open Europe to the Turks; their troops had reached as far as the river Danube long before 1453. What it did was to link securely their European and Asian possessions, giving them a valuable base for further conquests. By the time Mehmet died (1481) Turkish armies had overrun the Balkans (now Greece, Yugoslavia, Bulgaria and Albania) and were threatening southern Italy.

The empire which ended that Tuesday was more than a Christian dam holding back the Muslim flood. For a thousand years it had been a vast storehouse of art and literature. Inside its palaces and libraries were the sculptures, the mosaics and, above all, the books of the Ancient World. At first these were unknown or forgotten in western Europe. From crusading times onwards, however, trade links between east and west helped to increase western knowledge and interest in the arts of Greece and Rome. Venice, Genoa and the ports of Sicily, in particular, sent numbers of ships to Byzantium and many Byzantine scholars and artists travelled west. Europeans also learnt the arithmetic, geometry and astronomy of the Egyptians and Babylonians from the Arabs who now controlled much of the African parts of the old Roman Empire.

The re-awakening of interest in the achievements of the Ancient World which these contacts helped to produce in known as the Renaissance (rebirth). The word is misleading because it suggests something sudden, as if the curtains were drawn back to let in light after the 'darkness' of the medieval world. The Middle Ages was not a time of complete ignorance. Students studied law, Latin literature and the Scriptures. Monks produced beautiful and brightly coloured manuscripts. Artists painted lovely religious pictures. Craftsmen carved the wonderful designs and figures still admired in our churches and cathedrals. Neither was the literature of the Ancient World entirely unknown.

Even so, large areas of knowledge were neglected. Scholars of the Middle Ages knew little history or geography. Asia and Africa were mystery continents; physics, chemistry and medicine were treated as kinds of magic. Alchemists spent years trying to turn ordinary metal into gold. Doctors cast spells over their patients. Sorcerers believed they could find elixirs (mixtures) which would make them live forever. Nobody studied animals or birds properly and the superstitious thought witches, ghosts and dragons existed.

Medieval people took too much for granted. Renaissance scholars and artists, on the other hand, started to look more closely at man and nature. They asked questions and refused to believe everything they had been told. A cold, critical wind began to blow on old ways of life and thought, on Church, manor, guild and monastery, and even on the World and Universe. As a result nothing was quite the same again.

The Medici

The reawakening first affected Italy. There were several good reasons for this. For many years great cities such as Genoa and Venice had traded with Constantinople. Hence it was natural that their sailors and merchants should know Byzantine scholars and artists. Long before Renaissance times Byzantine painters had decorated the cathedral of St Mark's in Venice with Roman and Greek-style mosaic pictures. In addition, many Italians lived near impressive Roman ruins; it was, after all, 'their past' which was rediscovered. Most important, there had grown up in Italy during the Middle Ages a few wealthy independent cities, dominated by rich families who had time to study and collect books and art treasures.

This Renaissance began in a small way, just as an avalanche can be started by a few rocks. An Italian poet, Petrarch (1304–74) and his friend Boccaccio (1313–75) searched for Greek, Latin and Hebrew manuscripts lost since the fall of the Roman Empire. Because they were looking for the 'human' literature of the Greeks and Romans instead of the 'divine' works of the Church these men and their followers were called Humanists. Petrarch's investigations took him to many places, outside Italy, including Germany and Flanders. The work of both writers encouraged rich, educated men to form libraries of such books; Nicholas V (Pope 1447–55), for instance, collected over 5,000 manuscripts to found the Vatican Library at Rome. Interest revived in the Greek language and many Greek books were translated or copied. Boccaccio himself made the first translation into Latin of Homer's *Iliad* and *Odyssey.*

Kings and nobles eagerly followed this new fashion. In earlier times a prince's fame had depended mainly on how successful he was in war. Now he was expected to have artists and scholars at his court. It was the beauty of his palaces, as well as the strength of his castles, which was admired. It Italy the greatest of these Renaissance princes were members of the Medici family who ruled Florence during the fifteenth century. Although cruel and unpopular, they spent vast sums of money encouraging art and science.

The seeds fell on fertile ground. Florence was already famous for its artists and writers; Petrarch, Boccaccio and another famous poet, Dante, had lived there. With Medici help, the city now gave more beautiful painting, sculpture and architecture to the world than any since ancient Athens. The first Medici ruler, Cosimo, built a Renaissance style palace in the mid-fifteenth century. In it he entertained some of the greatest princes of his day, including the Holy Roman Emperor (ruler of Germany) and the Pope. His son, Lorenzo, employed many clever artists and showed such good taste that he was called 'Il Magnifico' (the Magnificent).

Few cities have ever contained so many talented men at one time. A typical example was the remarkable Leonardo da Vinci (1452–1519). There was little he could not do. He produced plans of all sorts of machinery, including a helicopter, a clockwork car and a submarine. Yet he also painted the 'Last Supper' in such as way that one seems to be looking not at a wall painting but into another

Leonardo da Vinci's wall painting 'The Last Supper'. Leonardo used a new technique for applying oil painting to walls but it was not successful and so it is in bad condition

room. His portrait of a woman, the 'Mona Lisa' is so lifelike that her skin seems living flesh, and her curious smile has fascinated admirers ever since.

Two other great artists, Botticelli (1444–1510) and Michelangelo (1475–1564) also came to Florence to work for the Medicis. Botticelli's 'Birth of Venus' and Michelangelo's paintings on the ceiling of the Sistine Chapel in Rome are far different from the flat and unreal figures seen in medieval paintings. Both these artists were able to show every detail of muscle and hair, every fold of dress or play of light and shadow. Michelangelo combined painting with sculpture, and his statues show a knowledge and appreciation of the human body not seen since the days of the Greeks. His carvings included the magnificent Medici tomb in Florence.

Printing

The spread of the 'new' knowledge was helped by the invention of printing. Hand-written books, though often beautiful, took a long time to produce. When Cosimo de Medici wanted to found a library it took 45 scribes nearly two years to copy 200 books. And because books were scarce only a few really rich men could afford them. Thus the spread of knowledge was limited in ancient and medieval times.

Block printing — the carving of a single page on a wooden block — had been known in Europe for some time. Unfortunately these blocks took a long time to make and were no use afterwards. The real breakthrough came when Johan Gutenberg (1397–1468), a German from Mainz, found a way of making movable metal type. The exact date of this discovery is uncertain. Gutenberg was said to have been

working on a 'secret process' in 1439. His style of printing was certainly known by 1460. Earlier, Laurens Janszoon, a Dutchman, had made separate wooden letters but these were never exactly alike, however skilled the carver. Metal type, on the other hand, was made by pouring molten metal into a matrix (mould), which never varied.

Printing helped to satisfy the growing demand for books from well-to-do people. It also encouraged the production of cheaper paper. Vellum and parchment were too expensive to be used in large quantities. The Chinese method of paper-making had been known in Europe since the twelfth century. Now it was adapted to feed the busy printing presses. Linen or rags were first boiled into a pulp. Then a square sieve was dipped in the mixture and shaken until the wet fibres stuck together. When dry, these sheets were the size and shape of the tray. Later they were squeezed in a press and brushed with chemicals to make them less absorbent.

Michaelangelo's paintings on the roof of the Sistine Chapel in Rome. They took him four years to complete

Page printed by William Caxton at the 'Sign of the Red Pale', Westminster, 1490

Printing helped to standardise spoken language too. William
Caxton, who introduced printing into England, learned that a man
who asked for 'eggies' in a Kent public house puzzled the landlady
because local people called them 'eyren'. Caxton decided to use
dialect spoken in London and the Court for his books and so helped
it to become standard English. His wooden press at the 'Sign of the
Red Pale' in Westminster printed the first book in England, the
Sayings of Philosophers (1477). During his career he published
nearly a hundred books, including Chaucer's *Canterbury Tales*.

Savonarola

There was an unhappy side to the Renaissance. Questioning long
established customs and ways of thought could lead to disobedience,
violence and disorder. Greater freedom could mean the freedom to
harm others. Even love of beauty might become an excuse for a

greedy man to steal art treasures. The Medici, after all, were brutal and pleasure-loving as well as clever and sensitive.

In an essay called *The Prince*, Niccolo Machiavelli (1469–1527) described the rulers of his time. He analysed their cruelty and treachery; he explained how right and wrong no longer mattered to them. If an action was successful it was good; if unsuccessful it was bad! Machiavelli did not approve of such behaviour but he decided it was impossible to rule successfully without it. The invading French and German armies he had seen devastate his homeland, convinced him that only tyrants like the Medici could save Italy from foreign domination. Princes, he claimed, must show no mercy. A victorious rebel for example, should kill his opponents even if they had surrendered! Probably because the essay was written as a letter to a Medici, Machiavelli wisely kept it secret until his death. Unfortunately, readers of the book have usually condemned Machiavelli, not the princes he wrote about. To this day the devil is sometimes called 'Old Nick' because of Niccolo Machiavelli, and cunning, ruthless politicians are described as Machiavellian.

It was not surprising that such wickedness and luxury should turn some against the Renaissance. In Florence the prior of the monastery of St Mark's, Girolamo Savonarola (1452–98), began to preach sermons condemning the new ways. He prophesied that a terrible disaster would fall on Italy unless men became less worldly and more religious. Savonarola's ugly face, his hooked nose and flashing eyes, had an almost hypnotic effect on those who heard him preach. Furthermore, his warnings came just as the King of France, Charles VIII, had invaded Italy. French troops were already marching towards Florence, when, in September 1494, Savonarola preached on the text from the Bible, 'And, behold I, even I, do bring a flood of waters upon the earth'. To his congregation it seemed he had foreseen the 'flood' of enemy soldiers, burning and killing. They decided he was a prophet of God.

For the next three years Savonarola was the most powerful figure in Florence. Piero de Medici, Lorenzo's successor, was overthrown and the prior went in person to see the French King. He told Charles his invasion was meant to punish the people for their wickedness. At the same time, he warned him, to leave Florence in peace or he would no longer gain victories. The King was impressed. He stopped his soldiers damaging the city and contented himself with carrying off some art treasures.

Savonarola helped to set up a fairer government in Florence. He also tried hard to make the citizens live better lives. Gambling houses were closed and children encouraged to spy on grown-ups and report immoral behaviour. People were ordered not to wear ornaments and to 'cleanse' their homes of luxuries. At a huge bonfire in the Square an enthusiastic crowd burned perfumes, mirrors, false hair, musical instruments, carnival masks, paintings and books, including ones by Petrarch.

It seemed as though Florence had turned its back upon the beauty as well as the wickedness of the Renaissance. But in Rome the Pope,

Alexander VI, was displeased. He ordered Savonarola to come to Rome for questioning. When Savonarola said he was too busy Alexander excommunicated (expelled from the Church) him for disobedience. It was believed at the time that this terrible sentence meant he would go to hell when he died. Soon afterwards a Franciscan friar challenged Savonarola to walk through flames to prove his special powers. The prior refused, and when another man took his place the episode ended in a downpour of rain. Those who had once hailed Savonarola as a prophet quickly turned against him. He was tortured, hanged and burnt while still alive on 23 May 1498. The Church seemed as powerful as ever. Yet only nineteen years later another monk was to defy it and not burn.

More about the Renaissance
Books
G. Bull, *The Renaissance* (Hart-Davis), available with four tapes.
Caxton and the Early Printers (Cape: Jackdaw)
E. R. Chamberlin, *Everyday Life in Renaissance Times* (Batsford)
E. R. Chamberlin, *Florence in the Time of the Medicis* (Longman)
J. Gage, *Life in Italy at the Time of the Medici* (Batsford)
E. Harmey and J. Hampden, *Books: from Papyrus to Paperback* (Methuen)

Visual aids
The Italian Renaissance (Educational Audio Visual Ltd)
The Renaissance (Hulton Educational)
Lorenzo de Medici (Common Ground)
Leonardo da Vinci *(film)* (Rank)
Michelangelo (Common Ground)
William Caxton (Visual Information Services)
Story of Printing *(film)* (EFVA)
Story of Paper Making *(film)* (EFVA)

Visit
Many Art Galleries contain examples of Renaissance painters' work and most sell small postcard reproductions which are useful for any individual or group projects.

To write and find out
1 Imagine the modern world without printing. Make a list of activities which would be impossible or drastically reduced.
2 Compile short biographies of the painters and sculptors mentioned in this chapter.
3 The siege of Constantinople was one of the first battles to be seriously affected by the use of artillery. Find out more about the history of early guns.
4 When did Turkey cease to be ruled by a Sultan? Find out more about the history of the Turks in Europe. What modern European countries had part or all of their territory occupied by the Turks in the past?

End of a reformer. Savonarola is burnt in the square at Florence 1498

2 Christians and Spices
World Discoveries   1415-1492

Preserved in Hereford Cathedral in England is a *Mappa Mundi* (World Map) made in about 1300. It shows the earth as a disc with Jerusalem at its centre. Round the Holy City are the three corners of the world imagined by men of the time—Europe, the region of light, Asia, the region of mystery and Africa the region of darkness. These continents are surrounded, in turn, by an ocean as vast and limitless as outer space.

The Hereford document was copied from a Roman map. with one important difference. The original map showed two circles, one for each hemisphere. *Mappa Mundi* has only the northern circle, possibly because the southern one was blank, or maybe because the monks who drew it wished to ignore a part of the globe where men knew nothing of Christ! Consequently, *Mappa Mundi* gives the impression that its makers believed the world was flat.

Whatever ordinary folk thought, no educated man in the Middle Ages ever doubted that the earth was a sphere. Some described it as a ball, or compared it with the yolk of an egg. One thirteenth century writer even suggested a journey round it. 'If there were no obstacles' he wrote,' a man could go round the earth as a fly crawls round an apple'. Another worked out that a man covering twenty miles a day could walk round in four years, sixteen weeks and two days.

Some parts of the globe seemed more attractive than others. Few Europeans were interested in Africa with its deserts, scorching sun, wild beasts and even wilder men. Asia seemed to them far more fascinating. The riches of China and India, in particular, had been brought to the West since the Crusades (1099 onwards), and Marco Polo's journeys (1275—95). The rare luxuries of the East excited the minds of merchants and travellers, as well as filling their pockets.

India was a paradise, it seemed, with sweet-scented bushes, strange coloured birds and tall forests which touched the sky. Precious stones, spices, and a mountain of solid gold were to be found there. Its inhabitants were thought of as queer pagans, some cannibals, some with the heads of dogs. They would need to be taught about Christ. China was more wonderful still. It had a gigantic harbour, Zaitun, and its capital, Quinsay, was enclosed by 100 miles of walls. A wise Khan ruled over it, descendant of the prince who had welcomed Marco Polo.

'Mountains of gold' would be difficult to bring to Europe but gems, spices and carpets took up little space. 'Spices' could mean nearly a hundred different commodities, from pepper, sugar and dyes to perfume and glue. They were in great demand in the West where they could be sold at high prices. Since Crusading times the spice trade had operated by sea from China and India, up the Red Sea and over-

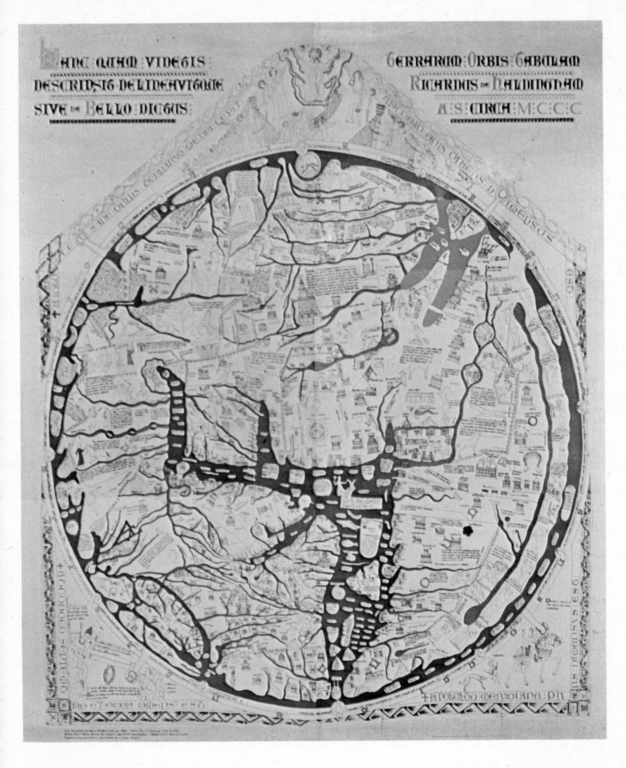

land to the Mediterranean. From there, the merchants journeyed in Venetian or Genoan ships to Europe. The Turkish capture of Constantinople had hindered, not stopped, such trade. But the Italian

An early view of the world. The *Mappa Mundi* in Hereford Cathedral

monopoly made goods from the East very expensive in Spain, Portugal and the other countries of western Europe. Neither Spain nor Portugal wanted a sea war with mighty Venice. Both faced the Atlantic, over whose desert of water the sun set every evening. Here possibly was an alternative route to the East.

As man's geographical knowledge increased, merchants, seamen and geographers began to talk of reaching India, either by going round Africa or right round the world. 'If there were no obstacles' the medieval scholar had wondered. How many obstacles *were* out in that grey mist of waters?

Tools for the job

Among the piles of manuscripts brought from Constantinople was one by the fourth century Greek astronomer' Ptolemy. Called *Geography,* it contained information about the shipping routes used by Greek and Roman sailors, from the Canary Islands in the west to Ceylon and China in the east. The book was not always correct. Although ancient seamen used latitude and longitude, Ptolemy's estimate of a degree of latitude was too short. Consequently, 'his' world was much smaller than the real one! Furthermore, his information mixed fanciful travellers' tales with accurate reports. In spite of these errors, Ptolemy's work was a great help to fifteenth-century ocean voyagers.

Until that time it was rare for a ship to be out of sight of land for long. A captain carried only a compass, a lead-line and perhaps a coastal chart called a portolan. Compasses had started as magnetised iron needles stuck in floating chips of wood. In the fifteenth century they usually consisted of a needle balanced on a card marked with the points of the compass. A 'lead' was a piece of metal, hollow at one end, which was thrown overboard fixed to a line. Regular knots in the line marked off the depths in fathoms, and tallow in the open end collected sand or stones from the bottom. With such an instrument it was possible for sailors to know not only the depth of water but also the nature of the sea-bed.

Sixteenth-century compass

For long ocean voyages a ship's master needed far more. First he had to 'fix' his position on a map. To find latitude he measured the height of the Sun or Pole Star above the horizon with a quadrant or cross staff. The difference in angle since the last reckoning could be measured in degrees of latitude. Longitude was more difficult. A navigator used 'dead reckoning', that is, he worked out how far and in what direction he had travelled each day. Before chronometers (very accurate clocks) were perfected in the eighteenth century this could never be done with certainty.

One simple way of estimating speed was to throw a piece of wood overboard at the bow and time it as it passed the known length of the ship. Another involved fitting a knotted line to the wood so that the knots could be counted as they ran out. This is why a ship's speed is still reckoned in knots. If the helmsman changed course he marked it on a pegged board. At best such calculations were rough and ready. Changes in speed, side drift and compass errors might put a vessel miles off target. And no ship's master could ever be sure of following the same route twice. The Solomon Islands, for example, were discovered in the sixteenth century but 'lost' for the next two hundred years.

Although technical aids of this sort were essential blueprints for a successful voyage, they would have been little use without a suitable ship. Early square-sailed vessels, which could only run with the wind, generally carried rowers for moving against it. But an oared galley was no use for long journeys because its crew took up valuable cargo space, besides needing much food and drink. As early as the twelfth century Arab sailors had fixed a triangular sail along the deck (a lateen) so that the vessel could tack (zig-zag) against the wind. In the fifteenth century three-masted ships were developed and this meant that ships could carry both square and lateen sails. Some explorers, particularly the Portuguese, voyaged in ships called caravels which at first carried only lateens. Later models carried a mixture of the two. Whichever was used, such vessels could generally move in any direction regardless of the wind.

Fifteenth-century astrolabe

New routes for old

The Portuguese started to explore the African coast in 1415. Most of their expeditions were organised by Prince Henry, the king's son, who was so interested in exploration that he became known as 'the Navigator'. Henry consulted experts, collected information from Arab traders, and is said to have established an observatory and college for seamen at Sagres in Portugal. At first the objective was not India but the gold of the Guinea Coast. Gradually, as slave trading and fishing made the trips profitable, the dream of reaching India took hold of men's minds. For eighty-four years hardly a season passed without caravels leaving Lisbon, the Portuguese capital. Braving high waves, treacherous currents and the harmattan wind which carries dense clouds of sand off the African coast, the Portuguese slowly colonised a coastline half the length of the globe.

In 1415 the Canary Islands were discovered. Five years later Madeira was colonised and its first vineyards planted. The dangerous Cape Bojador—probably the modern Cape Juby—was rounded after twelve years' effort. By 1448 Prince Henry had sent fifty caravels southwards, but when he died in November 1460 there was still no sign of the turning point to India. Nevertheless his death did not stop the exploration. In 1475 a Portuguese captain named de Sintra came to a coast where the thunder of the surf reminded him of the roaring of lions. He called its tall peaks 'Sierra Leone'—the mountains of the lioness. Seven years after de Sintra's voyage another Portuguese captain entered a river whose fresh water extended twenty miles out to sea. He had found the river Congo.

It was 1487 before Bartholomew Diaz rounded the southern tip of Africa. Thankfully he landed and erected a large cross on the headland. Back home he told King John II of the 'Cape of Storms' which had nearly sunk his ships. The king was more optimistic. He knew that the way to India lay open and renamed the tip of Africa 'Cape of

Good Hope'. At last, three ships, *St Gabriel*, *St Raphael* and *Berrio*, were prepared at Lisbon for the voyage to India (1497). When all was ready, the sailors went with their commander, Vasco da Gama, to a solemn service in the cathedral. Then they walked to the beach, followed by chanting priests carrying candles and watched by silent sometimes weeping crowds. From this 'beach of tears' they sailed on 8 July.

For 3,800 miles the caravels ploughed through the Atlantic, creating a record by being ninety-six days out of sight of land. They rounded the Cape after three unsuccessful attempts and on Christmas morning da Gama named the land they were passing 'Natal' (birth), in honour of Christ's birthday. It remains the name of a South African province to this day.

What the Portuguese needed now was a guide to take them across the Indian Ocean. The sailors offered caps, bells and red trousers to the natives, without success. Finally, after many landings on the East African coast, they contacted Ahmed Ibn Majid, the most famous Arab pilot of his day, who agreed to take them. After twenty-five days at sea lookouts sighted tall mountains. On 20 May 1498 the three ships dropped anchor in Calicut harbour, India. Da Gama sent a sailor ashore. He is supposed to have been greeted with the remark 'May the devil take you. What brought you hither?' Da Gama always maintained he had come for 'Christians and spices'. The European conquest of the East had begun.

Vasco da Gama, from a painting on the wall of his palace at Goa, India

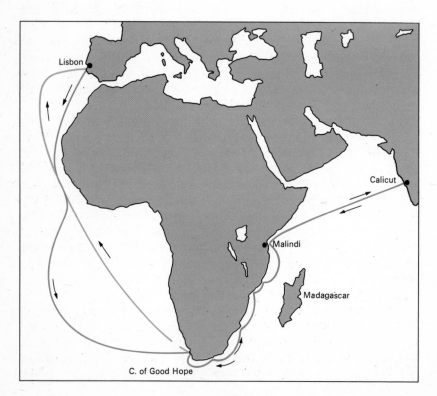

Vasco da Gama's sea route to India 1497–98

Lost Atlantis

The Portuguese had found one way to the East. To men of the time there seemed another—west across the Atlantic. It was an old dream, inspired by countless tales and legends. Far out in those stormy waters, it was said, lay a floating island called Antilla or Atlantis. Years before, several bishops and their congregations were believed to have fled to this spot to escape barbarian attacks. Their descendants now lived in happiness and peace. If found, Atlantis might be used as a stepping stone to Cathay (China) and Cipangu (Japan). It was an exciting idea which attracted both priests and merchants. Certainly there seemed no reason why Asia should not be reached across the Atlantic.

One man interested in such a route was Christopher Colomb (usually known by his Latin name Christopher Columbus), the son of a weaver in Genoa, Italy. As a young man he had travelled a great deal, although he was never a full-time sailor. In 1478 he married the daughter of one of Prince Henry's captains. From her he probably heard tales of the eastern sea route to India. In later life he claimed that from the age of twenty-eight he longed to conquer 'the Indies'. It is possible also that he sailed with one or two Portuguese masters on the 'Africa' runs.

In 1484 Columbus suggested a western voyage to King John of Portugal, only to find that he was more interested in the African route. When John said no, Columbus went to Spain. After many delays he persuaded the councillors of the deeply religious Queen Isabella to let him look for the 'lost' Christians. In April 1492 the Queen ordered Columbus to take three ships and 'discover and acquire islands and mainland in the ocean sea'. The great search was on.

The voyage to the 'Indies'

Three ships, the *Santa Maria, Nina* and *Pinta,* and ninety men sailed from Palos with Columbus on 2 August 1492. Throughout the voyage the weather was almost too good; its very calmness made some men wonder how they would find a wind to blow them home. Nobody knows exactly what happened on the voyage but the long hours were probably spent in various ways, such as painting and tarring the ship's hull, mending spare sails, roasting salt meat over a wooden firebox and washing down dried peas with water or wine. As it got warmer they slept on deck. When becalmed they probably went for a swim.

Each long day was divided by chants from a boy who stood near the helmsman and turned the sand glass every half hour. At dawn he sang,
Blessed be the light of day,
And the holy cross we say.
At dusk, the sailors heard,
God give us a good night and good sailing,
May our ship make a good passage
Sir, Captain and Master and Good Company.

Columbus sets sail. A drawing made during his lifetime

Puzzling sights often met their eyes. Sometimes great trailing bands of brown and yellow seaweed floated by. Flocks of birds passed overhead on their autumn migration from North America. Day after day the lookouts scanned the horizon, often mistaking cloudbanks for land. Some men grumbled at the length of the voyage, saying that as they had not found Atlantis they should turn back.

After thirty days' sailing, a cliff appeared in the moonlight. The captain of the *Pinta* lowered his sails and fired a gun as a signal to the *Santa Maria*, rolling and pitching behind. By noon on 12 October 1492 they were at anchor in a large bay, watched by naked men on the beach. Carrying the royal flag of Castile (a Spanish province) the

An 1892 full-size model of Columbus's *Santa Maria*. No drawings were ever made of the ship so it is probable that this replica is inaccurate

Captain-General, as he was styled, was rowed ashore, wearing a green velvet suit, purple stockings and a red cloak. Kneeling down, he thanked God and named the island San Salvador (Holy Saviour). It is now called Watling Island. He then visited Cuba and Haiti, but lost the *Santa Maria* which was run aground by a drunken helmsman.

Columbus returned home with six Indians, a parrot, some fish and a small amount of gold, probably obtained in Cuba. On other voyages he found a number of West Indian islands, including Haiti, Guadaloupe and Antigua. In 1495 he landed in South America near the mouth of the river Orinoco. Yet when he died in 1506 he was a disappointed man. He had not seen Cathay, the land of the Great Khan described so well by Marco Polo. He had not, like da Gama, found a sea route to India.

Future ages did not look on him as a failure. As early as 1494 some scholars suspected the truth about the 'islands and mainlands in the ocean sea' discovered by Columbus. One wrote: 'When treating of this country one must speak of a new world.' It was true. Christopher Columbus had stumbled on an unknown continent.

More about the great discoveries
Books
H. Brinton and P. Moore, *Navigation* (Methuen: Outlines)
C. A. Burland, *Leif Ericsson and the North Atlantic* (Hulton)
Columbus and the Discovery of America (Cape: Jackdaw)
H. E. L. Mellersh, *The Story of the Great Seafarers* (Pergamon)
P. Richardson, *The Expansion of Europe 1400-1600* (Longman)

Visual aids
Columbus (Visual Publications)
The Navigators *(film)* (Paul Hoefler Productions)
Columbus (Common Ground)
Seaway to India (Visual Publications)
Age of Exploration *(four films)* (Rank)
Christopher Columbus *(film)* (Gateway)
Discovery of America (EAV)

Visits
Science Museum, London
Maritime Museum, Greenwich

To write and find out
1 Consult your science teacher to see if it is possible to make some of the navigational instruments described in this chapter.
2 From authentic drawings or models make your own model of a sixteenth century ship.
3 Find out why sailing ships took such a roundabout route across the Atlantic. Compare life on one of Columbus's ships with travel on a modern liner.
4 What areas of Africa are still ruled by the Portuguese? Find out what is happening in them at the moment.

3 The New World
Discovery and Colonisation   1492-1530

Columbus was not the first European to reach the New World. Viking sailors visited North America about five hundred years before him, after setting up colonies in Greenland and Iceland. About A.D. 1000 one of their chiefs, Lief Ericsson, left Greenland and made the first known crossing of the North Atlantic, which Vikings called 'The Whale's Bath'. The coastline on which he landed, probably Newfoundland or Labrador, was named 'Vineland'. Nobody, of course, realised that his discoveries were part of a continent extending the length of the globe.

In 1497 two Venetians living in Bristol persuaded the English king, Henry VII, to allow exploration of this North Atlantic route. John Cabot and his son Sebastian took fifty-four days to cross the Atlantic in the tiny fifty-ton *Mathew*. They landed in Nova Scotia, possibly near Cape Breton. Like Columbus, the Cabots thought this land was Japan, China or some nearby islands. But they saw no signs of eastern gold or spices, noting only dense shoals of fish off their 'Newfoundland'.

The English king gave the explorers £10 and a pension of £20 a year. John Cabot did not live to enjoy this reward for he disappeared on a voyage next year. On a later expedition Sebastian explored the North American coast as far south as the modern state of New England (USA); he may even have entered Hudson Bay. Two Portuguese brothers also reached Greenland, Labrador and Newfoundland, but their king showed little interest, preferring to develop the African trade route instead.

Meanwhile a merchant from Florence in Italy, Amerigo Vespucci, went on several voyages to the South American coast where he visited Brazil. Amerigo Vespucci was a keen geographer and wrote interesting accounts of his travels. His books became very popular, so America was named after him. This was rather unfair, although he was one of the first to realise that America formed an almost continuous land barrier between Europe and Asia.

Magellan's voyage

Columbus thought Japan was 3,000 miles from Europe. It is really three times further away. As explorations continued, men realised that an even greater ocean than the Atlantic barred their way to the East. In 1513 a Spaniard, Vasco de Balboa, crossed the Isthmus of Panama and became the first European to sight the Pacific. He strode into the water until it reached his waist, held his sword high above his head and claimed the ocean for Spain.

Quarrels over ownership of the new lands had already flared up between Spain and Portugal. In 1493 Pope Alexander had divided

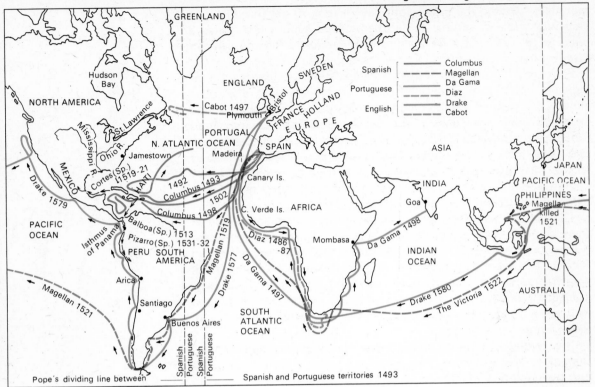

World voyages 1487–1522

the unknown world between the two. Later, Pope Leo X was so pleased by the gift of an elephant from the Portuguese that he declared they could have any land reached by sailing east. Naturally such statements were too vague to satisfy either country. Each began to send expeditions to seize the richest lands before the other got there.

This was the reason for the voyage of Ferdinand Magellan, a Portuguese seaman in the service of Spain, who sailed from Seville in September 1519 with five ships and 265 men. His orders were to reach the Molucca Islands which were thought to be near South America. Magellan himself believed that it was possible to sail round South America into the Pacific.

From the Cape Verde Islands the ship crossed the Atlantic at its narrowest part and then followed the South American coast as far as the river Plate. Here in Patagonia they encountered huge cannibals with painted faces, who performed acrobatics and pushed arrows down their throats. During the winter troubled flared up between the Portuguese commander and his touchy Spanish sailors. Magellan acted firmly, hanging some ringleaders of a mutiny. Sixty years later his gallows was found by the English seaman, Sir Francis Drake.

In the spring of 1520 the fleet set off through the hundreds of reefs and mountainous islands at the southern tip of South America. This 'Magellan Strait' as it is called today, is a grim spot, with dangerous swirling currents and freezing gales roaring through gaps in the mountains. During the thirty-eight days it took to get through, one ship was lost and another turned back. After such a trip it was a relief to sail into the wide Pacific. Only gradually did the seamen discover that this ocean had its own particular kind of terror.

For nearly four months Magellan's ships steered towards a seemingly endless horizon. They sailed over shark infested seas, and knife-edged coral reefs, through typhoons which uprooted trees and fired coconuts like cannon balls on the empty islands they passed. Good food was short. Men ate biscuits full of insects, sawdust, leather and rats. They drank yellow, stinking water. Scurvy, a disease caused by lack of fresh fruit and vegetables, made their gums swell until they could not eat. At least nineteen men died of starvation or sickness before the Southern Mariana Islands were sighted.

The first known crossing of the Pacific by Europeans ended at Sebu in the Philippines in March 1521. It was followed by a tragedy. A local chief who gave the starving sailors food and supplies asked for help in a tribal war. During a skirmish the Spaniards wore thick breastplates so the natives fired poisoned arrows at their legs. Magellan was struck several times and finally killed by a spear thrust in the face. Sadly, the expedition's navigator, Sebastian del Cano, took charge.

The two remaining ships, *Trinidad* and *Victoria,* sailed round Borneo to the Moluccas. The *Trinidad's* captain then decided to turn back. He was later captured by the Portuguese. Cano, however, brought the *Victoria* safely across the Indian Ocean and round Africa and home. Only fifteen out of those who set out completed this first voyage round the world on 6 September 1522. Their achievement was a mighty one. They had *proved* the world was round.

Aztec and Inca

Close on the heels of the explorers came the 'conquistadors'—the conquerors. Most large West Indian islands and the Gulf of Darien area had been settled by the Spanish within twenty years of Columbus's first landing. Some of them imported African slaves, horses and cattle, and settled down to farm. Others went to the American mainland to seek wealth and adventure. Here they found a land far stranger than any lost Atlantis. Stone Age civilisations like those of the Aztecs of Mexico and the Incas of Peru lay deep inland.

The Aztecs were a warlike tribe who had only just conquered their neighbours. Basically, they were simple farmers whose main crop was maize. They used only picture writing, had no iron tools, no wheels and no animals for carrying or pulling. Aztec settlements resembled ancient Mesopotamiam cities—large temples and pyramids were surrounded by baked earth houses.

The Aztec world was a mixture of beauty and savagery. Its capital, Tenochtitlan, rose almost magically from the waters of a lake. Standing on sunken wooden piles, many 'streets' were canals, as in modern Venice. Aztec gods had beautiful names—Plumed Serpent (Quetzalcoatl) and Humming Bird (Huitzilopochtli). But their priests taught that such gods demanded constant human

Valley of Mexico

LAKE TEXCOCO

Tenochtitlan

Causeways

Dyke

0   10
Miles

POPOCATEPETL
(SMOKING MTN)

sacrifices. Girls were flayed alive, young men cut open. Only a large supply of blood, it was believed, would please Huitzilopochtli in particular.

The Incas were also conquerors. Successful wars had given them control of a large empire, stretching from what is now northern Ecuador to central Chile. Although they were skilful workers in gold, silver and copper and could weave cotton and wool, their language, Quechua, had no writing. In a primitive way they were fine engineers. A network of roads and cable bridges criss-crossed their territories. The Inca capital, Tiahuanaco, was possibly more impressive than Tenochtitlan. Thirteen thousand feet above sea level, its great stone pyramids and gateways were set beside a lake from which rose snow-capped mountains. Incas worshipped a Sun God, whose earthly representative, the emperor, lived in a palace faced with solid gold! The peasants grew root crops, particularly potatoes, and wherever possible used the llama (an animal of the camel family) for carrying things. Both they and the Aztecs had never seen a horse until the Spaniards landed.

Excited by tales about the Aztecs' gold and silver, a conquistador, Hernan Cortes, left Cuba with a small force in 1519. Once ashore he destroyed his ships so that there could be no turning back. Then he led his men out of the steamy, hot jungles of the coastal plain, up to the frost and cold of the high Mexican plateau. Four hundred Spaniards with fifteen horses and ten cannon were about to destroy a civilisation.

The conquests

The odds against success seemed high, but the clever Cortes had cause to feel confident. He knew, for example, that the Aztecs had many enemies who could be used as allies. One tribe, the powerful Tlaxcalans, were hostile at first. But once their painted warriors had been mowed down by Spanish gunfire, they joined the invaders. Again, Cortes knew the Aztecs were expecting Quetzalcoatl to return to earth at about that time. Thus it was possible for the Spanish to pose as gods.

Montezuma, the Aztec emperor, had no doubt that the white-faced strangers were from heaven. Instead of fighting he sent messengers with gifts, begging the intruders to go away. It was no use; the greedy soldiers were not likely to turn back after seeing such riches! Soon they were in the Aztec capital, living in the royal palace with the feathered 'god-king' as their prisoner.

After a short stay, Cortes left the city to defeat an expedition sent from Cuba to arrest him. He returned to a dangerous situation. Some of his men had behaved badly, demanding extra food, melting down gold idols and murdering Aztecs during a solemn religious feast. Before long, certain Aztec nobles began to plot the Spaniard's downfall. When Montezuma tried to calm a mob outside his palace a stone flew from the crowd and killed him. The emperor's death was the signal for thousands of warriors to hurl themselves on Cortes and his men.

Montezuma II, Aztec king of Mexico

Tlazcalans fighting alongside their Spanish allies against Aztec warriors

Night had just fallen when the fighting started. The Aztecs, decorated with animal skins and feather head-dresses, charged to the screech of war pipes and beating of drums. Showers of arrows and stones filled the air. Screaming, dancing savages could be seen in the light of fiery sparks thrown from the nearby volcano, Popocatopetl. Cortes's men, heavily outnumbered, relied on their skilled swordsmanship to save them. Step by step, they cut their way through the Aztec mob, out of the city and along a broken wooden causeway. A temporary bridge was thrown across the gap but it collapsed, drowning many men. Eventually the main force crossed on sunken guns and waggons, except one huge Spaniard who leapt to the shore, using his lance as a vaulting pole!

Quite a number were not so lucky. Some were stabbed or clubbed to death. Others were taken prisoner, stripped naked, led up the terraces of Huitzilopochtli's temple and cut to pieces before the eyes of their comrades. By morning about half the conquistadors were safe. The rest were floating dead in the lake, or waiting to be slaughtered by the temple priests.

A grim Cortes swore to be revenged on the Aztecs. Next year he returned with more Indian allies and specially built boats to cross the lake. He broke all the causeways, cut off supplies of food and water and fought his way in. The Aztecs held out for eighty days, suffering about 250,000 casualties. When Tenochtitlan finally fell it was completely destroyed; even the rubble from its buildings was thrown into the lake.

Pizarro of Peru

Ten years after the conquest of Mexico the Incas were overthrown by an even more ruthless conquistador, Francisco de Pizarro. Atahualpa, the Inca emperor, was seized treacherously by Spaniards who had pretended to be his friend. When he pleaded for his life he was told to fill his prison cell with gold as a ransom. Seventy cubic yards of gold had been stacked in the chamber before Pizarro killed him and allowed his soldiers to loot. The Spaniards seized millions of pounds of valuables; Pizarro even shod his horse with silver.

In Spain, the conquistadors were not highly regarded, possibly because of their cruelty. Cortes, in particular, felt bitter about his treatment when he returned home. Once he claimed the honour of standing on the steps of the Spanish king's coach. Disdainfully, Charles V asked who he was. 'I am the man who has given you more provinces than your father had towns,' Cortes replied angrily, for he, Pizarro and others had given Spain one of the largest empires in history.

More about the conquest of the New World

Books
C. A. Burland, *Inca Peru* (Hulton)
C. A. Burland, *Montezuma* (Hulton)
J. Dorner, *Cortes and the Aztecs* (Then and There) (Longman)
Conquest of Mexico (Cape: Jackdaw)
P. Francis, *The Spanish Conquest of America* (Pergamon)
L. F. Hobley, *Exploring the Americas* (Methuen: Outlines)
B. Ross, *Mexico, Land of Eagle and Serpent* (Methuen: Outlines)
J. Soustelle, *Daily Life under the Aztecs* (Penguin)

Visual aids
Magellan (Visual Publications)
The Incas of Peru (Hulton Educational)
Magellan (Hulton)
Hernando Cortes (Common Ground)
Aztecs and Their Way of Life (Encyclopedia Britannica)
Incas and Their Way of Life (Encyclopedia Britannica)
Cortes (Encyclopedia Britannica)
Pizarro (Encyclopedia Britannica)
Bilbao (Encyclopedia Britannica)
The Ancient New World *(film)* (Churchill)

To write and find out
1 Compare Magellan's route around the world with modern sea lanes. Consult a geography book or get some pamphlets from a travel agency.
2 Write a story describing your adventures as one of Cortes's men. One conquistador, Bernal Diaz, did write a book about the Conquest of Mexico. See if you can find extracts from it in books on this subject.
3 Which modern countries occupy the territories once ruled by the Aztecs and Incas?

Tudor Triumph
The England of the Wars of the Roses   *1399-1485*

No country was destined to benefit more from those great voyages than England. For centuries it had been on the outer edge of European civilisation. Within two centuries these new discoveries were to place it astride the world's chief trade routes. In the fifteenth century few Englishmen realised what was happening. Instead they wasted their time fighting amongst themselves.

Their quarrel was an old one. In 1399 the Duke of Lancaster had seized the throne from Richard II and become Henry IV. When Richard died at Pontefract a few months later the matter seemed settled. Unfortunately one branch of Richard's family, the Yorkists, neither forgave nor forgot. Faced by warlike Lancastrians like Henry IV and his son Henry V, their plots and rebellions came to nothing. But after Henry V's death in 1422, the crown passed, in the words of an old chronicler, to 'a simple man without any crook or craft or un-truth'. Henry VI inherited few of the qualities which had enabled his father to win the Battle of Agincourt against the French (1415). Deeply religious and peace-loving, 'the royal saint' founded Eton College and King's College, Cambridge. He also lost the throne stolen by his grandfather.

Initially Duke Richard, the Yorkist leader, hoped to become king without bloodshed. This was possible because for some time Henry and his wife Margaret had no children. Indeed, when the king began to show signs of madness Richard was appointed Protector. The King's recovery and the birth of a son, Edward, changed the situation. A desperate Richard gathered his forces and at St Albans (1455) defeated and wounded the king. The fighting which followed is called the Wars of the Roses because the Lancastrian badge was supposed to be a red rose and the Yorkist a white one. The title is misleading for the Lancastrian badge was a white swan whilst the Yorkists had several badges besides the white rose.

'The Royal Saint', Henry VI

Edward IV

The Battle of St Albans settled nothing because parliament refused to make Richard king. Four years later he rebelled again, only to be killed in battle at Wakefield (December 1460). The joyous Lancastrians put a paper hat on his severed head and stuck it on the walls of York.

Within months the tables had been turned. Richard's son Edward proved an even more dangerous opponent. Tall and handsome, with a broad chest and great strength, he was, wrote Sir Thomas More, 'very princely to behold, of heart courageous . . . in war sharp and fierce'. First he beat the Lancastrians at Mortimer's Cross. Then, in spite of his ally, the Earl of Warwick, being defeated he joined him and entered London in triumph. Leaving the capital, the two chased the retreating Lancastrians to Towton where they fought the biggest battle of the war (March 1461).

'That day there was a great conflict, which began with the rising of the sun, and lasted until the tenth hour of the night,' reported Warwick's brother. The Yorkists fought their way up hill, to where their enemies were blinded by driving snow. They were outnumbered but won when reinforcements arrived and attacked Henry's men on the left. Eleven Lancastrian lords fell on the battlefield. Hundreds of their men who fled into the valley were drowned in a swollen stream. Henry and Queen Margaret escaped to Scotland. In November Edward became king, even though Henry VI was still alive.

Meanwhile, Henry's wife, Margaret, continued to stir up trouble, even after her husband, the King, was captured. When Warwick, styled 'the Kingmaker', quarrelled with Edward, Margaret helped by the King of France, persuaded the Earl to change sides. The marriage of Warwick's daughter to Henry VI's son was the signal for a Lancastrian uprising against Edward. Taken by surprise, the Yorkist king fled to the Netherlands.

Once again the Lancastrian success was shortlived. Although Edward returned with only 2,000 men, he defeated Warwick's army in a thick fog at Barnet (14 April 1471). The 'King-maker' died in the battle. Queen Margaret, meanwhile, had her army cut to pieces at Tewkesbury in a fierce fight amongst hedges, bushes and trees. The triumphant Edward returned to London in a savage mood. On the night he arrived Henry VI was murdered in the Tower. England now had a far different ruler from the 'Royal Saint'.

Henry Tudor

Edward died suddenly in April 1483, leaving two young sons, Edward V and the Duke of York. His brother Richard, ignoring their claims to the throne, made himself king. The two boys were sent to the Tower of London and never seen again. These 'princes in the Tower' were certainly murdered, although by whom is not known for certain. The story that Richard had them suffocated may be true. In 1674 their bones were supposed to have been found under a stairway.

Rumours and suspicions about the princes helped Richard's enemies to plot his downfall. The surviving Lancastrian leader, Henry Tudor, was related to Henry VI. His claims to the throne were weaker than several Yorkists, but the best of any Lancastrian. As a boy he had been taken abroad by his uncle. When Richard seized the crown a group of Lancastrian lords rebelled only to be beaten before Henry could help. Two years later the Tudor himself landed in England.

Night was falling on 7 August 1485 as the small force came ashore at Milford Haven, in Wales. If it is true that Henry read his men the 46th Psalm it was appropriate. In its later English version the psalm begins,

God is our refuge and strength,
A very present help in trouble.

The staircase in the Tower of London where the bodies of the little princes were supposed to have been found in 1674

There was no doubt the rebels faced plenty of trouble. They had come to challenge a warrior king in his own land. Richard III was an experienced soldier whereas Henry had never fought a battle. As he advanced into the heart of England the Lancastrian leader must have wondered whether he was marching to destruction.

Even so, certain things were in his favour. Two of his generals, his uncle Jasper Tudor and the Earl of Oxford, were good soldiers. More important, several leading Yorkists had quarrelled with Richard. In particular Henry hoped that the powerful Stanley family who dominated north-west England and north Wales would join him. Both Sir William and Lord Stanley had changed sides during the Wars of the Roses so they might betray their new master. And even if Henry was defeated, the Welsh hills would provide good cover for his escape.

Bosworth Field

Richard suspected the Stanleys' loyalty and arrested Lord Stanley's stepson as a hostage. Apart from this move, he showed few signs of worry as he rode proudly through the countryside surrounded by lords and knights. By 21 August four armies, those of Richard, Henry, and the two Stanleys, had camped around the Plain of Radmore (red moor) near Market Bosworth in Leicestershire. Next morning Richard drew up his men on Ambion Hill. The Stanleys lay to north and south, watching and waiting. Because neither Richard nor Henry could rely on them each kept his troops in marching, not battle order. Only with this formation could they hope to deal quickly with a flank (side) attack.

A volley of arrows from both sides signalled the start of the battle early on 22 August 1485. Oxford immediately led his rebel forces

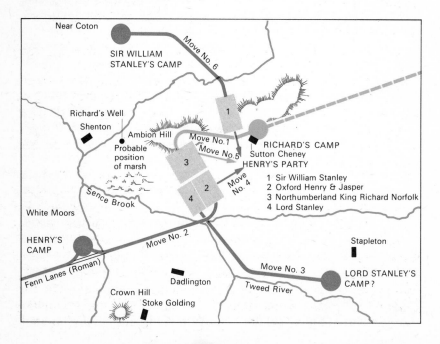

Plan of the Battle of Bosworth, August 1485

HENRY'S PARTY

1 Sir William Stanley
2 Oxford Henry & Jasper
3 Northumberland King Richard Norfolk
4 Lord Stanley

Henry VII—founder of the Tudor dynasty

up the hill in close order. A fierce hand-to-hand fight resulted in which several of the King's leading men were killed. After an hour or so Richard saw Sir William Stanley's men moving to attack him. Realising he had been betrayed he became desperate. Henry Tudor was guarded by only a few soldiers. Richard decided to try to win the battle by killing him. Stopping to drink at a stream still called Dickon's Well, Richard spurred forward, cut through his enemy's bodyguard, unhorsed a standard bearer and closed with Henry himself. Nobody gave the Lancastrian much chance. In fact, he held out long enough for Sir William's men to arrive and kill Richard.

As news of the King's death spread, the royal troops either fled or surrendered. Henry dismounted, fell on his knees and thanked God. One of his men found Richard's crown and placed it on his head. The body of the first English king to die in battle since 1066 was slung naked over a horse 'as an hog or another vile beast' and carried to Leicester for burial. During the next few months not many Englishmen believed that 'Henry VII' would last long. Yet the man who won at Bosworth reigned twenty-four years and every later British monarch, is descended from him.

Polydore's England

What sort of country had Henry gained on the battlefield? The Wars of the Roses had not affected the lives of the people as much as we might expect. Many lords died, it is true. But there was only thirteen week's fighting during thirty-two years and none of the battles, except Towton, was on a large scale. Compared with the sufferings of the French during the Hundred Years' War, the English were lucky. 'England enjoyed the peculiar mercy' wrote a foreigner, 'that neither the country, nor the people nor the houses were wasted, destroyed or demolished; but the . . . misfortunes of the war fell only upon the soldiers, and especially upon the nobility.' It was therefore a peaceful and prosperous land by the standards of the time.

An Italian, Polydore Vergil, left a detailed description of early Tudor England. Britain, he wrote, was divided into four parts, England, Wales, Scotland and Cornwall. It had 'many hills . . . with most delectable valleys'. A rich soil produced good crops and the seas around its shores teemed with fish. The countryside was alive with stags, goats, fallow deer, hares, rabbits, pigs and oxen. Rooks, ravens, jackdaws and many other birds filled the air. Large flocks of swans glided on the Thames.

In spite of seeing many fields of wheat and barley, Polydore reckoned there was more cattle- and sheep-farming than anything else. Since such work needed relatively few men, the countryside seemed rather empty compared with Italy. Those English people who did appear were a fine sight, according to Polydore. The men were generally tall, with fair hair and grey eyes. They were very brave in battle but rather lazy. The women were said to be of a snow-white beauty. All the people loved fish, fowl and beef and perhaps for this reason lived to great ages; people 110 years old were not unknown it seemed. The King, whom Polydore knew well, was 'slender but well built and strong; his height above average. His appearance remarkably attractive, especially when speaking; his eyes small and blue; his teeth few, poor and blackish, his hair . . . thin and white; his complexion sallow'.

The English, apparently, disliked large cities. They preferred to live in 'valleys' or 'little towns'. Bristol and Southampton, it was true, were thriving ports; York was important and Oxford and Cambridge had famous universities. But in Polydore's opinion only London, with a population of 50,000, compared with Milan, Rome, Venice or Florence. Its main streets were most impressive; in Cheapside alone he counted fifty-two goldsmiths' shops. A forest of spires rose from London's ninety-seven churches; St Paul's, the city's cathedral, was crowned by one 500 feet high. London's famous bridge, with its nineteen arches, lines of houses and great wooden piles filled with stones, was one of the wonders of the fifteenth-century world.

Farming

This account, although slightly exaggerated, seems to have been fairly accurate. England's population in 1485 was probably something over two million. Its chief industry was farming, both arable (growing crops), and sheep- and cattle-breeding. Crop-growing methods had hardly changed since Saxon times. In the south and central midlands where most of the people lived, village arable land was usually formed into three large fields. These fields were, in turn, divided into (furlong) strips, which were shared between peasants so that each family's strips were scattered. A common scheme was to sow one field with winter corn, wheat or rye, and the second with spring crops, barley, oats, beans or peas. One entire field was left unused (fallow) each year so as to rest the soil.

This 'open field system' had many disadvantages by modern standards. Leaving the fallow field meant that one-third of the arable land was wasted each year. All the villagers, whether good or bad farmers, had to work together at the same pace. A manor court decided the date for sowing each year. Cross ploughing—useful to help fertility—was not possible with such narrow strips. The small amount of food produced left hardly any for cattle fodder in the winter. Consequently a proportion of livestock were killed each year; our word 'bonfire' comes from the fires of their bones made in the autumn. On the other hand, the system was fair. Besides sharing good and bad land, it left areas of 'commons' which villagers could use for grazing cattle, cutting firewood and so on. It also allowed for co-operative ploughing at a time when few farmers were rich enough to possess their own plough and team of oxen.

The better-off farmers were called yeomen, others were either husbandmen or labourers. Agricultural methods had remained unchanged for centuries. Ploughs were pulled by oxen (bullocks). Seeds were thrown on the ground (broadcast) whilst boys walked behind banging wooden clappers to keep the birds off. Main crops were harvested in August, usually by teams consisting of four men and a boy. A good team could cut and stack about two acres of corn a day. Women and young children walked behind picking up every scrap of wheat (gleaning). Threshing was done with a flail—two pieces of wood loosely fixed end-on with a strip of leather.

Other tasks included cutting firewood, trimming hedges, weeding, clearing ditches, picking fruit, salting meat for the winter and sharpening tools. Women helped in the fields at busy times, as well as rearing the children. They also cooked and preserved food, brewed beer, made sweets and dipped rushes in hot fat to make candles.

The three-field system of farming

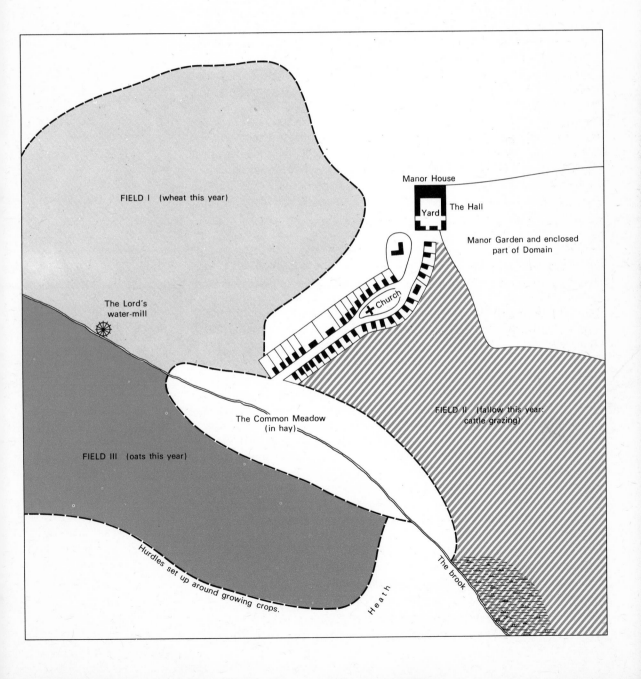

The cloth trade

Next to arable farming in importance came the production of wool and the manufacture of woollen cloth. Since the early Middle Ages England's chief trade had been the export of wool. Cloth made from English wool was popular on the continent so a trading company, the Merchants of the Staple, shipped this wool to Europe via Calais. In the later Middle Ages merchants realised that if they turned the wool into cloth in England instead of sending it to Flanders they could increase their profits. This cloth export was organised from London by 'Merchant Adventurers' and usually went to Antwerp.

The switch from exporting wool to making cloth altered the pattern of English industry. Existing looms were insufficient to cope with the increased demand, and England's weavers were few. Their methods were old-fashioned, and in the towns they were hampered by guild laws which restricted profits, hours of work and the numbers of apprentices. So village after village took up spinning, weaving or dyeing. Old cloth towns such as York, Coventry and Bridgnorth, declined in wealth and size. 'New' towns, such as Halifax, Leeds and Wakefield, expanded. Rich merchant clothiers organised their trade over a wide area so that wool grown in one county might be spun in a second and woven in a third. Some supplied weavers with looms as well as the raw material. A few clothiers became very rich. John Winchcombe, known as 'Jack of Newbury', made a fortune supplying a rough cloth, called *kersies*.

Enclosures

Not everybody benefited from these changes. Landowners wishing to increase food production, or to breed sheep, often enclosed their land with fences to keep out wandering animals. Such enclosures caused hardship and distress. Ordinary farming folk were supposed to receive fields equivalent in size to their old strips. But many had no legal claim to land which their families had farmed for centuries, and so got nothing. Even those who did receive fields lost the use of the common land which was now enclosed by the lord for his own use.

The effect of sheep-farming was worse in some cases. It required fewer hands than arable farming and sometimes peasants were told to leave after the harvest, pull down their houses and sow the strips with grass. Occasionally an entire village disappeared in this way. Recently aerial photography has revealed the outlines of many such 'lost' villages including one at Wharram Percy in Yorkshire. The King and his ministers did not like enclosure because it deprived the country of farmers who made good soldiers. Indeed yeoman and soldier almost meant the same thing. As the poet Geoffrey Chaucer had written in his *Canterbury Tales*:

This Yeoman wore a coat and hood of green,
And peacock-feathered arrows, bright and keen
And neatly sheathed, hung at his belt the while
For he could dress his gear in yeoman style.
His arrows never drooped their feathers low—
And in his hand he bore a mighty bow.

Many parliamentary Acts contained complaints about the 'empty' countryside. The Isle of Wight—essential for the defence of England —was once described as 'desolate and not inhabited but occupied with beasts and cattle'. Desolate or not, this was the price to be paid for England's wealthy woollen cloth industry.

More about fifteenth-century England

Books

M. C. Borer, *People of Tudor England* (Parrish)

K. Davies, *Henry Percy and Henry VII* (Then and There) (Longman)

A. P. G. Macdonald and I. L. MacDougall, *British Battles,* vol. 1 (Macmillan)

E. K. Milliken, *Lancastrian and Tudor* (Harrap)

M. Raine, *The Wars of the Roses* (Pergamon)

Richard III and the Princes in the Tower (Cape: Jackdaw)

M. and C. H. B. Quennell, *History of Everyday Things in England, 1066-1499* (Batsford)

Visual aids

Expansion of Trade and Wars of the Roses (Visual Publications)

The First of the Tudors (Visual Publications)

The Three Field System *(film)* (Gateway)

Tudor England (Visual Information Services)

Textile Industries (Common Ground)

England's Wealth from Wool *(film)* (EFVA)

Tudor London (Educational Productions)

Visit

Westminster Abbey, London

Guildhall, London

The Tower of London

The London Museum

To write and find out

1 Mark on graph paper two lines, illustrating the successes and failures of each side in the Wars of the Roses.

2 Find out more about the Princes in the Tower. Who do you think had them murdered? Read *We Speak No Treason* by Rosemary Jarman (Collins).

3 London Bridge had a long and interesting history. Find out all you can about it. See Chapters 14 and 22 in this book.

4 Find out more about the open-field system. Draw a diagram to illustrate how it worked.

5 Find out more about the early English woollen cloth trade. The Guildhall at Lavenham in Suffolk contains much interesting material concerning the industry in that area and there may be similar museums in your part of the country.

5 The Merchant King
Henry VII   1485-1509

Emperor Maximilian I

Henry VII hoped his victory would end the feud between Yorkists and Lancastrians. Before Bosworth he had promised to take Elizabeth, a daughter of Edward IV, as his wife. Three months after his impressive coronation he married the tall, golden-haired Yorkist princess. Some of his enemies were not converted, and continued to plot against him. During 1486 Henry had to tour the country putting down riots and disorder. Next year certain Irish lords who favoured York claimed they had found Edward IV's nephew, the Earl of Warwick. But in fact the twelve-year-old boy they crowned king in Dublin was Lambert Simnel, the son of an Oxford tradesman.

Although the real Warwick was a prisoner in the Tower of London, enough people believed in the imposter to make an invasion of England by German mercenaries (soldiers fighting for money) and Irish troops possible. Henry had been warned and met them at Stoke in June 1487. In some ways the battle resembled Bosworth. Parts of Henry's army ignored the fighting, playing a waiting game as the Stanleys had done. But this time the King of England was victorious. The Germans fought well under their brave leader, Martin Swart. The Irish were poorly equipped, having only darts, knives or knotted ropes for strangling. They were, a chronicler recorded, cut down like 'dull and brute beastes'. Swart and most of the Yorkist leaders were also killed.

When captured, Simnel admitted he was not Warwick. Henry, instead of executing the pretender, made him work in the royal kitchens. Several years later Simnel served wine to the very Irish lords who had crowned him king. 'My masters of Ireland,' said Henry with a smile, 'you will crown apes at last.'

A profitable failure

It was not only at home that Henry faced problems. Across the Channel France was becoming more powerful. Its king, Louis XI, had nearly doubled the amount of French territory during his reign (1461–83). Much of this land was taken from his own semi-independent nobles. His son, Charles VIII adopted the same policy. In 1490 he invaded Brittany, where Henry had lived in exile. After defeating a Breton army, Charles offered to marry the country's ruler, Anne, ignoring the fact that she was already formally married to the German Emperor Maximilian.

Henry felt he must save Anne. After all, the conquest of Brittany might be followed by an attack on the English base at Calais. In case France proved too strong for England alone he asked Spain for help. The Spanish monarchs, Ferdinand and Isabella, had already quarrelled with France about the ownership of certain border territories.

They agreed by the Treaty of Medina del Campo (1489) to become England's ally in a war against France. It was this treaty which arranged for the marriage of Henry's son Arthur to Ferdinand and Isabella's daughter, Catherine, which eventually took place in 1501. Unfortunately Arthur died soon afterwards so Catherine was engaged to his brother, Prince Henry.

Henry asked for £100,000 from parliament to fight the war. He also sent troops to Brittany. They achieved little and by December 1491 Anne decided reluctantly to wed the French King. The Spanish, meanwhile, spent more time attacking the Moors who had been settled in southern Spain for centuries than sending armies to help Henry. Deserted by his allies, the King should have given up. Instead he boldly revived English claims to the French throne and prepared to invade France. Thousands of troops were assembled at Portsmouth, where three new breweries were needed to quench their thirst. In October 1492 Henry himself crossed the Channel to lay siege to Boulogne with 26,000 men. The bluff worked. Charles, who was planning his Italian invasion (see Chapter 1), had few troops available to deal with the English. After only nine days of fighting peace was signed at Etaples. Charles gave Henry an annual pension, besides promising not to shelter or help any Yorkist pretender.

The English, who would have liked a showdown with the French, sailed home disappointed 'in great fumes, angry and evil content that the occasion of so glorious a victory . . . was refused'. Parliament, too, was so annoyed it delayed confirming the treaty. England's crafty King, on the other hand, was satisfied. Besides the French pension, he had saved nearly half the war tax voted by parliament. It had been a profitable 'failure'!

Perkin Warbeck

The chief Yorkist claimant to the throne after Simnel's defeat was Perkin Warbeck, son of a customs officer at Tournai, Belgium. While in Ireland, he had been persuaded by some Yorkists to pose as Richard, Duke of York, one of the 'princes in the Tower', whom he resembled in appearance. When he returned to the Netherlands, Margaret, Duchess of Burgundy, a sister of Edward IV, saw him and declared he was indeed her 'lost' nephew.

Whatever Margaret might say or do, Henry felt sure that if Perkin invaded England it would be from Ireland, not the Netherlands. In theory Ireland had been ruled by English kings since Henry II's reign (1154–89). In practice the English governed little more than a small area around Dublin called the Pale. For control of the rest of the country they usually relied upon the support of Irish lords. Since most of these were Yorkists, Henry decided to ignore them and try to rule more directly from England. First he declared his baby son, Prince Henry 'Lieutenant of Ireland'. Then Sir Edward Poynings was sent with an army to enforce the prince's authority. By December 1494 the Irish parliament had been compelled to pass 'Poyning's Law' which stopped them making any law without the English government's permission.

Perkin Warbeck spent some years both in Ireland and Scotland trying to stir up trouble for Henry. The Scots king, believing the pretender really was the Duke of York, allowed him to marry his cousin, and promised military help. In September 1496 a Scottish army crossed the English border and devastated the countryside. Henry replied by planning a counter-invasion of Scotland which had to be cancelled when the Cornish rebelled against his war tax (June 1497). Three months later Warbeck himself entered England where he was defeated and captured. After his execution (1499) relations between the two countries improved. Indeed, in 1503 King James IV of Scotland married Henry's daughter, Margaret. It was their descendants who ruled England as the Stuart kings and queens from 1603.

King and Council

Soon after Bosworth, Henry told his parliament that he had gained the crown through the 'right judgment of God given in battle'. Whether true or not, he kept it by wise and efficient government.

Although an English king of those times had to be obeyed, he was expected to seek the advice of his nobles and gentry (gentlemen). Henry governed with the help of a council of about twenty men. These rarely met together, for Henry preferred to consult them individually or in groups. To discuss important matters, the King, his Council and Lords (including lawyers and clergymen) met as a *Magnum Concilium* (Great Council). Occasionally the Commons were summoned. This assembly consisted of two knights from each shire (county) and two representatives from each borough (town with a charter of self government). The Commons were also called to give permission for new laws and taxes. Since both were rare, it is not surprising that Henry's parliaments only met for a total of sixty-nine weeks during his twenty-four-year reign.

Commons members gathered in the chapter-house or refectory (dining room) of Westminster Abbey until 1547, when they moved to St Stephen's Chapel in the royal palace at Westminster. Knights from the thirty-seven shires were elected by farmers owning land worth forty shillings or more a year in rents. Burghers (town representatives) were chosen in various ways, usually by the richer merchants and tradesmen of the town. The Commons chairman, known as the Speaker, was supposed to be elected by the members. In fact he was appointed by the King in order to make certain they approved of royal policies.

Parliamentary laws were administered by various courts, ranging from the three main ones (King's Bench, Common Pleas and Exchequer) to county magistrates' courts. All met four times a year, with holidays fixed to avoid seed and harvest time. The king appointed judges who travelled from one county town to another, trying serious offenders. Minor cases were dealt with by justices of the peace (j.p.'s) who were appointed by the government. Officially justices' courts met only four times a year—at Quarter Sessions. In practice, j.p.'s were responsible for law and order all the time.

The lady kneeling at the front on the right is Queen Isabella of Spain. She sent Columbus to the Indies and was the mother of Henry VIII's first wife, Catherine of Aragon

The appointment of unpaid justices had been started by Henry III (1216–72). Both Edward IV and Henry VII increased the work they had to do. A justice of the peace controlled local working conditions and fixed maximum wages for different trades. He saw to the repair of roads, licensed ale-houses, stopped 'unlawful' games, and even arranged for the ransoming of local sailors captured by pirates. Such a system was popular with English kings because of its cheapness, and the officials themselves enjoyed the prestige and power. In the days before modern taxation, police or army, England could not have been governed effectively without them.

Henry's most famous court, the Star Chamber, was not created by him. It consisted of members of his Council who met at Westminster Palace in a room with star shaped ornaments on the ceiling. The Star Chamber was supposed to speed up decisions in quarrels between rich and powerful persons. Its judgments were usually based on common sense rather than a strict interpretation of the law. Henry frequently asked it to investigate plots against him. It could not inflict death, and most of the punishments were fines.

Finance and trade

An English king of the sixteenth century was expected to live 'of his own', that is, run the country out of his own income. Only in times of crisis would parliament help him financially. Henry was fascinated by money. He copied Edward IV and put his royal revenue in a department called the Chamber, rather than the Exchequer with its old-fashioned and inefficient methods. Here he kept a careful eye on all transactions; one set of royal account books for 1504–08 still exist and show that he examined and signed every page. As a result he rarely needed extra taxes. 'The kings, my predecessors,' he once remarked, 'weakening their treasure, have made themselves servants to their subjects.' The first Tudor never allowed this to happen to him.

A great deal is known about Henry's income which was made up from various sources. A parliamentary grant—supposedly one-fifteenth of the value of all movable objects in the counties and one-tenth in the towns—produced about £39,000 a year. Customs duties on wool, and fees paid to the king on the death of a lord or the marriage of his children, made the final total about £110,000 p.a. In addition, Henry sometimes made his richer subjects lend him money (forced loans) or 'give' him certain sums out of their love for him (benevolences)! He also heavily fined lords who broke his laws against livery (wearing of badges or uniform by a lord's servants) or maintenance (attempting to settle a law-suit by force).

It was said of Henry: 'Being a king that loved wealth and treasure, he could not endure to have trade sick.' He was, in fact, a first-class businessman. As a private person Henry hired ships to merchants, loaned money at high interest rates and even sold materials. As ruler he tried to help English trade by signing trade treaties with foreign countries.

The *Magnum Intercursus* (1496) established fair arrangements for

Henry VII lies beside his Queen.

Their magnificent tomb is in Westminster Abbey

the English wool trade with the Netherlands. Parts of the Medina del Campo Treaty gave English and Spanish merchants equal rights in each other's country, at least for a time. Various Navigation laws, ordering certain goods to be imported only in English ships, were passed to prevent English shipbuilders and sailors being unemployed. The Mediterranean trade—wine from Crete, currants from the Middle East, glassware from Venice—was expanded with the King's encouragement. When Venice objected, Henry put heavy duties on Venetian wine entering England.

The King had less success in his struggle with the Hanseatic League, a trading alliance of about eighty German ports, with its own army and navy. Much English trade, particularly wool, passed through their hands. Moreover, Edward IV had given their London agents special privileges because the Hansa had helped him. Henry persuaded Denmark to make war on the Hansa but it was defeated. He also hoped that his Navigation laws would deprive the Germans of English trade. Actually there were not enough English ships to carry all the English goods to Europe. Whether he liked it or not Henry knew his merchants could not do without Hanseatic vessels.

Army and navy

Unlike some continental rulers, an English monarch of those times had no regular army or police. Soon after he became king Henry formed a bodyguard of red-coated 'Yeomen of the Guard', and this unit still exists today. One hundred of these Yeomen Warders (Beef-eaters), plus eight hundred men garrisoned at Calais, were the only professional soldiers always available. For defence against invasion or rebellion young men were called up in each county. This 'militia' was later commanded by a lord lieutenant. For overseas expeditions, the king generally hired soldiers from his lords. In 1497 for example, Henry paid one shilling and sixpence a day for armed horsemen and sixpence a day for archers. These troops mustered (assembled) at an agreed place and were paid sixpence for every twenty miles they had to travel.

Henry also inherited a Yorkist 'navy' of four ships. To these he added the *Regent, Sovereign, Sweepstake* and *Mary Fortune.* Finest of all was the *Regent* which had four masts and 225 cannon. This armament was less formidable than it sounds for most of these guns fired a shot no larger than a musket ball. The *Regent* was an armed merchantman, a floating platform for fighting men rather than a cannon-firing warship. She was too large for the Southampton harbour of those days so Henry founded a naval dockyard at Portsmouth.

In wartime, the King enlarged his navy by hiring merchant ships, usually at the monthly rate of a shilling a ton. He paid the masters 3*s* 4*d* a week, trained seamen 1*s* 3*d* and boys 6*d*. In time of peace Henry reversed the process and allowed merchants to hire his 'warships' for commercial voyages. In this way he made even his navy pay.

A strong monarchy

Henry was respected but not loved. His skill at finance, his cunning and efficiency gave him a high reputation. Yet beside his spectacular son, Henry VIII, he seems drab and dull. Even so, he was not quite the inhuman miser some have suggested. From his splendid coronation onwards Henry had the Tudor knack for 'playing the king'. His clothes were always very fine; even his dogs wore silk collars. His banquets were noted for gorgeous dishes, like 'perch in jelly dipped' or 'castles of jelly' and 'peacockes in hackle'.

Henry, besides being a loving husband, was certainly less bloodthirsty than his fellow monarchs. Simnel, for example, would probably have been executed had he rebelled against any other ruler of the time. Elizabeth's death in 1503 left the king lonely, so he considered marrying various ladies. On one occasion envoys were sent with instructions to report on the Queen of Naples's complexion, hair, colour of eyes and 'to approach as near to her mouth as they honestly may to . . . feel the conditions of her breath, whether it was sweet or not'. Obviously the old king did not spend all his time thinking about money! When he died on 21 April 1509 at Richmond palace he was buried under a magnificent marble tomb in Westminster Abbey. In death, as in life, he was a true sixteenth-century king.

The full extent of his achievement became clear after his death. Henry, his son, succeeded him without the slightest dispute or disorder. The English monarchy was strong and secure once more.

More about Henry VII

Books
Nearly all those listed for Chapter 4, also:
R. Lockyer, *Henry VII* (Longman: Seminar Studies in History)
Peoples of the Past, Series D (Oxford University Press)
D. Pitt, *Henry VII* (Oxford University Press)
C. Williams, *Life in Tudor England* (Batsford)

Visual aids
Henry VII (Visual Publications)
Tudor Britain *(two film strips)* (Visual Publications)

Visits
As for Chapter 4.

To write and find out
1 Write a story imagining that Lambert Simnel had become King. What do you think would have happened to him?
2 From the figures given in this chapter calculate the cost of employing 1,000 of Henry's soldiers for four weeks.
3 Henry was considered lucky in war. Do you agree? Give reasons.
4 See how many Tudor Rose designs there are in old buildings in your district. Any inns in your neighbourhood called 'The Tudor Rose' or 'The Rose and Crown' refer to Henry VII. So does any 'Red Dragon'. Do you know why?

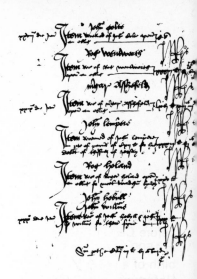

Above: The Royal Account Books for 1506. Henry VII signed each entry
Below: A Yeoman Warder of the Tower of London, in his Tudor uniform

6 'A Very Accomplished Prince'
Henry VIII   1509-1521

Henry VII was given a memorable funeral. Five horses, draped in black, pulled the hearse which was escorted by archbishops, bishops, lords and barons. The old King's richly decorated armour and battleaxe, his helmet with gold crown and spear sheathed in black velvet, were carried in the procession. On 10 May 1509 the victor of Bosworth was laid to rest in Westminster Abbey.

He was succeeded by his seventeen-year-old son, Henry VIII. Most paintings of Henry show him when he was fat and middle-aged so it is easy to forget how magnificent 'Bluff King Hal' seemed when young. 'His majesty', wrote the Venetian ambassador a few years after his accession, 'is . . . extremely handsome . . . very accomplished, a good musician, composes well, is a most capital

A joyful Henry VIII jousts before Catherine of Aragon in 1509 to celebrate the birth of a son. Unfortunately the royal prince lived only two months

horseman, a fine jouster, speaks French, Latin and Spanish, is very religious. . . . He is extremely fond of tennis, at which game it is the prettiest thing in the world to see him play.' No man was better qualified to play the 'Renaissance prince'.

In many ways Henry resembled his grandfather, Edward IV. Tall and strongly built, he was an athlete who could fight, hunt and drink with the toughest of his courtiers. At jousting, in particular, he was said to have 'no respect or fear of anyone in the world'. Like the Yorkist Edward, he could be ruthless and savage. Henry boasted that there was no head in his kingdom so noble 'but he would make it fly' if its owner defied him. One of his first actions was to execute Empson and Dudley, two of his father's most hated tax-collectors, simply to please the people. One of his last acts was to sign the death warrant of the Duke of Norfolk. The headman's axe and hangman's rope were never far away in Henry VIII's reign.

Two weeks before his coronation Henry kept a promise made to his father and married Catherine of Aragon. It was against Church law for a man to marry his brother's widow, so Pope Julius II gave special permission. Years afterwards Henry was to remember the warning in the Bible: 'And if a man shall take his brother's wife, it is an unclean thing . . .; they shall be childless.' For the moment he seemed content, as he and his young queen spent the midsummer days of 1509 mostly hunting, feasting and dancing.

Henry's first war

Apart from marrying Catherine, Henry did little which would have pleased his father. Henry VII had told his son to avoid war at all costs. This wise advice was ignored by the vigorous young man who longed to win honour and glory on the battlefield.

The European situation offered plenty of opportunities for war. Two royal families, the Valois kings of France and the Habsburg emperors of Germany, were struggling to dominate Europe, using Italy as a battleground. The Valois Louis XII ruled the best organised kingdom on the continent. France was far more powerful than in the days of the Hundred Years War. The old medieval divisions into dukedoms and provinces had been replaced by a 'nation state', in which all the people of one language and nationality were ruled by a king with his own army.

The Habsburg emperor, Maximilian, reigned over larger but more scattered territories. Germany was divided into small states, the more important of which were ruled by Electors (princes) who took little notice of the man they had chosen 'Holy Roman Emperor'. Indeed, Maximilian's most lasting successes were scored through marriage not war. By marrying Mary of Burgundy (1477) he gained her rich possessions in the Netherlands. Their son, Philip, married a Spanish princes with the result that Maximilian's grandson, Charles, became King of Spain as well as Emperor. Thus by 1519 Habsburg marriages had ringed France with hostile territory.

There was not much doubt which side Henry would support. France was England's traditional enemy. French ships could threaten

'An accomplished prince.' Henry VIII in his prime

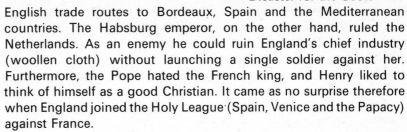

Lands controlled by the
Habsburg and Valois
families in 1520

English trade routes to Bordeaux, Spain and the Mediterranean
countries. The Habsburg emperor, on the other hand, ruled the
Netherlands. As an enemy he could ruin England's chief industry
(woollen cloth) without launching a single soldier against her.
Furthermore, the Pope hated the French king, and Henry liked to
think of himself as a good Christian. It came as no surprise therefore
when England joined the Holy League (Spain, Venice and the Papacy)
against France.

In the summer of 1513 Henry crossed to France with an army and
large numbers of personal attendants. At Thérouanne the young
King, in full armour and mounted on a horse hung with bells, met the
Emperor. Old Maximilian charmed him by offering to serve under his
command. On 13 August the two nearly trapped the enemy at
Guinegate (near Courtrai). Ordered to escape, the French cavalry
fled so quickly that the skirmish is known as the 'Battle of the Spurs'.

Flodden

While the English king was campaigning on the continent he missed a
far greater victory at home. France's Scottish allies invaded England
in the summer of 1513. English troops, commanded by the Earl of
Surrey (later Duke of Norfolk), met them at Flodden, near Berwick
in September.

The Scottish King James had taken up a well defended position
on a hill, so Surrey split his force in two and got behind him. The
King realised the danger too late. When his troops tried to reach the
safety of another hill there was confusion. Handicapped by rough
ground and harassed by English gunfire the Scots broke ranks just
as Surrey's men closed with them. In such conditions they were
unable to use their chief weapon, the spear, effectively. Large
numbers were massacred by the deadly English axemen.

Defeat was turned to disaster when the brave but rash James led
his nobles in a desperate charge into the English ranks. Both he and
his son were cut down a few yards from Surrey's flag. Many bishops
and nobles fell with their King and over 11,000 soldiers were left
dead on the battlefield. The triumphant English celebrated by getting
drunk on captured Scottish beer. To this day the bagpipes of Scottish
regiments play a lament 'The Flowers of the Forest' which tells of the
terrible defeat which deprived Scotland of an adult monarch for
many years to come.

Catherine sent James's bloodstained coat to Henry who showed
it proudly to Maximilian. The crafty emperor, however, had already
started negotiations with the French behind his back. Fortunately for
Henry, Louis decided that English armies were more dangerous than
Habsburg plots. He offered to double the pension granted originally
to Henry VII and he also married Henry's sister Mary. The English
King returned home triumphantly. In the rejoicing few realised that
the war had cost all Henry VII's fortune.

It seemed Europe might enjoy peace for a while. Unfortunately,
Louis died two months after his marriage (1515), and was succeeded
by his nephew, Francis I. The new king was as typical a Renaissance

prince as Henry himself. Clever and athletic, with a bushy black beard and long nose, he was cruel, wildly extravagant and brave to the point of foolishness. Within a year of his accession he crossed the Alps, smashed a Swiss army hired by the Italians (Battle of Marignano) and made himself master of northern Italy. Three years later when Maximilian died, he tried to bribe the Electors to make him emperor. When they chose his greatest enemy, the Habsburg Charles, instead, a European war was certain.

The glorious peacock

One of the men who encouraged Henry to interfere in continental affairs was Thomas Wolsey, his chief minister for sixteen years. Wolsey's story is one of 'rags to riches'. He was born in Ipswich, the son of a butcher, went to Oxford and became a priest (1498). In those days a poor man could rise quickest in the Church, where brains counted as much as wealth or high birth. Clergymen were in demand as secretaries and advisers, partly because they could read and write and partly because, being unmarried, they could not found troublesome families! From the start the ambitious young man looked for powerful friends and his ability was soon noticed, as chaplain to the Archbishop of Canterbury and then to the governor of Calais.

Few men have risen so quickly. In 1507 Wolsey was appointed a royal chaplain and two years later, Dean of Lincoln. After the French war he became, a cardinal, Archibishop of York, and Lord Chancellor. He never became Archbishop of Canterbury because the holder of that office, William Warham, outlived him. Nevertheless, in 1518 the Pope made him legate, or papal ambassador, in England. By 1520 the butcher's son from Ipswich lived in palaces and dreamed of becoming Pope himself one day.

There was nothing particularly religious about the 'glorious peacock' as he was called. When young he had lived with an innkeeper's daughter; giving her two children. When cardinal, he made himself rich by taking bribes. What probably annoyed people even more was his pride. Wolsey ate alone, sitting under a cloth of state like a king. He gave magnificent feasts, dressed in gorgeous clothes and made his personal clergy wear silk. Visitors were nearly always kept waiting, and then made to stand 'an arrow's length' from him. He even carried an orange filled with a sponge of vinegar to keep off the smell of poor people.

Cardinal Wolsey

The Great Harry, **pride of Henry VIII's fleet**

Wolsey's palace at Hampton Court, given to Henry VIII in a desperate attempt to regain the King's favour

Henry VIII—a portrait
painted in the style of
Hans Holbein

In 1519 the Venetian ambassador told his government: 'This cardinal is the person who rules both the king and the entire kingdom.' But this was not quite true. The King knew he had nothing to fear from a man who was so unpopular with people and nobles. Time was to show that Henry had made Wolsey and Henry could break him!

Great Harry's navy

Henry VIII was deeply interested in ships and the sea. As well as founding naval dockyards at Deptford and Woolwich, he set up a special board (committee) to run the navy and encouraged the formation of a guild of pilots which—as the Corporation of Trinity House (1546)—still looks after buoys and lighthouses around the British Isles. He was never happier than when aboard one his warships, dressed as a sailor and holding 'a large whistle with which he whistled almost as loud as a trumpet'.

In 1512 he ordered 'a great ship such as never was before seen in England', to be made. This was the *Henri Grace à Dieu* (Henry by the Grace of God), usually known as the *Great Harry*. This very tall vessel with four masts and 186 guns was afloat by 1514, ready to be inspected by her proud owner. How it took to rough weather is hard to say. Henry rarely allowed his favourite warship to put to sea! Unlike his father's *Regent*, it existed to impress foreigners, not to make money. Other monarchs owned similar 'prestige' ships at that time—France, the *Grand Francois,* Scotland, the *Great Michael* and Sweden, the *Elefant.*

Henry started a ship-building revolution in England by having guns placed low down in the hulls of warships. Shipwrights were not happy about this because it meant that these guns must stick out through the sides. They knew that such holes had to be cut through the wales (horizontal beams) which were the ship's main strength, and that the lowest ones would be near the waterline. Henry ignored such objections. Eventually a master shipwright, Peter Baker, devised a special gun deck to support the rows of cannon. This is why the side of a boat are called the gunwales.

Eventually the 'Father of the Royal Navy' possessed ninety warships of various sizes, from little two-gun rowboats to ships like the *Great Harry*. In 1545, however, Henry saw his new battleship, *Mary Rose,* heel over and sink in a few minutes because its lower gun-

ports, only sixteen inches above the waterline, were flooded. The shipwrights had not been so silly, after all.

Defender of the Faith

Throughout his reign Henry liked to have learned men around him. His own teachers had favoured the New Renaissance Learning, so many famous Humanist scholars were welcomed at his court. Two of the best known were Englishmen. John Colet (1467–1519) had travelled in Italy where he had been influenced by Savonarola's teachings. Back home, he gave lectures on the Bible which sometimes disagreed with Church doctrine. In 1509 Colet founded St Paul's School, London, in which Greek was first taught publicly in England.

Sir Thomas More (1478–1535) went to Oxford University and then became a lawyer. Wolsey introduced him to the King's service and Henry quickly grew fond of his clever conversation. Sometimes he was invited to the royal apartments for a serious talk. On other occasions, Henry would honour More's Chelsea house with a visit and they would walk and talk together in the garden, by the river.

More's most celebrated book is *Utopia* (The Land of Nowhere) published in 1516. In it he described an ideal state on an imaginary island 'where no man has any property' but 'all men zealously pursue the good of the public'. Utopians fought no wars and built no prisons; criminals were made to do useful work and were not tortured or executed. In his book, More condemned many of the evils of his day, such as war, religious intolerance and enclosures in the countryside. Governments, he thought, 'are a conspiracy of the rich who . . . only pursue their private ends'. Far better to live in his Utopia where 'no man is poor, none in necessity, and though no man has anything, yet they are all rich; for what can make a man so rich as to lead a serene and cheerful life . . .?' Yet his own 'never-never' land was sometimes dull and inhuman. Both sexes wore the same clothes, incurably sick people were killed off and everyone had to attend lectures before breakfast.

The most notable foreign scholar to come to England was Desiderius Erasmus (1466–1536), a Dutchman who gave lectures on Greek at Cambridge. Erasmus criticised the follies he saw around him, particularly the ways of the Church, with its luxury-loving popes and cardinals, its monks who were merely 'impudent pretenders', and its priests who often cared more for church ceremonies than Christian beliefs. 'You honour the bones of St Paul hidden in a shrine,' he wrote, 'but you do not honour the mind of St Paul hidden in his writings.' Such remarks pleased the German protestants who had rebelled against the Pope's Church (1517), and they often used Erasmus's fine Latin translation of the New Testament. For all his criticisms, however, Erasmus wanted the Church improved, not destroyed. Because of this he never became a protestant and condemned Martin Luther's revolt against the Pope (see Chapter 7).

Henry was also shocked by Luther's actions which roused all his hatred of heresy (disbelief in the Church's teaching). With the help

Thomas More—'the man for all seasons'

of Thomas More and others, the king wrote a book condemning Luther. A copy was sent to Rome in 1521 and the Pope was told that Henry would like the title 'Defensor Fidei' (Defender of the Faith) as a reward. Leo X agreed, so 'FID DEF' has been engraved on most British coins ever since. In spite of such titles, the affair soon became less dignified. Luther called Henry a liar, claiming he had not written the book himself. Henry reproached the Electors of Saxony for protecting 'a wretched monk who dared to throw filth in his face'.

More about Henry VIII
Books
R. K. Battson, *Modelling Tudor Ships* (Model and Allied Publishers)
R. Bolt, *A Man for all Seasons* (play: Heinemann)
G. A. R. Callender and F. H. Hinsley, *The Naval Side of British History* (Christophers)
Cardinal Wolsey (Cape: Jackdaw)
M. Checksfield, *Portraits of Renaissance Life and Thought* (Longman)
F. Hackett, *Henry VIII* (Cape)
R. D. Jones, *Erasmus and Luther* (Oxford University Press)
A. P. G. Macdonald and I. L. MacDougall, *British Battles* (Macmillan)
A. F. Pollard, *Henry VIII* (Longman)
Sir Thomas More (Cape: Jackdaw)
Tudor England (Longman Project Kit)

Visual aids
Henry VIII (Visual Publications)
Henry VIII (Common Ground)
'A Man for All Seasons' *(filmstrip based on Bolt's play)* (Educational Productions)
Erasmus *(film)* (Nederlande Onderwijs)
Revival of Learning *(film)* (Coronet)

Visits
Tower of London
Hampton Court Palace
St George's Chapel, Windsor
Framlingham Castle and Church, Suffolk, contains tombs and relics connected with the Norfolk family and the victor of Flodden.

To write and find out
1 Write your own *Utopia*, that is, an essay explaining how you would improve the world you live in.
2 Try and see the film, or a stage performance of, Robert Bolt's *A Man for All Seasons* which tells the story of Henry VIII's relationship with Sir Thomas More.
3 Write an account of the battle of Flodden, either as an English or Scottish soldier. At what battle nearly two hundred years earlier were the Scots victorious?
4 Wolsey founded 'Cardinal College', Oxford. What is it called today?

7   'On this I take my stand'
The Reformation   1517-1554

Martin Luther was a teacher of religion at Wittenberg University in Germany. In October 1517 he pinned a notice on the door of Wittenberg Castle, protesting at the sale of indulgences (pardons) in the town by Johann Tetzel, a Dominican friar. Indulgences were the Church's way of reducing a penance (punishment) given for breaking one of its rules. Originally they were granted to men who went on a crusade. By the sixteenth-century such pardons could be bought for both living and dead sinners.

Martin Luther

In this case a German prince had been appointed Archbishop of Mainz on condition he paid the Pope a large sum of money. To collect this sum he was given permission to sell indulgences providing he gave half his profits to help build St Peter's Church in Rome. Luther disliked people 'buying' forgiveness. 'If Christ . . . says "Do penance"', he wrote, 'he wants the entire life of the pious to be one penance.' Years ago, he remarked, crusaders had risked their lives for an indulgence. Now Christians lost only their money, and of course, the poor were at a disadvantage.

Luther hoped his protest would right a wrong. He thought the Pope would disapprove of an impudent friar who had told ordinary folk, 'As soon as the gold in basin rings, Right then the soul to Heaven springs'. What he probably did not expect to start was a religious revolution.

Luther the monk

Martin Luther (1483–1546) was born at Eisleben, Germany, the son of a copper miner. When young he had shown no particular interest in entering the Church. At university he lived a gay life, had many friends and played musical instruments. Then, at the age of twenty-three, a strange experience made him change. Walking in the country one day he was caught in a violent storm. Out of a dark sky, lightning struck close enough to knock him down. Luther, who had always believed in devils and witches, took this as a sign from God.

Soon afterwards he became an Augustinian monk. 'Encircled by the milling forces of the terror and fear of death,' he wrote, 'I made vows (promises).' Probably this was not quite as sudden as it sounds. Certain events—the sight of a plague-ridden village, the death of a friend—had already caused him to think seriously about the purpose of life. Nevertheless, it was on that stormy afternoon a decision was made which later caused a far greater storm in Germany.

Luther took his new career very seriously. He studied hard, spent hours at prayer and went without food for days on end. 'If ever a monk got to Heaven by monkery, I would have got there too . . . if it had gone on much longer I would simply have martyred myself to death,' he said later. Unfortunately, such 'spiritual exercises', as they were called, did not satisfy the young man. Doubts about his faith continued to torment him. In 1510 Luther visited the Pope's court in Rome and saw the riches and wickedness of men who claimed to serve God. 'If Christ had been poor, why was the Pope so rich?' he wondered.

Such experiences made him question the Church's teachings. Was it possible to obtain salvation (eternal life) by being good, or was each person doomed or saved regardless of how they lived? Did salvation come through baptism, fasts, pilgrimages and regular attendance at Mass, as the Church maintained? If not, was there another way in which a sinful man could be forgiven by God?

The head of the priory where Luther lived tried to help. On his recommendation the monk became a teacher of the Bible at Wittenberg University. As Luther studied the New Testament his problems began to be solved. In the writings of St Paul he made contact with another questioning mind. St Paul, too, had been critical of the Church in his day. His Epistles (letters) often criticised practices he considered were against Christ's teaching. Gradually most of Luther's difficulties passed away. Only the problem of God's mercy remained. In St Paul's letter to the Romans it stated that Christ had come to give 'justice' to the world. In Luther's opinion this word suggested punishment, not forgiveness.

One day, sitting at his desk in the monastery, Luther realised that a judge pardons as well as punishes. St Paul's words could mean that God would show mercy after all! This comforting thought, added to St Paul's belief that 'The righteous shall live by faith', formed the basis of Luther's later teaching. God, he claimed, would pardon all who believed in Christ, no matter how many kind deeds they did, or masses they attended. 'Good works will never make a good man, but a good man does good works; bad works will never make a bad man, but a bad man does bad works,' he explained. A man's only hope was to have faith. This alone could lead to salvation.

It seemed simple but it was the reason why Joan of Arc and Savonarola had been burned. They too, had bypassed the Church on their way to God!

Luther the rebel

All might have been well for the Church had Luther's protest been ignored. But Tetzel was a Dominican friar and Luther was an Augustinian. The rivalry between the two brotherhoods caused many Dominicans to rush to Tetzel's defence. Their fierce attacks, and Tetzel's demand that Luther should be burned, revived all the reformer's hatred of what he had seen in Rome. Gladly he took up the challenge against those who defended such wealth and luxury. Tetzel, he remarked, would do better to burn geese for he knew more about them than he did about religion! Both in public debate and in print Luther clashed head on with his enemies. Soon his books were being read all over Germany. The Reformation, like the Renaissance, might never have happened without printing.

In the heat of battle Luther attacked more than indulgences. The Church taught that in the Mass (modelled on Christ's last supper with his disciples) the bread and wine (eucharist) actually turned into the body and blood of Christ (transubstantiation). Luther refused to believe this, although he thought Christ's spirit was present during the service. This denial, which made Luther liable to the death penalty, was followed by further revolutionary statements. The Church, according to Luther, needed neither Pope nor clergy. Every man of true faith was in a way his own priest. Monasteries should be closed and vicars allowed to marry. In addition, congregations should take more part in services, singing hymns instead of listening to the chanting of the monks. This proved too much for Pope Leo X who gave Luther sixty days to change his views. If he failed to do so he was to be excommunicated.

Quite soon the matter became a political as well as a religious quarrel. Throughout Germany Luther was treated as a national hero. One Catholic agent reported to the Pope: 'Nine tenths of Germany are crying "Luther" and the other tenth are at least crying "Death to to the Roman Court".' As Holy Roman Emperor, Charles V felt he must do something. He ordered Luther to meet him at a town called Worms. The reformer came guarded by German knights. He boldly refused to change his mind, saying of his beliefs: 'On this I take my stand. I can do no other. God help me. Amen.'

Charles was in a difficult position. Besides being Emperor, he was King of Spain and ruler of lands in Italy and Holland. Although he disliked Italian Popes as much as any prince, he recruited most of his soldiers and raised much of his money from Catholic states outside Germany. Thus he could hardly lead a 'German' religious revolt. He, too, condemned Luther. With the two greatest European rulers against him, the rebellious monk should have suffered the fate of Savonarola. But Luther was in Germany, not Italy. Frederick, the Elector of Saxony, disliked both Pope and Emperor. He gave the rebel his protection, hiding him in Wartburg Castle where he took the name of 'Knight George'. It was the Pope's Bull (decree) against Luther which was burned, not Luther himself. The break with Rome was complete.

The Pope's Church

Why was Luther's protest so effective? Why did the Reformation happen in his time and not earlier?

The Papacy (Pope's court) was the richest monarchy in Europe. Renaissance Popes lived like princes, spending freely and employing great artists to beautify their cathedrals and palaces. Cardinals and archbishops lived in similar luxury. To pay for such grandeur, large sums of money were required. Taxes on each family, called Peter's Pence, were collected yearly in all Christian countries. Exemptions from a particular Church law (dispensations) were sold as well as indulgences. Church officials were also allowed to buy their positions. We have already seen how the Archbishop of Mainz was appointed.

In the same year as Luther's protest, Pope Leo sold no less than 2,000 jobs.

This was not the only scandal. Bones of saints, pieces of Christ's Cross and other sacred objects were put up for sale. Such relics were often fakes. One man reckoned that all the wood sold as part of the True Cross of Christ would make a large boat! Wittenberg church alone housed thirty-three pieces as well as remains of the 'holy cradle'. 'The Lord desireth not the death of a sinner but rather that he shall pay and live,' joked one rich fifteenth-century priest. Merchants, peasants, even poor clergymen, resented such money-grabbing.

If dislike of the Papacy was common long before Luther's time, so was heresy. In England, John Wycliffe (1320–84) had already disputed the Pope's leadership. Even if he was head of the Church, Wycliffe argued, he was only second in command to Christ. Wycliffe's followers, called the Lollards (mutterers or mumblers) by their opponents, did not believe in transubstantiation and disobeyed Church commands by translating the Bible into their own language.

Wycliffe was allowed to die in peace. His less fortunate followers were persecuted and his own body was dug up and thrown in a river. On the continent John Huss of Bohemia was burned in 1415 for preaching Lollardry. His disciples, the Hussites or Moravian Brethren, remained strong in what is now Czechoslovakia, where they fought a successful war against Catholic armies. High in the Alps, the Waldenses (followers of Peter Waldo), were less warlike, but they did not believe in transubstantiation and disliked the worship of saints. All these movements had sown the seeds of doubt long

St Peter's Church, Rome. The method used to collect money for its building sparked off the quarrel between Luther and Tetzel

before the sixteenth century.

Even so, it was politics rather than religion which sparked off the Reformation. Ever since the Middle Ages monarchs and princes had quarrelled with the Papacy. All Popes claimed to be above kings, whilst many monarchs regarded the Pope as an interfering foreigner. In medieval England, Kings Henry I, Henry II and John had defied the Church at various times. In Germany the Emperor Frederick II had a long quarrel with the Church in the thirteenth century. By 1517 countries with strong monarchies, France, Spain and England for example, did not always let the Pope have his own way. Divided Germany with its small dukedoms found resistance more difficult.

As a result, the Germans suffered more than most from Papal interference. Every year the Imperial German Diet (parliament) received thousands of complaints about the Church from princes, knights, merchants and peasants. Furthermore, Germany was a dis-ordered country, troubled by petty wars. Luther had thrown his match into a smouldering fire.

Wars of religion

Luther was concerned with saving souls, not changing govern-ments. Indeed, he thought it a sin for a subject to disobey his prince. Unfortunately, his own disobedience had set a bad example.

Among the thousands who now became Protestants, were some more extreme than their leader. Wittenberg Town Council abolished Mass altogether and allowed mobs to damage churches and attack priests. Religious fanatics roamed Germany, many claiming to be in personal contact with Christ. The Anabaptists (believers in adult baptism) were particularly extreme. Announcing that a true Christian could not sin, whatever he did, they predicted that Christ would soon return to earth. One Anabaptist, Thomas Müntzer (1490–1525) went further and taught that only the poor would be saved. Discontented peasants, often more angry about high prices, lower wages and new laws than religious matters, joined him. Soon rebel armies were on the march in Germany, killing the rich and destroying their homes.

The Emperor Charles formed a league of German princes to fight the peasants. At Frankenhausen (1525) Müntzer's army was defeated and he was beheaded. Other Anabaptist groups, led by a certain John of Leyden, defended the town of Münster for nearly a year against Catholic troops. During the siege John went mad, announced he was King of the Earth and married over a dozen wives. When the town fell in 1535 nearly all the inhabitants were slaughtered and John was tortured to death with red hot tongs. Luther may not have approved of such a horrible revenge. Yet he had written a book in which he called rebellious peasants 'mad dogs' and advised the authorities to 'knock down, strangle and stab' them.

It was not only poor men or cranks who rebelled. Princes who disliked the Pope's interference, or fancied seizing Church property in their lands, began to consider founding their own protestant church. Over the years the idea of a 'national' church, a German church for the Germans, grew up. Something Luther disliked—

government control of the Church—developed from the Reformation.

Luther died in February 1546 just as Charles V was going to war with these Protestant princes. But warfare could not destroy such a powerful movement. By the Peace of Augsburg (1555) the two sides agreed that each state must follow the religion of its ruler. Thus for the first time in Christian history a man's religion was decided by his prince, not the Pope. Luther's burning faith had helped create new, enthusiastic churches. In doing so it had destroyed the idea of a united Christian Europe. A religious 'iron curtain' now divided the continent.

Zwingli and Calvin

Luther was not the only reformer to found a new church at this time. Ulrich Zwingli (1484–1531), a Swiss soldier, taught that Christ was not present in the Mass because he could not be on earth and in heaven at the same time. This had so horrified Luther that it prevented any chance of an alliance between their followers. Some Swiss cantons (provinces) accepted this teaching; others remained Catholic. Zwingli himself was killed in a war between the two sides and Switzerland, like Germany, became a divided land over religion. Another reformer, Martin Bucer, preached that each man and woman is doomed or saved from birth (predestination). A similar idea was taught by John Calvin, the most influential reformer apart from Luther.

Calvin was a French lawyer and priest who settled in Geneva, Switzerland in 1541. Here he wrote, *Institutes of Christian Religion*. In this he explained his views on church teaching and organisation. Perhaps because of his legal training, Calvin took more interest in church discipline than Luther. He suggested that a 'true' church should consist of preachers, teachers, elders and deacons, all elected by their congregations. A governing committee, the Consistory of clergy and laymen, and 'a Venerable Company of Pastors' were to pass laws and see they were obeyed.

At Geneva Calvin persuaded the Town Council to put his ideas into practice. Serious attempts were made to create a model religious community. The city was split into parishes whose councils were responsible for worship, education and the care of the poor. Schools were set up, the sick looked after and the streets cleaned regularly. Profiteering by shopkeepers was discouraged. Calvin even tried to devise an efficient sewage system.

In some ways the reformer's rule was less pleasant. Consistory members patrolled the streets so that 'their eyes might be on the people'. Dancing and games were forbidden; hotels and inns were closed for a time. Theatres showed only religious plays. Laughing was frowned upon and non-Christian first names were condemned. Those who did wrong were tried by the Consistory each week. Punishments varied from fines and penances to whipping and death. A girl who put irreligious words to a psalm tune was beaten. An important town councillor who dared to describe Calvin as a bad man was made to walk through the streets dressed only in a shirt and carrying a candle. A boy who struck his parents was beheaded.

How his enemies saw him. A nasty caricature of John Calvin by a Catholic artist. The cheek is a boiled chicken's leg, the nose a plucked pullet and the mouth and chin pieces of dead fish

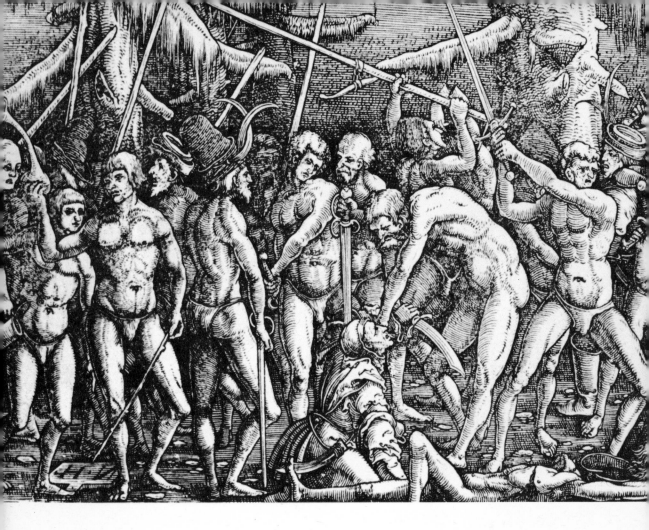

And when Michael Servetus, a reformer with different views from Calvin, came to the town he was arrested and burned.

On the other hand, Calvinism brought faith, spiritual happiness and education to millions of Christians as it spread to Switzerland, Holland, Scotland, parts of France and Germany. Calvinists often showed more self discipline than Luther's wild peasants and unruly knights, probably because they were as well organised as their Catholic enemies. If Luther had lit the fire, Calvin taught men how to control it.

A massacre during the German Peasants' Revolt, 1525

More about the Reformation
Books

J. Atkinson, *Martin Luther and the Birth of Protestantism* (Penguin)

L. W. Cowie, *The Reformation* (Hart-Davis), available with four tapes

C. J. Davey, *The Monk Who Shook the World: Martin Luther* (Lutterworth: Faith and Fame series)

R. D. Jones, *Erasmus and Luther* (Oxford University Press)

Martin Luther (Cape: Jackdaw)

J. S. Millward, *Portraits and Documents of the Sixteenth Century* (Hutchinson)
G. Mosse, *The Reformation* (Holt)

Visual aids
Reformation and Counter-Reformation (Visual Publications)
The Reformation (Common Ground)

To write and find out
1 Draw a Reformation 'tree', showing how Protestant 'branches' broke away from the Catholic 'trunk'. Make a list of the various Christian sects and churches in Britain today.
2 Find out more about the Catholic Church. Pamphlets issued by the Catholic Truth Society explain its organisation and beliefs in simple terms.
3 Find out more about John Wycliffe. See 'The Middle Ages' by R. J. Cootes in this series.
4 Imagine you are a citizen of Geneva in the time of Calvin. Write a letter to a friend outside the town explaining what life is like.

It was a tense occasion despite all the outward show. French and English soldiers were more used to meeting each other in battle. They were quick to take offence or to laugh at one another. The two young monarchs were proud and jealous. At their first meeting Francis, 'merry of cheer, brown coloured, great eyes', embraced Henry. On another occasion, when Henry playfully put his hand on Francis's neck and said, 'Come you shall wrestle with me', the French King threw him to the ground. Several courtiers were needed to hold Henry back!

Talk of peace between the two countries was as temporary as the pavilions and tents. No sooner had the meeting ended than Henry met Emperor Charles V, near Gravelines (France). At this conference, first moves were made towards signing a treaty making Henry and Charles allies against France (1522). The emperor also promised to marry Henry's daughter, Mary.

Pavia

Henry's second French war was unpopular with rich and poor alike. Some peasants summed up the general feeling when they remarked that, in spite of all the fighting and expense, Henry VIII 'hath not one foot of land more in France than his most noble father had'. As a result England took hardly any part in the dramatic events which followed in Europe.

Francis invaded Italy once again but at Pavia (February 1525) suffered a disastrous defeat. Caught between the main imperial army and troops attacking from Pavia itself, the French fought well until their King foolishly led a charge in front of his own artillery. With the French guns forced to stop firing, enemy squadrons were able to wipe out the French cavalry. Francis himself was dragged from his horse and taken prisoner.

Such a victory made Charles feel he was strong enough to do without England. He dropped the idea of marrying Mary and ignored Wolsey's hint that Henry might now be given the vacant French throne. An angry Cardinal Wolsey retaliated by offering France peace in return for an increased pension for Henry. In May 1526 the Holy League of Cognac (France, Florence, Venice and the Papacy) was formed against the Emperor with Henry as its 'protector'. Francis, meanwhile, gave up all his claims to Italy in order to obtain his release (Treaty of Madrid).

Charles's triumph did not last long for he was beset by numerous problems. Francis returned home determined to renew the war. In Germany the Protestant revolt grew worse every day, and the Catholics looked to the Emperor to crush it. In the east a Turkish army slaughtered the Hungarians at Mohacs (1526) and threatened Vienna—a city within the Holy Roman Empire. Even Charles's own troops mutinied and looted Rome for several days (the Sack of Rome, 1527). It was clear Charles could not fight all his enemies at once. Next year, even though Francis had again been beaten in Italy, Charles gave him fair terms (Peace of Cambrai).

The English had already rioted at the thought of a war with Spain which would ruin the cloth trade. Wolsey, not the king, was blamed, and peasants in Kent suggested pushing him out to sea in a boat full of holes. Actually, the cardinal was about to 'sink' for a different reason.

The royal divorce

For some time Henry had been thinking of taking a new wife. He wanted a son to rule after his death, yet of Catherine's seven children only a daughter, Mary, had lived. By 1527 it was obvious that Catherine was past child-bearing age and Henry was asking himself whether he was being punished for having broken Church law.

This problem—the 'King's Great Matter'—was made more urgent by Henry's love for Anne Boleyn. Anne came from a wealthy merchant family, related to the Dukes of Norfolk. Returning from France to the English court, her black hair and eyes, pale face and fascinating ways soon attracted the King. The depth of his feelings are revealed in letters which still exist. In one, Anne is described as 'the woman

The queen Henry rejected —Catherine of Aragon

Armour made for
Henry VIII in 1540

in the world I value most'. In another Henry writes of himself as
'having been for a whole year struck with the dart of love'. It was a love
that had important consequences for England.

Wolsey had often boasted of his influence with the Pope. The
King now expected him to prove it by persuading Clement VII to
declare his marriage unlawful. The cardinal stood to lose either way.
If he failed he would be ruined. If he succeeded a member of the
family which hated him most would become queen. In fact he stood
no chance of success. Since the Sack of Rome, Pope Clement had
been the prisoner of Charles V, Catherine's nephew. Charles saw the
'divorce' as nothing but a plot against his family. There was no
doubt he would never allow the Pope to grant it. Only a French
victory in Italy could free Clement, and this became impossible after
Francis made peace.

The Pope decided to play for time by sending Cardinal Campeggio
to England to try the case. Knowing his mission was doomed from
the start, Campeggio travelled as slowly as possible. When he did
arrive he suggested Catherine should enter a convent but she refused.
At Blackfriars, before the King, Wolsey and Campeggio, the Queen
denied that she had ever had intercourse with Arthur and claimed
therefore that she was the King's true wife because her first marriage
was 'incomplete'. She then ignored the court and walked out,
cheered by her ladies-in-waiting.

Nothing could save Wolsey after that, and his enemies gathered
for the kill. He was accused of breaking the law of *Praemunire* (1392)
which made it illegal for a priest to bring papal bulls (orders) into
England and with them use authority which rightfully belonged to the
King. Wolsey could hardly have failed to break this law for he was
papal legate and previously Henry had never worried about it.
Now, there was nothing the proud Cardinal could do except beg
forgiveness. At first he was dismissed from most of his offices,
although he remained Archbishop of York. It is possible this is the
worst that would have happened to him had he not written to the
Pope urging him to persuade the King not to marry Anne. When news
of this interference leaked out the King ordered him to be arrested
and sent to the Tower.

This time the executioner was cheated. Arriving at Leicester Abbey
on his journey south, Wolsey was too ill to ride his mule. 'Father
Abbot', he told his host, 'I am come to leave my bones among you.'
Two days later he was dead.

'The King's Great Matter'

Wolsey had glowed brightly, like a shooting star, and then disappeared. Little was left to remind men of his years of power.
Certain law reforms, a palace or two, a few colleges and schools
recalled the good he had done. Otherwise there remained only the
bad example of his pride, wealth and dishonesty. Two men, Cranmer
and Cromwell, arose to wield his power over Church and Parliament.

Thomas Cranmer (1489–1556), a Cambridge scholar and priest,
first came to Henry's notice when he suggested that the universities

should be asked their opinion regarding the lawfulness of the King's marriage. Henry liked the idea and Cranmer was made a royal chaplain and attached to the household of Anne Boleyn's father. He was also sent to the continent to visit foreign universities. Here he met several protestant princes, as well as pleading personally with the Pope. Apart from falling in love and secretly marrying, Cranmer gained little from his travels, since some foreign professors agreed with Henry and some did not. Yet on his return he was made Archbishop of Canterbury (1533). Such a sudden rise to power and influence was not of Cranmer's choosing. Unlike Wolsey, he was a timid, unambitious man who preferred study to politics.

Meanwhile the King's Great Matter had ceased to be a subject for learned discussion since Anne was pregnant by Henry. In January 1533 the two lovers were secretly married so that if a son was born he would be heir to the throne. Three months later Cranmer held a court at Dunstable, which declared that Catherine had never been Henry's wife. The unfortunate lady retired to Kimbolton Castle, Huntingdonshire, where she died in 1536. Anne Boleyn was crowned queen in Westminster Abbey at Whitsun 1533. Few English people liked her for Catherine had been very popular. Of the ceremony, an eyewitness wrote: 'All the world was astonished, not knowing whether to laugh or cry.' On 7 September the new Queen gave birth to a daughter, the future Queen Elizabeth I.

Cranmer had given the King his 'divorce'. Thomas Cromwell (1485–1540) helped the King attack the Church he had already defied. Cromwell was a tough man of the world, a 'jack of all trades' who had been at various times a soldier, banker, businessman and lawyer. During his youth he had lived in Europe where he had seen the 'Machiavellian' ways of its rulers. Back in England his path to power had been laid by Wolsey, whom he served as secretary. Cold, clever and ruthless, no more suitable person could have been found to shape the 'new' England which began with the summoning of the Reformation Parliament in 1529.

The King wanted three things from his members of parliament. First, the people's help in his quarrel with the Pope. Second, the support of the English clergy. Third, he hoped by his actions to persuade or bully the Pope into recognising his marriage. The last was impossible for Clement failed to free himself from the Emperor's influence. The first two were achieved partly because England hated a foreign Pope and also because of the brilliant way Cromwell handled Parliament.

The English clergy soon surrendered. Henry discovered, as if for the first time, that priests at their consecration (appointment) 'make an oath to the Pope, clean contrary to the oath they make us (the King), so that they seem his subjects, not ours'. Fearing they would be charged with *Praemunire*, they humbly begged Henry's pardon and were fined £118,000 altogether. At the same time, Parliament abolished papal taxes in England (Act of Annates) and agreed that Henry was 'Supreme Head of the Church of England' (Act of Supremacy 1534). Under the new system, English men were ordered

Anne Boleyn, described by Henry VIII as 'the Woman in the world I value most'

to call the Pope, the 'Bishop of Rome'. Government officials, in-cluding Sir Thomas More, who still regarded the Pope as Head of the English Church, were executed.

Thomas More had once said of Henry, 'if my head would win him a castle in France, it should not fail to go'. In the end it was chopped of for the 'wrong' beliefs!

The end of the monasteries

The King now switched his attack from priests to monks. At that time monasteries owned one quarter of England's land, and their annual income was greater than the royal revenue. Since Henry needed money in case his quarrel with the Pope led to foreign wars or rebellions at home, such wealth was tempting. Cromwell had helped Wolsey to destroy several small monasteries so that their money could be used to found colleges at Ipswich and Oxford. Possibly because of this experience, he suggested closing all of them.

There was no doubt monastic reform would please many English-men. For centuries monks had been unpopular. Clergymen often disapproved of their way of life. Bishops grumbled that they had no power over them. Ordinary folk complained that they lived unholy lives. Scandals involving monks were enlarged and exaggerated by their enemies. Although it was true that unsuitable young men were sometimes forced or persuaded to become monks, it was forgotten that the majority lived good lives.

In January 1535 Cromwell was made 'Vicar General' of Henry's new Church of England. He at once sent teams of lawyers on 'visitations' to monasteries. The questions asked were not unusual:
Was divine service properly conducted at correct times?
How many attended?
Who was exempt?
Did women visit the monastery by backways or otherwise?
Were meals over-rich?
Did the brothers dress extravagantly?
The difference was that this time the questioners were interested in closure, not reform.

Bad reports were not long in arriving. Monks with several wives

One of the monasteries closed by Cromwell—the ruined Fountains Abbey in Yorkshire

and six or seven children, monks who stole church silver, and even one who made profits out of piracy were discovered. Large numbers of lazy 'hangers-on'—stewards, bailiffs, ploughmen—filled many monasteries; certain lords used monasteries as free 'hotels' for months on end. Good works such as teaching, healing, copying books and farming, were ignored. The lawyers had found what Cromwell wanted. A parliament which pretended to be surprised quickly ordered 270 smaller monasteries to be shut. Then Henry and his ruthless minister waited to see how Englishmen would react.

The Pilgrimage of Grace

Most of England stayed quiet, although there was a small rising in Lincolnshire which was quickly suppressed. In Catholic Yorkshire, however, where fifty-three religious houses had been closed, an army of discontented 'pilgrims' assembled, led by Robert Aske. Calling themselves the 'Pilgrimage of Grace for the Commonwealth' and marching with a banner showing Christ on the Cross, they captured York (October 1536). There might have been a serious battle with the royal army had it not been a rainy autumn in which 'each side could not come at the other' across the flooded countryside. The King's commander, the Duke of Norfolk, was short of men. He decided to play a waiting game and invited the rebel leaders to see the King in London.

Henry hid his rage and said he would consider the Pilgrims' demands. But no sooner had Aske disbanded his forces than the King broke his promise. A number of rebels retaliated by attempting to take Hull and Scarborough. They failed and were captured. Now the rebels saw a different side of their King. Henry ordered, 'dreadful execution to be done upon a good number . . . by hanging them up in trees as by quartering them'. Aske was hanged in chains at York. Over 200 others, including the Abbots of some Yorkshire monasteries, were also executed. The most serious rebellion of the reign was over.

The failure of the Pilgrimage of Grace showed once more the power of the Tudor monarchy. It also signalled the closure of the larger monasteries (1537–39). Most abbots wisely became bishops or retired with pensions. Those at Reading and Glastonbury defied the king so they were hanged. All movable monastic property was taken by the Royal Exchequer. Cattle were sold and abbey servants sacked with half a years' wages. Land was rented or bought by rich farmers. At Canterbury Thomas Becket's shrine was destroyed. Two large cases of jewels and twenty-four waggons loaded with treasure were taken away by the king's officers. An important part of English life since the Middle Ages disappeared almost overnight.

Although the monasteries had gone, Henry's Parliament in 1539 passed the Statute of the Six Articles which maintained Catholic beliefs and worship. So severe were the punishments laid down for any who broke these articles that Protestants called this Act the 'whip with six strings'. England was still really a Catholic country but her Pope was a Tudor.

Jane Seymour, Henry's favourite wife, who gave him his only son

Wives and wars

Henry had courted Anne Boleyn for six years. His marriage to her lasted only three. The new Queen was arrogant and domineering. She quarrelled with Henry as well as disappointing him again by giving birth to a dead boy (January 1536). Cromwell, who detested her, managed to persuade the King she had been unfaithful. Following a fake trial, Anne was beheaded (May 1536). A week after a French swordsman had cut off Anne's head, Henry married Jane Seymour, a childhood friend. Jane was Henry's favourite wife. She gave him a boy, Edward (October 1537) only to die soon afterwards. Henry was heartbroken. 'Divine providence', he wrote to the French King, 'hath mingled my joy with the bitterness of death.'

Two years later Cromwell arranged for the lonely King to marry Anne, daughter of the Protestant Duke of Cleves in Germany. Whether Henry really called her a 'Flanders mare' when he first saw her is doubtful but he certainly found her unattractive and divorced her soon afterwards. He also blamed Cromwell for the affair and had him beheaded in 1540 for 'encouraging heresy'. So ended the career of the King's cleverest minister. Long before his reign ended Henry regretted this particular execution for it deprived him of much expert advice.

The King's fifth wife was Katherine Howard. Unfortunately, his intense love for this girl disappeared when he discovered she had been unfaithful. Katherine suffered the same fate as her cousin, Anne Boleyn, and several of her lovers were slaughtered too (1542). Eighteen months after her execution, Henry married his sixth and last wife, Katherine Parr. She was destined to outlive the King.

Apart from unhappy marriages, the king's last years were spent in wars with Scotland and France which plunged England deeper into debt. The Scots were defeated at Solway Moss in 1542. Their King, James V, died soon afterwards, leaving the throne to his baby daughter, Mary. In 1544 an army led by the Earl of Hertford (Jane Seymour's brother, later Duke of Somerset) raided Scotland, burning Edinburgh and Leith. Meanwhile Henry himself invaded France in alliance with the Emperor. Boulogne was battered by sixty-pounder guns and forced to surrender. Then events followed a familiar pattern. Charles V concluded a separate peace with France, thus leaving England to fight alone.

Henry returned home immediately for he feared this meant an invasion of England. The people rallied loyally, supplying both men and money. Troops marched from all over the southern counties once the beacon lights had flickered their warning from hill to hill. The old King stationed himself bravely at Southsea where a landing was expected. In fact, the matter was decided at sea in confused battles off Southsea, Seaford and Shoreham. Henry hoped to see his new warships destroy the enemy as he watched from the beach. He did see the *Great Harry* emerge undamaged from a fierce attack by galleys but the *Mary Rose* sank in a few minutes. It was left to small English rowboats, armed with two or three guns, to defeat the French who were short of supplies and afflicted by disease.

Anne of Cleves, the German princess whom Henry found unattractive

Katherine Howard, Henry's fifth wife and the second to be executed for unfaithfulness

By the time the war ended there was little to remind those who met Henry of his athletic youth. Although he still went hunting and hawking he was very fat, with a bad leg which made mounting a horse difficult. As his death approached in the winter of 1546, the dark corridors and candle-lit rooms at Whitehall Palace were the scene of a struggle for power between the Catholic Howard family and the Protestant Seymours. Thanks to Howard plots, the King nearly executed Queen Katherine Parr. She talked herself out of danger and the Howards themselves fell. Surrey, Norfolk's son, was beheaded. Norfolk was due to die on 28 January 1547. He survived because King Henry VIII died early that morning.

When Prince Edward was told his father was dead he clung crying to Princess Elizabeth's skirts. Great, terrifying Harry had been replaced by a nine-year-old boy.

More about Henry VIII's reign

Books
Most of those listed for Chapter 6, also:
Henry VIII (Pitkin Pictorial)
Henry VIII and the Dissolution of the Monasteries (Cape: Jackdaw)
J. Ridley, *Thomas Cranmer* (Oxford University Press)

Katherine Parr, Henry's last wife, who outlived him

Visual aids
Some of those listed for Chapter 6, also:
The Monastery (Common Ground)
Life in Tudor Times (Common Ground)

Visits
As for Chapter 6

To write and find out
1 Write a life of Henry VIII assuming he died in 1529. Make sure you leave out the right events. How different a view of him would result?
2 Collect information about Henry's wives. Numerous reproductions of their portraits are available and an interesting illustrated booklet can be compiled.
3 There are many buildings and ruins connected with Henry's Dissolution of the Monasteries. Index Publishers of 27/8, Finsbury Square, London E.C.2. produce each year *Historic Houses, Castles and Gardens in Great Britain and Ireland* which contains a complete list. Perhaps there is a ruined abbey in your own district?
4 Conduct an 'investigation' of a Tudor monastery, asking your own (relevant) questions.
5 Imagine you are Henry VIII or Anne Boleyn—whichever is appropriate. Write the other a love letter, showing knowledge of the 'King's Great Matter'.

9 The Boy King
Edward VI 1547-1553

Henry VIII had been cruel, selfish and extravagant. He defied the Pope, forced great changes on England and made the country bankrupt with his wars. He crushed both friends and enemies without pity. No man was a more typical sixteenth-century ruler, caring little for individuals and behaving as God's representative on earth. The great square figure, legs apart, hands on hips, which stares at us from many of his portraits, casts a long shadow over English history.

In spite of his faults, both rich and poor remembered Henry with affection. He gave England the strong government its people desired. The beheadings, burnings and hanging which horrify us today were few compared with those ordered by other European kings. Neither does it seem they were resented by a tough and brutal people. When disorders, plots and rebellions followed his death, most Englishmen were certain they had lost a great king.

The new ruler was slightly small for his age, with fair hair and grey eyes. He was a rather serious boy who understood Greek and Latin well, and kept a diary. Only once is he known to have laughed publicly, although he seems to have enjoyed parties and games. Because of Edward's age, Henry had appointed a Council to rule until he grew up. This was headed by a 'Lord Protector', the Duke of Somerset, Edward's uncle.

Edward VI shown in his gold coronation medal 1547

From the start Somerset faced serious foreign dangers. Henry's old rival, Francis I, had died in March 1547. His successor, Henry II, proved to be just as arrogant and troublesome. Besides demanding the return of Boulogne and Calais he plotted against the English in Scotland and Ireland. Scotland, in particular, became almost an extra province of France with Protestants persecuted and French troops occupying key points in the country. Somerset was a soldier, so he chose a soldier's solution. In the autumn of 1547 he crossed the border into Scotland with 17,000 men.

The Protector found the enemy entrenched at Pinkie, east of Edinburgh. Their right flank was protected by a marsh, their left by the sea, whilst a river lay in front. These advantages were thrown away by the Scots. Forgetting his troops were poorly equipped, their commander decided to cross the river and attack the smaller English forces. In the battle which followed the Scottish ranks were shattered by English cannon-fire. After nearly 6,000 had been killed the survivors fled. When the news of 'Black Saturday' reached the Scots government they sent the young Queen Mary to France in case the English forced her to marry Edward. Somerset placed garrisons in some Scottish castles, distributed large numbers of Protestant Bibles and returned home in triumph.

The Prayer Book rebellion

Even though only nine years' old, the new King was a keen Protestant, ready to argue with grown-ups about religion. Consequently Edward's reign saw the birth of an English Protestant Church.

The new policy took various forms. Henry VIII's 'whip with six strings' (the Six Articles of 1539) was repealed (cancelled). Chantries (foundations which provided money so that masses could be said for the dead) were dissolved and their funds used to found 'Edward VI' grammar schools in various places. Catholic bishops found themselves imprisoned or forced to retire. Reformers like Martin Bucer were allowed to come to England. And in 1549 Cranmer issued a revised Prayer Book written in English instead of Latin. This was not entirely new. Henry VIII had liked to hear English spoken in church. In 1535, for example, he had given permission for Miles Coverdale's English translation of the Bible to be published. Before his death worshippers were used to hearing the Creed, the Ten Commandments and the Lord's Prayer in their own tongue. But in the 1549 Prayer Book no part of the service was in Latin.

Reactions to the new Prayer Book reflected the general confusion caused by the Reformation. Some Catholic priests stuck firmly to the old ways, celebrating the full Latin mass. Protestant clergymen went to the other extreme. Wooden tables were substituted for stone altars in their churches, ornaments and statues removed, wall paintings of saints and Bible stories covered with whitewash. A minority even grumbled because Cranmer's Prayer Book retained the words of the mass for those who wished to believe in transubstantiation.

The moderate majority cared little for such disputes. They were horrified at losing familiar statues, and puzzled when English prayers replaced the Latin ones they had known since childhood. In Devon and Cornwall the new services were described as 'Christmas Games'. Peasants and gentry alike demanded the return of the Latin mass because, they claimed, they could not understand English! What started as a protest movement quickly became a rebellion. An army, which rushed to the West Country, beat the rebels, relieving Exeter after a six week siege (August 1549). In Oxfordshire a smaller rising was crushed easily and the discontented priests who led it were hanged from their own church steeples.

Trouble at Mousehold Heath

Religion was not the only cause of discontent. Throughout Henry VIII's reign enclosure had been widespread, especially on land which had belonged to monasteries. Many landlords did not care how their land was farmed providing it made a profit. For this reason they often preferred sheep-rearing, because of the expanding cloth trade. Flocks of sheep replaced fields of corn throughout Oxfordshire, Buckinghamshire, Northamptonshire and Leicestershire. In other places richer farmers consolidated smallholdings into large estates, or exceeded the number of animals allowed to graze on the village common land. All these changes had the effect of depriving villagers of either home or work.

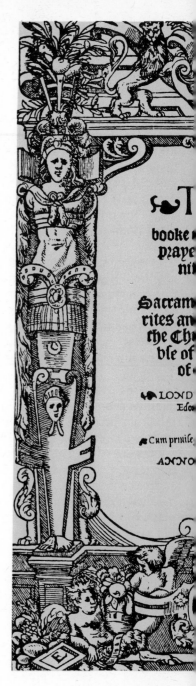

Front page of a book which caused a rebellion —the Protestant Prayer Book of 1549

E

ommion
admi-
n of

and other
nonies of
after the
hurche
nd.

OFFICINA
echurche.

rimendumfolum.

4 9. Menfe

Somerset had personal experience of this problem for he had bought large estates during the previous twenty years. Following the example of the two previous kings, however, he issued orders forbidding further enclosures as well as putting a tax on sheep. With these acts in mind, certain Norfolk peasants probably thought Somerset would support them when they began breaking the fences of unpopular landlords (August 1549). Led by Robert Ket, the movement grew rapidly until nearly 12,000 labourers gathered on Mousehold Heath, near Norwich. It was a sit-down strike rather than a rebellion, with law and order kept by Ket and his assistants.

The sympathetic Protector might have agreed to Ket's demands. Unfortunately, John Dudley, Earl of Warwick (later Duke of Northumberland) persuaded the Council to declare the gathering a rebellion. At that moment 1,500 foreign soldiers had arrived in England, ready for garrison duty in Scotland. Warwick led these professionals to the camp, and when Ket's men refused pardon because they said they were not rebels, he attacked, and killed many of them. Ket himself was hanged at Norwich castle.

Somerset was already unpopular because he had been forced to execute his brother, Thomas Seymour, for plotting to marry the fifteen-year-old Princess Elizabeth. The upheavals in Norfolk and Devon led to his fall. Warwick was a strong-willed, unprincipled man. He convinced his fellow councillors that neither rebellion would have happened had he been Protector. Somerset was promised his life if he resigned, but later he was beheaded on a false charge of conspiracy (January 1552).

Edward had never really liked his uncle; the serious-minded soldier lectured him too much. He showed no sorrow when he died, merely recording in his diary: 'The Duke of Somerset had his head cut off upon Tower Hill between eight and nine o'clock in the morning.' Many of his people were not so indifferent. They called Somerset 'the Good Duke'; some had dared shout 'God save him' as he was taken to the Tower. Certainly Northumberland, who flattered the boy King, was to prove a far more dishonest 'Protector'.

Good cloth and bad coins

Northumberland was as clever as he was cruel. In spite of having used Catholic lords to help overthrow Somerset, he soon decided that the best way to stay in power was to please the King with further doses of Protestantism. For this reason a revised Prayer Book was issued in 1552. This moved much further towards a Protestant Church. The Mass was left out altogether and replaced by a communion service which was merely an 'act of remembrance' of the Last Supper. Private confession to a priest was replaced by a general confession spoken during the service. The beautiful language of this Prayer Book was that of Cranmer, who also helped to prepare Forty-two Articles of belief for English Protestants.

Genuine reformers were pleased. One called the unholy Northumberland a 'faithful and intrepid soldier of Christ'. Actually in foreign affairs the new Protector did nothing for their cause. He

THE ẜENDVR
WONDE'ETH
OF TIE FOR
LORD: EVER

ẜVPERẜTICION

ALL FLESHE
IS GRASSE

FEYNED
HOLINE

Henry VIII (the figure in the bed) bestows the crown upon his son Edward VI to the dismay of the Po[pe]

ended the war with Catholic France, selling Boulogne to the French King. He also withdrew the English troops from Scotland. This left the Scottish Catholics dominant once more. They promptly married their young Queen, Mary, to the French Dauphin (heir to the throne). England's weakness was obvious and only Henry II's decision to fight the Emperor left the country in peace.

Northumberland's weak foreign policy was due partly to difficulties

A silver testoon minted at the end of Henry's reign. These coins contained only one third silver and were called 'copper noses' because of their dark colouring

at home. England at this time was beginning to pay the price of Henry VIII's mistakes, as rising prices and unemployment caused economic distress. Between 1542 and 1547 Henry VIII had turned £400,000-worth of silver coins into £526,000, simply by putting a proportion of ordinary metal in each one. By this debasement of the coinage he made a profit. The people, used to a coin worth exactly its face value in silver or gold, remarked sadly that the new red-coloured coins were 'blushing with shame'.

There were good reasons to be worried. Foreign merchants reacted to the debasement by lowering the exchange value of the English pound. In 1542, for example, a pound had been worth twenty-seven Flemish shillings. Five years later it was rated at twenty-one and by 1551 a mere fifteen. This meant that more English goods, particularly cloth, could be bought for the same money.

In the years which followed merchants faced a dramatic rise in demand. Clothiers opened new workshops and took on more men. Extra ships, many of them belonging to the Hanseatic League, were chartered. English cloth poured into Antwerp until supply overtook demand. With warehouses full of unwanted goods, clothiers were forced to sack hundreds of men and sell at a loss.

The Duke of Northumberland, realising the danger, reduced the amount of coins in circulation by halving their value; shillings became worth sixpence and so on. It was the right medicine but in too large a dose. Sales of English cloth in Antwerp dropped by a quarter as its overseas price rose. Unemployment in England grew worse, leading to riots in many places.

Fortunately, Northumberland tried another 'prescription' to cure the nation's ills. He sent an expert financier, Sir Thomas Gresham, to Antwerp. Gresham knew that the flow of English cloth abroad would have to be regulated if the price was to remain in England's favour. This ruled out any more debasement of the coinage. It also meant that the cloth trade must be entirely in the hands of Englishmen because foreigners could not be controlled by Acts of Parliament.

Gresham advised Northumberland to do what neither Tudor king had dared do, that is to end the privileges of the Hanseatic League. The Hansa merchants, although less influential than in Henry VII's time, did not give in without a fight. Eventually they were beaten by heavy duties (taxes) on their exports. Gresham was able to regulate the amount of cloth entering Europe and so obtain a favourable exchange rate for the pound.

World trade

However vital to England in the mid-sixteenth century, trade with Europe was soon to lose its old importance. Northumberland was the first English ruler to realise the wealth to be made from trading links with other parts of the world. Until his time most Englishmen had been ignorant of the possibilities opened up by new discoveries. It was 1555 before a book was published in English describing Spanish and Portuguese voyages of the fifteenth century. This was not surprising for English sailors had taken little part in the search

for ocean routes. Only Cabot, of all the great explorers, had sailed under the English flag.

Northumberland appointed Sebastian Cabot, the explorer, and John Dee, a geographer, as government advisers on such matters. He also started trading with Morocco as well as organising trips to the 'Gold' coast of Africa (now Ghana). A more difficult problem was how to reach the Far East, because Portuguese warships guarded the Cape route. Dee favoured a North-east Passage round Asia, so the Company of Merchant Venturers was formed to equip an expedition to these parts. Each of the Company's 200 members gave £25 towards the cost, thus creating the first joint stock company.

In May 1553 Sir Hugh Willoughby and Richard Chancellor sailed with three ships. Willoughby reached Russian Lapland but he and his men died of cold during the bitter winter. Chancellor crossed the White Sea, reached the Russian port of Archangel and from there travelled overland to Moscow. He was well received by the Russian Tsar (emperor), Ivan IV, who resented paying the high rates charged by the Hanseatic League to get his goods into western Europe. Ivan encouraged trade between the two countries and seemed keen to buy English cloth. On his return, Chancellor formed the Muscovy (Russia) Company for this purpose.

The second expedition to these cold and dreary regions ended in disaster. Chancellor was shipwrecked and drowned while bringing the first ever Russian ambassador to England. The Russian scrambled ashore and eventually reached London, where his efforts to increase trade were not very successful. Nevertheless, the idea of trading with distant parts had caught on. In 1579 the Eastland Company took over the important timber, tar and rope trade with the Baltic countries from the Hanseatic League. In the Mediterranean, ships of the Turkey Company fought off pirates to reach the land of the Sultan. Despite danger and disappointment, the English were beginning to forge trading links which would one day give them an empire.

Nine day queen

All Northumberland's plans were soon threatened by Edward's ill health. In January 1553 the young King was troubled by a bad cough. By May he could not sleep and his legs were swollen. It was clear he was dying, probably from tuberculosis. The King's death meant the end of Northumberland unless he could stop Mary, Catholic daughter of Catherine of Aragon, from becoming queen.

Desperately, the Duke decided on a wild scheme to save his own skin. Edward was persuaded to make a will leaving the crown to the children of Lady Jane Grey, grand-daughter of Henry VIII's sister, and wife of one of Northumberland's sons. The reason given for excluding Mary and Elizabeth from the succession was that they were women. Even this weak excuse was contradicted by events. When it became obvious that Edward would die before Lady Jane had a child the will was changed to give the throne to Lady Jane herself.

Only Northumberland's strong personality gave the plan a chance of success. When Edward died on 6 July 1553 the news was kept

Lady Jane Grey—innocent victim of Northumberland's plot. She reigned only nine days

secret for three days. Only after the Duke had bullied the Council into agreeing to a monarch they knew had no right to the throne, was Jane proclaimed queen in London. Londoners' reaction to the news was discouraging. The proclamation was received without a cheer and one man had his ears cut off for shouting, 'the Lady Mary hath the better title'.

All might still have been well for Northumberland had he managed to seize Mary. Unfortunately for him, his agents failed to arrest her and she fled into areas controlled by the Catholic Norfolks (Norfolk and Suffolk). From this stronghold she wrote to the Council demanding the throne. Such bold actions ruined Northumberland's plans. He had forgotten that no daughter of Henry VIII was likely to sit and watch the crown taken from her. Mary's defiance made the timid councillors recover their nerve. As recruits joined her in large numbers at Framlingham in Suffolk the Council declared their loyalty to Mary.

By the time Northumberland reached Cambridge with his small army there was nothing to do but surrender. The Duke was now as humble as he had once been arrogant. He appealed for mercy, swearing that he had always been a Catholic at heart. This last minute 'conversion' did not save him. He was beheaded in the Tower of London (July 1553). England had its first woman ruler.

More about Edward VI's reign
Books
Most of those listed for Chapters 6 and 8, also:
G. Berry, *Discovering Coins* (Shire Publications)
J. and W. Gittings, *Tudor People* (Hulton). Contains lives of Cranmer and Lady Jane Grey
R. Hakluyt, *Voyages and Documents*, ed. J. Hampden (Oxford University Press)
The North West Passage (Canadian Jackdaw)

Visual aids
Edward VI (Visual Publications)
Sixteenth-century Occupations (Hulton)
North-East Passage (Visual Publications)

Visits
Tower of London

To write and find out
1 Find out all you can about the coins of Tudor times.
2 Find out as much as you can about the 'North-East' and 'North-West' passages. Draw on a map the more important voyages. Find out about Henry Hudson.
3 Compile a booklet about all the Kings of England named Edward. Which of them were also 'boy kings', that is, began to reign before they were eighteen.
4 From historical novels and history books find out more about Lady Jane Grey.

10 'Turn or Burn'
Mary's Reign 1553-1558

The new Queen was in some ways the best of the Tudors. Mary had her father's pride and determination without his cruelty. She was more frank and straightforward than Elizabeth, and her courage might have made her as popular as 'Good Queen Bess'. From her mother, however, she inherited two traits not shared by other Tudors—high principles and a fanatical Catholic faith. Had she reigned before the Reformation this Spanish side to her nature might not have mattered. Coming at the wrong moment in England's history, she alone of Tudor monarchs was remembered with hatred.

Mary was probably the keenest Catholic in England. She had watched her father's Reformation with horror. After his death much that she loved had been destroyed by Edward's ministers. Now she felt it her duty to restore the old Church in all its power and pageantry. Catholic bishops came out of the Tower, Protestant clergy were allowed to leave England. Mass was ordered to be celebrated in parish churches and both Edwardian Prayer Books condemned. Cranmer, knowing what to expect from the daughter of Catherine of Aragon, bravely went to prison. So did three Protestant bishops, John Hooper, Hugh Latimer and Nicholas Ridley.

Parliament unwillingly prepared to change. Few of its members were enthusiastic Protestants but fewer still wanted to return to rule by the Pope. They refused to abandon Mary's title of 'Supreme Head of the Church'; neither would they give back the monastic lands. It was November 1554 before they knelt with their Queen at Whitehall to beg the Pope's pardon for the quarrel started a quarter of a century before.

The Spanish match

It was the Queen's marriage, not her faith, which first caused trouble. Mary had spent a lonely and unhappy childhood, parted from her mother and rejected by a father she loved. As a grown woman she had been stopped from marrying, first by Henry and then by her brother. She was now thirty-seven years old, with fading good looks and signs of the illness which was to kill her. To find herself Queen increased her loneliness. Overwhelmed by the task before her Mary longed for a husband to help her govern and give her children.

The English people agreed she should marry; in their view, a woman ruler was an unknown, almost freakish thing. But they expected her to wed an Englishman, possibly Edward Courtenay, a grandson of Edward IV. A foreign marriage was out of the question, because it would mean in reality a foreign 'king'. Mary on the other hand disliked Englishmen in general, and Courtenay in particular.

When the Queen decided on Prince Philip of Spain, son of the

One of Mary's victims— the burning of Thomas Haukes, 1555

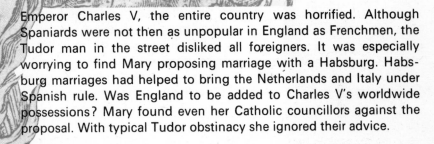

Emperor Charles V, the entire country was horrified. Although Spaniards were not then as unpopular in England as Frenchmen, the Tudor man in the street disliked all foreigners. It was especially worrying to find Mary proposing marriage with a Habsburg. Habsburg marriages had helped to bring the Netherlands and Italy under Spanish rule. Was England to be added to Charles V's worldwide possessions? Mary found even her Catholic councillors against the proposal. With typical Tudor obstinacy she ignored their advice.

Wyatt's rebellion

Some Englishmen did more than grumble. Three soldiers, Sir James Croft, Sir Peter Carew and Sir Thomas Wyatt, decided to stop the marriage by force. They were joined by the Duke of Suffolk, whose daughter, Lady Jane Grey, was under sentence of death in the Tower for her part in Northumberland's plot. Wyatt (1521–54) was an energetic, restless man. His reasons for rebellion were a mixture of prejudice and ambition. Service with Spanish armies had made him hate Spaniards. It is also possible he wanted to replace Mary with Elizabeth and restore the Protestant Church. Like all Tudor rebels, he maintained he was not really against his monarch. 'We seek no harm to the Queen, but better counsel (advice) and councillors,' he remarked.

The conspirators tried to rouse the country with rumours of a foreign invasion. They were not very successful. Suffolk found that people living in the Midlands did not really believe that far away Spain threatened them. Carew was too unpopular to gain much support in the West Country for he had taken a leading part in crushing the rebellion of 1549. Wyatt alone raised an army, mainly because he came from Kent where foreigners were known and disliked. By spreading tales of 'hundreds' of Spaniards landing at Dover he quickly recruited 4,000 men. Mary's general, Norfolk, was now eighty years old and obviously past his best as a soldier. His army was forced to retreat after 500 of his troops joined Wyatt.

In threatened London Mary again proved herself a Tudor. Knowing that some citizens were prepared to open its gates to Wyatt, she decided to meet the City Council at Guildhall. 'What I am ye right well know,' she announced proudly. 'I am your Queen, to whom at my

Mary I

Far right: The Martyrs'
Memorial, Oxford, erected
to commemorate the
burning of Cranmer,
Latimer and Ridley

coronation . . . you promised allegiance.' In a clear deep voice she condemned Wyatt and his followers as 'rank traitors'. Then she cunningly reminded her rich audience of what would happen if the rebels let loose a mob upon the city. 'And now, good subjects,' she concluded, 'pluck up your hearts, and like true men, stand fast against these rebels'. The assembly, we are told, 'wept for joy to hear her speak'. When the rebels arrived on 3 February 1554 they found the gates of London shut.

Wyatt had probably been promised help if he got into the city. He marched west to Kingston, crossed the Thames, and entered the suburbs through Knightsbridge. At first all went well. A royal attack at what is now Hyde Park Corner was beaten off, while in Fleet Street some defenders actually marched by Wyatt's column without a fight. But when he reached Ludgate he found it firmly closed. There was nothing to do but retreat. As he did so his rear column was wiped out by a cavalry charge. Surrounded at last in narrow streets, Wyatt fought desperately for over an hour before surrendering.

There was the usual end to such an adventure. With the Tower full of gentlemen awaiting execution, gallows were put up in various parts of the city. Suffolk's part in the rising caused his death and that of his innocent daughter, Lady Jane Grey. Wyatt was tortured to find out if Mary's sister Elizabeth had been involved in the plot. The future queen was sent to the Tower where she sat and wept, possibly remembering the fate of her mother, Anne Boleyn. The investigations proved that Wyatt had written to her. Fortunately no reply from Elizabeth was ever found, so she was sent to Hatfield House in Hertfordshire, under guard. By the time Wyatt himself died, heads, bodies, legs and arms disfigured the London streets. Only after these executions did Mary pardon 400 prisoners who were brought to Whitehall Palace with ropes round their necks.

Four months after Wyatt's rebellion. Philip married the Queen in Winchester Cathedral on the feast day of St James, patron saint of Spain (25 July). Nobody was very happy, for, whether they approved of rebellion or not, they still hated a marriage which tied England to Spain. And when Philip dragged England into war with France in 1557, causing the loss of Calais after 220 years of English occupation, many must have wished that the Queen had been less courageous four years before!

Holy bonfires!

In 1554 Mary invited her cousin, Cardinal Reginald Pole, to return to England as Papal legate. Pole had fled from England during Henry VIII's Reformation. He was an important churchman who had only narrowly missed being Pope. He was also an unworldly scholar whose absence from England for twenty-five years meant he was out of touch with religious developments. Neither Philip nor Charles V wanted him in England because, as a cardinal remarked, 'he does not understand the first thing about the conduct of affairs'. They were proved right for Pole's arrival in England helped strengthen Mary's belief that burning was the only proper end for a Protestant.

Philip had no objection to burnings in his own country. Nevertheless he was worried in case such executions sparked off another rebellion in England. He told Mary that most 'heretics' could, in fact, be executed for conspiracy or treason. Cranmer, for example, had been involved in Northumberland's plot. Mary and her cousin were too religious to heed such advice. In their opinion, the English must be saved from religious error. Better to burn a few bodies and so save thousands of souls from the far worse flames of hell. It was Mary and Pole who gave Protestants the grim choice either to 'turn or burn'.

The 'Marian persecutions' began with the burning of John Rogers, editor of a Protestant Bible, on 4 February 1554. Five days later Bishop Hooper suffered at Gloucester. After months of imprisonment and two trials at Oxford, Latimer and Ridley were burned in front of Balliol College, in October. Cranmer's case was more complicated. Mary's advisers were determined he should die but hoped he would confess himself a Catholic as Northumberland had done. The Archbishop was a gentle scholar, not a hero. Fear of the fire made him confess several times that he was wrong, even on one occasion that he was the chief cause of England's troubles since Henry VIII's time!

Confident he was a coward, the Archbishop's enemies drove him too far. When they demanded a public confession in St Mary's Church, Oxford, Cranmer stood up and proclaimed his Protestant faith, saying: 'I renounce and refuse, as things written with my hand, contrary to the truth which I thought in my heart, and written for fear of death and to save my life. And forasmuch as my hand offended, writing contrary to my heart . . . when I come to the fire it shall first be burned.' He was interrupted and hurried to the stake. Then, as an eyewitness recorded, 'as soon as the fire got up he was very soon dead, never stirring or crying all the while'. It was a noble end for a man who had started his career as the frightened servant of a ruthless king.

From the start Mary's 'holy bonfires' had the opposite effect to that intended. Before her reign those who called themselves Protestants in England had usually been greedy, selfish or cowardly men hoping either to gain a reward or escape punishment. The death of sincere believers made the name an honourable one at last. One man sang psalms until his lips were burned away. A young mother who gave birth to a child as she suffered lived long enough to see it hurled into the flames. And because the English executioners did not block up their victim's mouth, as was the continental custom, 'last' words were soon being repeated in hushed whispers. As he was tied to the stake, Latimer said to Ridley: 'We shall this day light such a candle, by God's grace, in England as shall never be put out'. His words have echoed down the ages, encouraging others in their Protestant belief.

Five years after Mary's death John Foxe published his *Acts and Monuments*. This long history of the Christian Church told of the sufferings of Protestant martyrs, particularly in Mary's reign. Copies were placed in parish churches by royal order and soon most well-to-do homes had one. For the next 200 years this *Book of Martyrs*

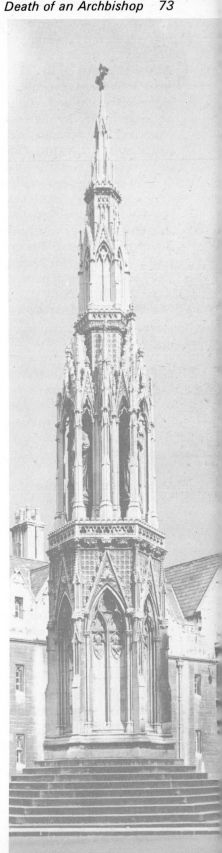

kept alive the memory of Mary's victims, as well as rousing hatred of the faith she loved.

Mary's death

Mary's marriage brought her little happiness. Philip stayed for eighteen months and returned again in 1557. After he became King of Spain in 1555 he showed little interest in his unhealthy and rather plain wife. Her love was not returned, and the child she longed for never came. In August 1558 she moved to Westminster Palace a dying woman. Philip, instead of coming to England to comfort her, sent his ambassador secretly to see Elizabeth!

News of Mary's last illness caused only relief and joy in London; the day before she died was called 'Hope Wednesday'. Unaware of this, the sad Queen who had burnt nearly 300 Protestants was dreaming of 'seeing many little children, like angels', as she passed away on 17 November 1558. Her cousin, Reginald Pole, died the same day. The policy of 'turn or burn' died with them.

More about Mary I's reign

Books

J. Foxe, *Foxe's Book of Martyrs*, ed. G. A. Williamson (Secker & Warburg)

A. Fletcher, *Tudor Rebellions* (Longman: Seminar Studies in History)

C. Morris, *The Tudors* (Batsford: Fontana)

W. C. Richardson, *Mary Tudor* (P. Owen)

J. Ridley, *Thomas Cranmer* (Oxford University Press)

G. Trease, *Seven Sovereign Queens* (Heinemann)

Visual aids

Mary (Visual Publications)

Visits

Oxford, which contains the Martyrs Memorial to Latimer and Ridley and St Mary's Church.

To write and find out

1 What other women have been sovereign queens of England, that is, reigned alone? How many have been married? Who reigned longest? Compile illustrated lives of at least two.

2 Draw a map of London at the time of Wyatt's Rebellion. One will be found in G. M. Trevelyan's *Illustrated Social History of England* (Longman), Vol. 2, although of a slightly later period.

3 A useful class project is to write a play dramatizing the more important events of Cranmer's life.

4 Make a time-line of the chief events in the life of King Philip II of Spain. This can be done with the aid of *Philip II* by Charles Petrie (Eyre & Spottiswoode). Concentrate on events *not* connected with England. Afterwards decide, possibly by a class debate, whether he really was the 'villain' and 'bogyman' he appeared to the English at the time.

11 Queen takes Queen
Elizabeth I 1558-1588

On the afternoon Mary died bells clanged in London steeples and the citizens feasted from tables set up in the streets. It was a date long celebrated as the 'Birthday of the Gospel', that is, the day England became a Protestant country. Within hours Parliament was told of 'a true, lawful and right inheritress to the crown . . . which is the lady Elizabeth'. Anne Boleyn's daughter was Queen at last.

The pale young woman with red hair and lively, expressive eyes who now ruled England had many qualities necessary to make a successful sixteenth century monarch. 'Young Bess' had grown up in a hard and dangerous world. Since her 'teens she had picked her way through plots and rebellions, learning to be careful of what she said and did. Less cruel than Henry VIII, she combined his royal courage and interest in learning with feminine cunning and caution. Elizabeth spoke several languages, loved music and enjoyed the company of scholars. Yet she could charm ordinary people as easily as her father. Indeed, no Tudor could 'play the king' better.

The problems confronting Elizabeth were far worse than those facing her father at his accession. Describing England in 1559, a court official wrote: 'The Queen poor; the realm exhausted . . .; divisions amongst ourselves; wars with France and Scotland; the French King bestriding the realm, having one foot in Calais and the other in Scotland.' It was a situation to worry an experienced ruler let alone a young woman just released from virtual imprisonment.

And whereas no foreign government had ever questioned Henry's right to the throne, the King of France reacted to Elizabeth's accession by proclaiming his daughter-in-law, Mary Stuart, Queen of England. This was because Catholics still regarded Henry VIII's marriage to Anne Boleyn as unlawful. In their view the Catholic grand-daughter of Henry VII had a better claim to the throne. European history for the next thirty years was to be influenced by the struggle between these two women.

The middle way

Some of the 'exhausted realm's' troubles were soon over. The French government faced near civil war between its own Catholics and Protestants. Consequently it had little time to concentrate on affairs abroad. French forces in Scotland were blockaded by the English fleet and forced to surrender. The Treaty of Edinburgh (1560) began nearly a century of peace between England and Scotland. It also led to a revolt by Scots Protestants who closed their monasteries and established a Presbyterian (Calvinist) State Church.

Meanwhile the English government tried to settle its own religious problems. The 'holy bonfires' of Mary's reign had turned thousands

The young Elizabeth is arrested after Wyatt's Rebellion. This was originally painted on a door at the Manor House, Little Gaddesden, Herts

of men and women Protestant. Even those who remained Catholic sometimes regarded the Pope as a scheming foreign prince. Nevertheless, to many the ceremonies and worship of the old Church often seemed more important than religious arguments amongst scholars. Elizabeth agreed with them. 'There is only one Jesus Christ,' she said 'and all the rest is a dispute over trifles.' Only the Pope's support of Mary, combined with a strongly Protestant Parliament, made Elizabeth reverse her sister's religious policy so quickly.

The Queen's lords and M.P.'s knew that the only alternative to Elizabeth was a Catholic monarch. For better or worse, they had to accept her. An Act of Supremacy (1559) was hurried through Parliament, declaring Elizabeth 'supreme governor in all spiritual and ecclesiastical things'. In other words, Elizabeth, not the Pope, was head of the Church of England. At the same time an Act of Uniformity ordered the Second Prayer Book of Edward's reign to be used in all churches. Priests who disobeyed this rule were to be sacked or imprisoned. Laymen who refused to go to church were to be fined. In future all services were to be conducted in English. On the other hand, many forms of worship were modified to make them acceptable to Catholics.

For Elizabeth these Acts represented a 'middle way' which she hoped would satisfy her subjects. Gone were the burnings and persecution of the previous reign. Mary's Archbishop of York was allowed to live in comfortable retirement on his estates. Only one Catholic bishop died in prison. Less than 200 clergymen lost their jobs. Even the fines were not always collected. Indeed, the setting up of a Protestant State Church brought true Catholics into the open at last. These 'recusants' gave up attending church, paid their fines and worshipped privately.

Recusants were not the only people dissatisfied with the Elizabethan Settlement. Keen Protestants were also unhappy. A Catholic, for example, could still believe that the bread and wine in Communion turned into the body and blood of Christ. The new Church was still governed by bishops whose authority some Presbyterians wished to abolish. In the years which followed a movement grew up to 'purify' the English Church of Catholic ways. Not all these 'Puritans' were extreme Calvinists, but most shared Luther's view that priests and bishops were not essential. Thus the Anglican (Church of England) Church was condemned both for being too Catholic and too Protestant!

The Dutch revolt

On the continent there was rarely a religious middle way. In France a struggle developed between Huguenots (French Protestants) and their Catholic government. Huguenots often lived together in fortified ports or towns. With typical Calvinistic discipline, they were prepared to fight for their faith. From one French Atlantic coast base, La Rochelle, their privateers even attacked Spanish shipping in the Channel.

In the Spanish Netherlands Protestantism took root in the northern provinces (now Holland) but not in those of the south (now Belgium and parts of northern France). By the 1560s Dutch Protestant worship went on in open defiance of the Spanish governor and Catholic statues and shrines were damaged or destroyed. Mary's former husband was now King Philip II of Spain, for his father, Charles V, had retired in 1555, leaving his son to rule Spain, and his brother Ferdinand as Holy Roman Emperor. Philip was a devout Catholic who once told the Pope he would rather lose both life and crown than rule Protestants. In 1568 a large Spanish army led by the Duke of Alva set out to crush the rebels in the Netherlands. Their ruthless and cruel activities began a war which did not end until 1648.

At first, Alva defeated the Dutch, driving their leader, William of Orange, out of the country. But Alva's dictatorial ways annoyed even Catholics who saw the free government of their towns threatened. An 'underground movement' began against his rule, spearheaded by Dutch 'sea beggars' who imitated Huguenot privateers in the Channel. The capture of Brill as a base for such operations in 1572 was the signal for a patriotic rebellion against the Spanish.

William re-entered Holland, where a new Spanish commander, the Prince of Parma, had been appointed. Parma was a brilliant soldier, skilled with horse and sword, an athlete who could jump 'the height of a horse'. He captured one town after another, killing those citizens who dared to resist. At Gembloux a garrison which offered to surrender was clubbed to death. At Maastricht 1,700 women's and children's bodies were counted in the streets after his men had finished. By 1585 most of the south was in Spanish hands and only the northern provinces remained undefeated.

Elizabeth's seadogs

Although Elizabeth had no wish to fight Spain, circumstances gradually drove the two countries apart. The Queen knew that if Philip beat the Dutch he would probably attack England. Furthermore, because the cloth trade had been almost ruined by the war, England no longer had commercial reasons for friendship with Spain. Consequently the English government decided to help the Dutch as much as possible without provoking Philip into war.

Elizabethan sailors were less cautious. Once their ships were far away from home they ignored Spanish and Portuguese claims to the New World. To them, the Pope's division of the globe between Spain and Portugal seemed stupid and unfair, especially as much territory had never been explored by either. Portugal, for example, claimed nearly 2,000 miles of the West African coast, from Arguim Island to Cape St Catherine (known as Guinea), although few of her explorers had ever ventured inland. Spain refused to allow foreigners to trade with any part of the Americas or the West Indies.

Such areas were, of course, too vast to be 'policed' by these jealous countries. In 1530 William Hawkins sailed to Guinea 'where he trafficked with the negroes, and took off them elephants' teeth'. Other Englishmen brought back gold and pepper. But when Sir

Mary Queen of Scots

John Hawkins began selling Negro slaves to Spanish West Indian plantations, his men were treacherously attacked by warships of Philip's fleet, at San Juan de Ulloa in the Gulf of Mexico (September 1568). Three English vessels were destroyed and many sailors killed. Only Hawkins and his cousin, Francis Drake, escaped with their ships. From that moment there was war between English and Spanish sailors in the New World.

Even before this news reached England, a diplomatic crisis occurred. Spanish merchantmen, carrying 450,000 ducats (about £100,000) to the Netherlands, were chased into Southampton by Huguenot ships. When Philip demanded the return of the money Elizabeth refused, because she feared it would be used to finance an invasion of England. Philip retaliated by seizing English property in Flanders. He also considered open war with England but decided against it in case English ships cut his Channel supply routes with the Prince of Parma. As an alternative he began to think of driving Elizabeth from the throne. After all, had not Mary Stuart, Elizabeth's rival, just arrived in England?

Murder at Holyrood

Mary, whose mother had been French, spent thirteen years in France following the battle of Pinkie (see Chapter 9). Here her close links with that country were further strengthened when she married the French king (1558). His sudden death in 1560 caused her to return reluctantly to Scotland (August 1561).

The young widow found a very different country from the one she had left as a child. Mary was a Catholic but large numbers of Scots had turned Protestant, led by the influential preacher, John Knox. Knox was a stern reformer, who had worked with Calvin in Geneva. He detested all Catholics and had spent eighteen months of his life as a galley slave in a French warship. Neither the Scots queen's faith nor her French relatives were likely to be popular with such a man.

At first Mary wisely accepted the situation. Knox was allowed to organise his kirk (church) of 'true believers' without interference and Protestants as well as Catholics were appointed to the Queen's Council. The reformer, it was true, had written a book entitled *First Blast of the Trumpet against the Monstrous Regiment of Women*. He disliked all female rulers and Mary in particular. Even so, the citizens of Edinburgh could not help feeling proud of their beautiful queen, whatever her religion. A happy and peaceful reign seemed likely.

In July 1565 Mary married Henry, Lord Darnley, a grandson of Henry VIII's sister. This union, although it strengthened her claim to the English throne, brought the queen little happiness. Darnley was said to the the 'lustiest, best-looking lad' in Scotland. Unfortunately, he was also spoilt, a drunkard and fond of other women. Possibly because he resented not being made king he neglected his official duties as well as his wife. Lonely and unhappy, Mary turned to her Italian secretary, David Riccio, for advice. Darnley began to grow jealous

The murder of Darnley. A sketch sent to Sir William Cecil in 1567. *Top left:* Darnley's baby son (later James I) with the words 'Judge and Avenge my cause, O Lord' *Left centre:* the square of houses attached to St Mary, Kirk O'Field showing Darnley's ruined house. *Below left:* the body of Darnley being carried away. *Top right:* Darnley and his servant lying dead.

In March 1566 Mary was sitting in her bedroom in Holyrood Palace, Edinburgh, surrounded by ladies-in-waiting and friends, including Riccio. Flickering candles and the firelight sent shadows whirling across the panelled room. Suddenly Darnley appeared in the doorway, drunk and angry. Behind him loomed the grim figure of Lord Ruthven, believed by the superstitious to practise witchcraft. He wore a helmet, and armour could be seen under his cloak. The two men rushed at Riccio who threw himself at the Queen's feet for protection. Tables were overturned; candles blown out in the uproar. Riccio was dragged screaming from the room and stabbed to death on the staircase.

The Kirk O'Field explosion

Fearing Riccio's murder might lead to a rebellion, Mary fled from Holyrood that night. A sober Darnley, horrified at what he had done, went with her. Once the fuss had died down the royal pair returned to

Edinburgh. Publicly Mary hid her feelings. Even in private she seemed fond of her husband, especially after their son, James, was born (June 1566). Behind the scenes, however, she was falling in love with a 'glorious, rash and hazardous young man', the Earl of Bothwell.

In 1567 Darnley fell ill with smallpox. He was brought to his house at Kirk O'Field near Edinburgh where the Queen saw him almost daily. On 9 February Mary cut short one of her visits to return to the capital for a wedding. At two o'clock next morning an explosion wrecked the house. Darnley and a man-servant were found dead in the garden. It seemed a tragic accident until it was discovered they had both been strangled.

If it was murder, who had done it? An old lady living in a cottage nearby said she had heard Darnley scream, 'pity me, kinsmen (relatives) for the sake of Him who pitied all the world'. If this was true he had been killed by somebody he knew. Other voices were heard in the dark streets of Edinburgh, shouting that Bothwell had killed the king (meaning Darnley). Posters appeared on walls making the same accusation.

✱ Mary announced, 'the murderer will shortly be discovered. . . . We hope to punish the same with such rigour as shall serve for example of this cruelty to all ages to come.' When she discovered that Bothwell, not an ordinary man, was responsible, however, she staged a farcical trial which found him not guilty (April 1567). Worse still, she married Bothwell three months after Darnley's death. This fatal move turned the Scots people against her. Why Mary did it is still a mystery. Perhaps she had fallen deeply in love with Bothwell. Perhaps she was frightened of him, or had suffered a nervous breakdown following the murders of Riccio and Darnley. Whatever the reason, the marriage soon ended her reign.

Within months a rebellion had led to defeat and imprisonment. Mary was forced to abdicate in favour of her son James. Bothwell escaped abroad, eventually dying insane in a Danish prison. After a while, Mary broke free, rallied her supporters but was again beaten. Riding for her life, the Scots Queen crossed the English border in May 1568.

The Northern Rebellion

Elizabeth refused to meet a woman suspected of murdering her husband. To help her ragged rival she sent only 'two torn shifts, two pieces of black velvet, two pairs of shoes and nothing else'. A Court of Inquiry was ordered to investigate Darnley's murder. 'When you are acquitted of this crime', Elizabeth wrote to Mary, 'I will receive you with all honour; till this is done I may not.'

Mary's Scottish enemies brought to the court eight letters, two marriage contracts and other documents which, if genuine, proved the Queen's guilt. Mary claimed that these 'Casket Letters' were forgeries. Nobody has ever discovered the truth. What was more certain was the effect of Mary's arrival in England. Those who feared she would become the centre of plots against Elizabeth were soon proved right.

Drake's *Golden Hind* homeward bound from her world voyage

The political situation in England increased the danger. The Queen's secretary of state, Sir William Cecil (later Lord Burghley) was engaged in a struggle with the Norfolk family. They represented the old feudal lords of an England that was passing. Burghley was typical of the new middle class to whom Henry VIII had given power and influence. He stood for the new Protestant England. He favoured expanding England's overseas trade. The Norfolks on the other hand still regretted that Catholic England was no more. They were anxious to keep the peace with the Catholic states of Europe and feared that Burghley's foreign policy would bring war with Spain.

The Norfolks also resented Burghley's high position. They hoped to ruin him as their relatives had destroyed Cromwell, a man of similar 'low birth', thirty years before. As a first step, they demanded that the Queen should recognise Mary's right to the throne after her own death. When she refused they plotted to marry the fourth Duke of Norfolk (grandson of the third Duke condemned by Henry VIII), to the Scots Queen, perhaps hoping this would increase their influence at court. It was a dangerous scheme, and when Elizabeth found out Norfolk's nerve failed and 'he fell into an ague (illness) and was fain to get to bed without his dinner'. Sure enough, the furious English Queen sent him straight to the Tower.

Young Norfolk's arrest set off a rebellion of those dissatisfied with Tudor rule. In particular, it roused northern Catholics who hated the government's 'new found religion and heresie'. Encouraged by the Earls of Northumberland and Westmorland, small troops of horse and foot soldiers seized towns and burned the homes and crops of Protestants. At Durham the cathedral was entered by Catholics who tore up Bibles and Prayer Books and openly celebrated Mass.

Government agents managed to carry Mary away before Northumberland's men could reach her. Then a large royal army moved into action. It found little to do. Few northern rebels were well armed. Many people had followed their lord through loyalty and were reluctant to fight. Most were poorly armed and equipped. The only serious skirmish was at Carlisle. Elsewhere rebel forces faded away as quickly as they had gathered. Northumberland was captured and beheaded. Westmorland fled abroad. A grim Elizabeth ordered the death of at least one man from each rebellious village. Their bodies, proclaimed the Queen, were to be on view 'till they fall to pieces where they hang'. As in the days of the Pilgrimage of Grace rebellion, Tudor power, based firmly in southern England, had again shown the weakness of the north.

When no action was taken against Mary, John Knox warned Elizabeth: 'If you strike not at the root, the branches that appear to be broken will bud again with greater force.'

Drake's voyage

Following the St Bartholomew's Day massacre of Protestants by French Catholics in 1572 another civil war weakened France for many years. As a result, Spain was England's chief opponent throughout Elizabeth's reign.

Far right: Execution of
Mary Queen of Scots in
Fotheringay Castle,
February 1587

While on the continent it remained a 'cold war', the high seas witnessed a very hot feud between English and Spanish sailors. In 1572 Drake landed at Panama, joined with runaway Negro slaves and captured a Spanish mule train carrying £20,000 to Nombre de Dios. Five years later he left England, apparently 'to explore the southern ocean'. Those who financed his voyage knew that 'the master thief of the known world', as the Spaniards called him, had other plans. As he ploughed across the Atlantic, Drake changed the name of his flagship from *Pelican* to *Golden Hind*. Every man on board knew what that meant. They were after Spanish gold, not new sea routes.

Only Drake's ship reached the Pacific; four others were broken up, sunk or driven back. Once through the Straits of Magellan, the *Golden Hind* started to raid Spanish outposts in Peru and Chile. At Callao, chief port of Peru, Drake sailed around the harbour cutting the almost unmanned Spanish warships adrift. His enemies thought he was mad. Actually he was making sure no one could chase him when he captured an even greater prize. A large galleon, the *Cacafuego* (Spitfire) was bound for Panama, loaded with treasure. Drake set off in pursuit, offering a gold chain for the first sailor to sight her.

· On 1 March 1579 near Cape San Francisco a shout from the ship's lookout told the crew the chain had been won. What followed was almost too easy. *Cacafuego's* captain, not expecting an enemy in such lonely waters, turned back to exchange news. The English moved alongside, fired a broadside of cannon balls and arrows, and boarded. Astonished Spaniards put up little fight. Within minutes Drake's men had rushed below. As they staggered up the stairways with chests and cases, it was obvious a vast treasure had been captured. Exact details will never be known, particularly as the matter was kept secret after Drake's return. But at least eighty pounds of

Drake's route round the
world 1577–80

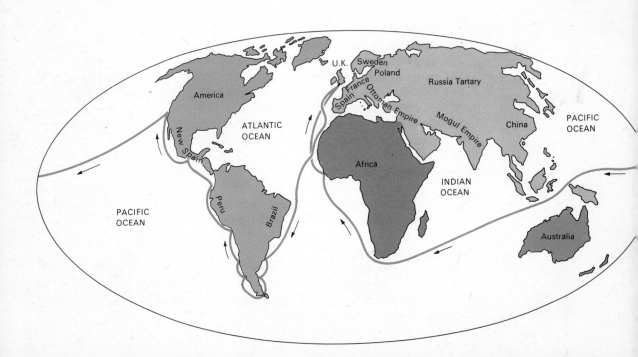

Bothwell

gold, twenty-six tons of silver, together with diamonds, emeralds, rubies and 360,000 gold pieces of eight were seized, as well as chests of silver table-ware and cloth of gold.

The *Golden Hind* completed its world voyage in 1580, ballasted (weighted) with gold and propelled by cloth of gold sails. Five loaded packhorses were needed to take the Queen's share of the treasure from Plymouth to London. Soon afterwards Drake was knighted by Elizabeth at Deptford.

Mary's death

In the years following this famous voyage relations between England and Spain moved towards breaking point. Parma's capture of Antwerp in 1585 brought enemy troops far too near England for comfort. As a result Drake's attack on Cartagena (near the Isthmus of Panama, now in Columbia) in 1586 was with the Queen's open approval. In the same year Elizabeth sent military aid to the Dutch. Her favourite, Robert Dudley, Earl of Leicester, was ordered to the Netherlands with an expeditionary force to help the northern provinces. He did little because his poorly trained troops stood no chance against Parma's infantry. He also annoyed the Queen by allowing the Dutch to make him governor-general of the Netherlands without her permission. The one memorable incident was the unselfish act of the dying Sir Philip Sidney, a famous courtier and poet, who gave his water flask to an ordinary soldier at the Battle of Zutphen (1586).

Throughout these years, all plots seemed to lead to Mary who sat, spiderlike, at the centre of every web uncovered by Burghley's spies. Had Elizabeth been a wife and mother this might not have mattered. But her determination that there should be 'a Mrs but no Mr in England' meant that Mary was heir to the throne. In 1571 Norfolk became involved in a wild scheme to dethrone Elizabeth and assist Spanish troops to land in England. The man behind the plot, Roberto Ridolfi, escaped abroad, but Norfolk was beheaded. Fifteen years later the Spanish ambassador in London encouraged a plan by Antony Babington and other Catholic gentlemen to kill Elizabeth. This also failed and the conspirators were executed. During the investigation letters were found hidden in beer barrels delivered to Mary's house which linked her with these traitors. The Scots Queen was put on trial at Fotheringay Castle in Northampton-shire, found guilty of treason and sentenced to death.

Burghley, the royal Council and Parliament all demanded that Mary should die. Elizabeth was reluctant to kill a fellow monarch and close relative. When she was persuaded to sign Mary's death warrant she changed her mind and refused to have it carried out. Finally, Burghley and the Council ordered the execution without Elizabeth's permission. A life of plotting and tragedy ended on 8 February 1587 when Mary went bravely to her death in the hall of Fotheringay Castle.

King Philip was not over-worried by Mary's death. Since he had at last decided to conquer England, it would be better if a Spaniard sat on the English throne!

More about Elizabeth I's reign

Books

P. Donahue, *Plymouth Ho! the West in Elizabethan Times* (Longman: Then and There)

Elizabeth I (Cape: Jackdaw)

A. Fletcher, *Tudor Rebellions* (Longman: Seminar Studies in History)

A. Fraser, *Mary, Queen of Scots* (Weidenfeld & Nicholson)

Mary Queen of Scots (Cape: Jackdaw)

J. Ridley, *John Knox* (Oxford University Press)

R. R. Sellman, *Elizabethan Seamen* (Methuen: Outlines)

The Spanish Inquisition (Cape: Jackdaw)

D. Titley, *Tudors and Stuarts* (Mills & Boon)

H. E. Wilbur, *Unquenchable Flame: The Life of Philip II* (P. Owen)

Visual aids

Drake (Visual Publications)

The Revenge (Visual Publications)

Elizabeth I (Visual Publications)

Sir Francis Drake *(film)* (Rank)

The Elizabethan Age *(filmstrips and record)* (EAV)

Queen Elizabeth I (Common Ground)

Mary Queen of Scots *(record)* (Philips)

Visits

Tower of London

Hatfield House, Hertfordshire

Edinburgh Castle

Holyrood Palace, Edinburgh, Scotland

To write and find out

1 Find out as much as possible about the history of your own parish church if it is an old one. Ask your local vicar to tell you about the Church of England, especially the way in which services have changed since Queen Elizabeth's reign. The Church of England 'Book of Common Prayer' contains many of the prayers and services originally devised by Cranmer.

2 Work on a class or group project concerned with 'England's sea-dogs'. Many historical novels, including *Westward Ho* by C. Kingsley, *Remember Vera Cruz* by Frank Knight (Macdonald) and *Beat the Drum* by S. Andrew Wood (Hodder & Stoughton) tell stories connected with the battle between English and Spanish seamen during this period.

3 Read as much as you can about Darnley's murder from the books in the above list. See if you can solve the main problem, which is whether Mary knew of the plot to kill him.

4 Compare modern circumnavigations—Chichester, Knox-Johnston etc., with Drake's voyage.

12 'God's Own Cause'
The Defeat of the Armada 1588

The Spanish King planned to overthrow Elizabeth and replace her with a Catholic monarch. His memories of England when he was Mary's husband made him certain the country was still Catholic at heart. Once his armies landed he believed its inhabitants would flock to support the new government. The Pope was not so sure. It was true that since 1570 Elizabeth, 'pretended queen of England', had been excommunicated by the Catholic Church. A later Pope had gone further and pardoned in advance any who might murder 'that guilty woman of England'. Nevertheless, the Papacy feared a conquest which would make the power of Spain even greater. Consequently, the Pope gave Philip's 'crusade' his blessing without much enthusiasm.

Philip knew the invasion would be expensive as well as dangerous. In 1585 the Marquis of Santa Cruz, Spain's leading admiral, had estimated that 500 ships would be needed, costing the equivalent of £20 million in modern money. The admiral wanted 100,000 men and suggested enormous quantities of food, such as 40 million pounds of biscuits and 3 million pounds of bacon. Overwhelmed by such figures, the Spanish King decided it would be cheaper to ferry Parma's army to England from the Netherlands.

Singeing the King of Spain's beard
Both Parma and Santa Cruz insisted that the English must be taken by surprise. Philip knew preparations for such an expedition, his 'Enterprise of England' as he called it, could not be kept secret.

At first spies' reports of shipbuilding in Spanish ports were laughed at in England. After all, both Parma and Philip still seemed friendly towards Elizabeth. When such warlike activities could no longer be ignored the Queen sent for 'her little pirate', Drake. 'Distress the ships within the havens (ports) themselves,' she ordered. Later she changed her mind about such an open attack in peacetime. Drake, who feared the Queen might do this, made sure he was at sea before her messengers arrived!

On 19 April 1587 'El Draque', as the Spaniards called him, appeared off Cadiz with twenty-three ships. Entering the narrow channel leading to the outer harbour, he found about sixty supply vessels at anchor. All were unprepared; most had no guns and some were without masts. These 'sitting ducks' were burned and destroyed. Next day the English sailors moved into the inner harbour in small rowing boats. They boarded and burned more Spanish ships, including a large merchantman belonging to Santa Cruz. By mid-day the harbour looked like 'a great volcano or that part of hell seen from the mouth', according to an eye witness.

ISSIMVS EQVES ANG

candide :fortifs .ac inuictifs Ducis .Draeck ad Vnum
be, duorum annorum, et menfium decem fpatio, Zeph
Anglinm fedes proprias, 4. Cal Octobr, anno á p
cum antea portu foluiffet fd, Decem: anni .157

'The Master Pirate of the known world', Sir Francis Drake

So far all had gone well for the raiders. But when Drake's men returned to their ships in the outer harbour they found that the wind had dropped. Pessimists had feared the English might be stranded; now the worst had happened. According to the naval theories of the time, the expedition should have been destroyed by Spanish galleys. In fact, the English gunners drove off every warship which dared to approach. After thirty-six hours a rising wind allowed the English to head out to sea. Drake had finished 'singeing the King of Spain's beard' without losing a man or a ship.

On his way home, Drake continued to 'distress' Spanish towns and ships. His most spectacular feat was the capture of the treasure ship *San Felipe*—the richest prize ever taken by an English sailor in Elizabeth's reign. His most important was the destruction of thousands of wooden barrels; later the Armada (the Spanish fleet) was to suffer as a result of barrels made of unseasoned wood which ruined its food and drink.

When Parma protested about the *San Felipe* incident, Elizabeth denied knowledge of it, even though royal dressmakers were fashioning her gowns from captured Spanish silk.

Final preparations

The attack on Cadiz seriously delayed the Armada, but it did not change Philip's mind. Ship-building was transferred to Lisbon, a port which even Drake could not attack. Early in 1588 the great Santa Cruz died. This was a severe blow to Spanish hopes. His replacement as commander—the Duke of Medina Sidonia, a cousin of the King—was no sailor. He did not want the job and remarked: 'I possess not one qualification for this post and believe myself the most unfit and unlikely candidate for it.'

Meanwhile, in the Netherlands, Parma grew more doubtful. Philip intended the Armada troops to seize the Margate area as a bridgehead for a thrust at London. His ships could then sail to Flanders and bring Parma's army across. Parma knew that there was no suitable port on that part of the Dutch coast from which an army could embark. Most large sixteenth-century galleons needed a depth of 25—30 feet of water to float safely. No such water existed close to the sandy shore off Dunkirk. Consequently a link between the Armada and Spanish troops in Flanders was impossible, unless a good port was captured.

Philip ignored this vital point. To him the expedition had become a religious crusade. He set a personal example by living like a monk, constantly at prayer. His soldiers and sailors were encouraged to do the same. Heads were shaved, ships named after saints, sails decorated with crosses. Even the sailors daily passwords were religious. Sunday's was 'Jesus' and the others were Monday 'Holy Ghost', Tuesday 'Most Holy Trinity', Wednesday 'Santiago' (St James), Thursday 'The Angels', Friday 'All Souls', and Saturday 'Our Lady'. Spain's astrologers had warned that 1588 would be a year of disaster. Philip did not believe them. God was on his side. How could he fail?

The English made less fuss. Their ships had cocky names like

Lion, Tiger, Dreadnought and *Revenge*. Nevertheless they also saw the war as a religious quarrel. Drake was a Protestant preacher's son who shared his father's hatred of Catholics. Hawkins told the Queen: 'God will help us, for we defend the chief cause, our religion, God's own cause.'

Fight in the Channel

When the Armada sailed from Lisbon on 20 May 1588* it consisted of 130 ships. About half of these vessels were genuine warships, the remainder were merchantmen carrying supplies. Spanish war-ships were not necessarily bigger than English ones as is often said. In fact, the largest ship on either side was the English *Triumph*. Neither was there much difference in numbers for the English could call on 102 warships of various sizes.

The Spanish ships probably looked larger because they stood higher out of the water than the low, fast English galleons built by Hawkins. Hawkins had been Treasurer of the Navy for eleven years. Assisted by two master shipwrights, Matthew Baker and Peter Pett, he had designed a warship nearly four times as long as it was wide, with special decks for the guns. Such a vessel could be handled by far fewer men than the older types, and was superior to most Spanish ships. Of the twenty-five which were ready by 1588 none was ever lost through storm, and only one was captured.

The Spanish were not short of guns. Philip had bought them from many countries, even England, whence a Sussex ironmaster smuggled them to Spain. Most had short muzzles which fired a shot nearly twice as heavy as that of any English ship. The English eighteen-pounder guns threw a lighter shot a greater distance. These were more use, because the English ships were unlikely to come to close quarters. They had no soldiers to take on the Spanish troops. Before the Armada sailed, Philip predicted, 'take notice that the enemy object will be to engage at a distance'.

Delayed by bad weather and the need to get fresh food supplies at Corunna, the Spanish fleet did not appear off Cornwall until 19 July. As the English coast appeared, Medina-Sidonia hoisted his personal flag, showing Christ on the Cross, and every ship fired a broadside which ashore must have sounded like distant thunder. With ship after ship looming out of the grey Atlantic mist it was time to light beacon fires. From hilltop to hilltop they flashed their warning across Cornwall and Devon and on to London. At the same time a speedy ship set off for Plymouth, where storms had driven the English after two unsuccessful attempts to find the enemy.

The English commander-in-chief, Lord Howard of Effingham, like Medina-Sidonia, was an important court official, not a sailor. He had been chosen by Elizabeth because as Lord High Admiral he had enough authority to control such proud and quarrelsome men as

*Note. In 1588 two calendars were in use. The Spanish had changed to the Gregorian; the English kept to the Julian or Old Style. Consequently there was a difference of ten numbers between Spanish and English dates for the Armada; for the Spanish it began on 29 July, for the English the 19 July. In this chapter the Old Style dates have been used.

Route of the ill-fated
Armada, 1588

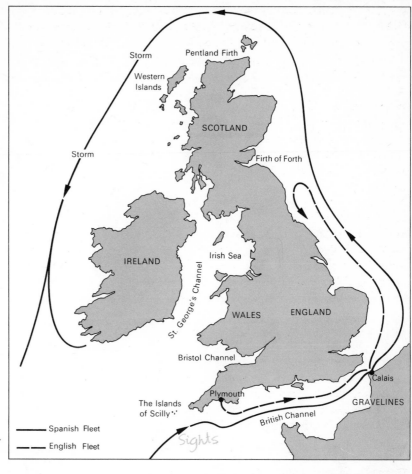

Hawkins, Drake, Martin Frobisher and Walter Raleigh. These experts
now told him that strong winds would not allow them to leave
harbour and engage the enemy. Many years later a Spaniard commented, 'their commanders were at bowls upon the Hoe at Plymouth'.
Even if this were true, they had plenty of time to finish the game!

The enforced wait meant that when the English fleet did put to sea it
was to the windward (rear) of the Armada. Medina-Sidonia was
impressed by the skill with which they kept this position. The English,
for their part, admired the enemy's firm crescent formation. This was
far more difficult in the days of sail than it would be today. Careful
adjustment of sails, and a varying rate of stroke for the oarsmen, were
necessary to keep the ships together.

When the English opened fire on 21 July their light shot did little
damage. Powerful warships stood protectively at either tip of the
crescent and if an English ship tried to get at the weak centre it
risked being surrounded and boarded. As a result, the darting English
resembled dogs snapping at a bull; they could hurt but not cripple
their opponent. On 23 July Hawkins's *Ark Royal* and Medina
Sidonia's *San Martin* exchanged shots. Neither was badly damaged.

So far the most serious injury to the Armada was accidental. One galleon was wrecked by an internal explosion. Another collided with a sister ship and had to be abandoned.

On 25th July a confused battle took place off the Isle of Wight. The English, not knowing the Spanish plan, thought they intended to land on the island. To prevent this they attacked the northern tip of the crescent nearest the shore. Actually Medina Sidonia passed many suitable landing places because his orders were to go to Margate. Day after day the huge fleet moved through the noise and smoke of battle. Nothing the English did could break their order. However, both sides were now running out of ammunition.

On 27 July the Armada came to anchor off Calais. Medina Sidonia

The Spanish Armada—a sixteenth-century painting

The Resolution of the Council of War of the English Commanders to fight against the Armada: '1 August, 1588. We whose names are hervnder written have determyned and agreed in counsaile to folowe and pursue the Spanishe ffleete vntill we have cleared oure owne coaste and broughte the ffrithe weste of us, and then to returne backe again, as well to revictuall oure ships (which stand in extreme scarsitie) as alsoe to guard and defend oure owne coaste at home; with further protestatione that, if oure wantes of victualles and munitione were suppliede, we wold pursue them to the furthest that they durste haue gone.' Signed by C..harles Howard, Lord— Howard ..of Effingham, Lord High Admiral—: George ..Clifford, Earl of— Cumberland: ..Lord— T..homas— Howard; Edmund ..Sheffield, Lord— Sheffield: ..Sir— Francis Drake; ..Sir— Edward Hoby; ..Sir— John Hawkins; and ..Captain— Thomas Fenner.

sent messengers to ask Parma what he intended to do. The Prince replied that he was helpless. Dutch ships swarmed along the coast and two ports, Walcheren and Flushing, were still held by Dutch and English troops. Not one Spanish boat could move safely; not a single soldier could get to the waiting ships. To go on to Margate would be to lose all hope of future contact. The Spanish and Portuguese seamen had done their best. They had brushed the English aside and sailed up the Channel. But it needed more than courage and skill to make an unworkable plan work.

Hellburners

Outside Calais the English admirals held a Council of War. What could be done? While the English ships kept at a safe distance they could do little damage, but if they closed in on the enemy it might prove disastrous. The best plan seemed to be to attack with fireships. These were usually old empty ships, filled with tar and gunpowder and set alight with their guns loaded. As there was no time to send to England for such vessels each shipowner in the fleet surrendered one of his vessels; Drake gave the 200 ton *Thomas*. Just after midnight on 28 July eight of these dreaded 'hellburners' were sighted by Spanish lookouts, 'spurting fire and their ordnance (guns) shooting, which was a horror to see'. The crisis of the battle had come.

Medina Sidonia had expected fireships. He had stationed sailors in small boats to push them away with long poles. But the 'hellburners' bearing down on them were much bigger than usual. When their guns started to explode the Spaniards rowed away, leaving their fleet unprotected. The result was panic. No danger was more dreaded in the days of wooden ships than fire. The Spanish captains ordered their anchors to be cut. Ships headed out to sea in all directions; one galleon was driven aground in the confusion. With the Armada's strict formation broken at last the English seized their chance. Off Gravelines a fierce, close range battle developed. This six day 'dog-fight' saved England from invasion and sealed the fate of Philip's 'Enterprise'.

Howard divided his fleet and allowed Drake to command the leading squadron. The Spanish and Portuguese fought heroically. Smoke and fire surrounded the ships. Masts and sails collapsed in tangled masses. Blood dripped from the decks as priests knelt beside dying men. Medina Sidonia's flagship was bombarded by three English ships. He refused to surrender and when there was no ammunition left for the cannon his men fired muskets. Gradually firing grew intermittent as one ship after another ran out of cannon balls. And as the battered Spanish ships drifted north, a strong wind began to drive them to the Zeeland sandbanks off the Dutch coast. It seemed the entire fleet would be lost, but at the last moment the wind changed. The Spanish disappeared into the haze of the North Sea. The English followed as far as the Scottish coast and then turned back.

For the next few weeks the Armada struggled to get home round the coasts of Scotland and Ireland. Most of the ships had torn sails, broken masts and holes in their sides. Nearly all were crowded with sick and wounded men whose only food was mouldy biscuits and foul water. Even so, the fleet stayed together until it reached the Orkneys. Then storms and mist caused whole squadrons to lose contact with each other. Groups of six or eight battered ships started to reach Spain in September. One or two were so badly damaged that they sank as they reached harbour. Fifty-three ships and one-third of the men never returned at all.

A great Queen

On 29 July Elizabeth had appeared amongst her militia at Tilbury, near London. Seated on a horse, wearing breastplate and sword, she proclaimed: 'I am come amongst you at this time, not for my recreation or sport, but being resolved in the midst and heat of battle to live and die amongst you all. . . . I know I have the body of a weak and feeble woman, but I have the heart of a king, and a King of England too, and think foul scorn that Parma or Spain, or any prince of Europe, should dare to invade . . . my realm'.

It was the sort of speech Tudor Englishmen loved to hear. No one knew then that the Armada was already sailing north, nor that the war would drag on for the rest of Elizabeth's reign. Yet few could have doubted that the Armada's defeat was the crowning moment of a great reign. The legend of 'Good Queen Bess' had been born.

More about the Armada

Books
The Armada (Cape: Jackdaw)
G. Robinson, *The Elizabethan Ship* (Longman: Then and There)
M. Lewis, *The Spanish Armada* (Pan Books)
C. W. Hodges, *The Spanish Armada* (Oxford University Press)

Visual aids
Some of those listed after Chapter 11, and:
The Spanish Armada (Educational Productions)

Visits
National Maritime Museum, Greenwich
Science Museum

To write and find out
1 Imagine you are an English/Spanish or Portuguese sailor taking part in the Armada battle. Describe your adventures and give your own opinion of the reasons for your side's success/failure.
2 Write a folk song telling the story of the Armada. Either set it to an existing tune or make up one of your own.
3 Find out about recent attempts to salvage Armada wrecks. There have been several of these, including the work in Tobermory Bay, Scotland and the discovery of the *Gerona* in the Giant's Causeway off the coast of Northern Ireland (1967).

13 Bess's Golden Days
Life in Elizabethan England

John Stubbs raises his remaining hand to bless Elizabeth, while another of her critics receives his punishment

The mature Elizabeth was not only supreme above all Englishmen. She was treated more like a goddess than a woman. Courtiers exaggerated her good qualities in words and music. Poets referred to her as 'Gloriana'. Painters showed her as a magnificently dressed doll, the face almost hidden by clothes and jewelry. During royal progresses (journeys) through southern England each summer, thousands flocked to watch and cheer her, to present 'humble petitions' asking some favour, or to offer presents. Even Elizabeth's unmarried state, which when she was young had seemed weird, now made the old 'Virgin Queen' appear wonderful.

Yet behind the doors of the palace, was an old, tired and lonely woman. 'To be a king and wear a crown is more glorious to them that see it, than it is pleasure to them that bear it,' Elizabeth remarked sadly towards the end of her reign. That it appeared glorious was due to the Queen's personality. Like her father, she acted the royal part well, winning the hearts of young and old, courtier and commoner. In 1589 a bored schoolboy scribbled the word 'Elizabeth' again and again in his textbook. In a margin he wrote:

The rose is red, the leaves are green,
God save Elizabeth, our noble queen.

Even the Queen's critics came under her spell. When John Stubbs had his right hand chopped off for daring to suggest Elizabeth should marry, he raised his left and shouted, 'God save the Queen'.

'The fourth sort'

In theory the lords were next in power and prestige to the monarch. In practice no Tudor had much love for this class. As a result noblemen were less important than in earlier times. Many baronial castles were in ruins or empty; private armies of 'retainers' no longer existed. The rebellion of the northern earls showed how weak lords had become since the Wars of the Roses.

Henry VIII had chosen men of humble birth to serve him—Wolsey, Cranmer and Cromwell. Generally Elizabeth did the same as far as her ministers and favourites were concerned. It became the custom to give high office to gentlemen, that is, men who owned property and were entitled to a coat of arms, rather than nobles. Tudor power was based on the support of this middle class of moderately well off people. In these times a pushing young man could often gain a fortune, although he might also lose his head!

Gentlemen were in a minority. One Elizabethan writer divided English society into Gentlemen, Citizens, Yeomen, and the 'fourth sort of men who do not rule'. The great majority were of this 'fourth sort'. Apart from certain rights under English law, they were expected

Longleat House—
England's first Renaissance-
style palace

to keep quiet, work hard and obey their 'betters'. Nobody thought they needed a say in governing the country, first because they owned no land or property and second because the Queen, Council and Parliament knew what was best for them.

Not that such people were ignored. Elizabeth's governments tried to organise trade and industry so as to get the best from the nation's resources. The Statute of Artificers (1563) graded work in order of importance. Agriculture came first, followed by the crafts associated with it—the making of tools and wagons, for example. The cloth trade was placed third with men of the professional classes (priests, lawyers and doctors) last. Because jobs were scarce, it was made difficult to enter crafts and professions. In most cases a seven-year apprenticeship was compulsory for craftsmen, while university candidates had to own some property.

Those who had regular jobs were fortunate. Throughout the sixteenth century the numbers of workless increased steadily. Numerous reasons were given to explain this unemployment. Many blamed enclosures or the dissolution of the monasteries. Others pointed to the debasement of the coinage, higher prices and the importing of foreign goods at the expense of English products. A few old men thought it was the result of lazy habits which had been unknown in their youth. There was probably some truth in all these explanations. Nevertheless, there was a deeper cause which could not be blamed on kings or landowners, dishonest ministers or greedy merchants. England, indeed the whole of western Europe, was changing its way of life and work, as trade increased and industry grew in importance. Above all, its population was increasing. The 'ragged rabblement of rakehells' who infested the towns and countryside, begging and thieving, were often the results of these changes.

The mature Elizabeth in all her glory

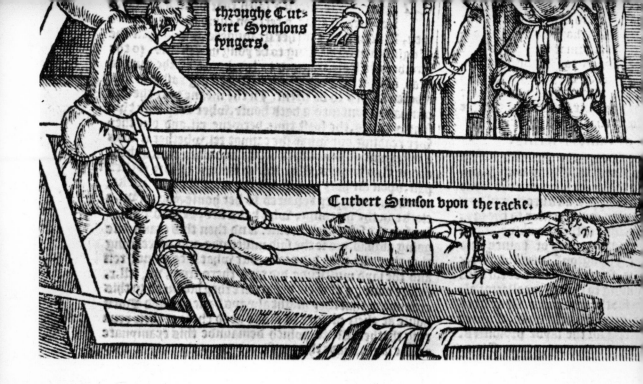

Inside the illustration:
throughe Cut=
bert Symsons
fyngers.

Cutbert Simson vpon the racke.

The Great Poor Law

By Elizabeth's reign there were far too many poor to live on charity alone. Norwich, for example, was reckoned in 1570 to have 2,000 beggars, that is, ten per cent of its population. In such conditions a man or woman turned easily to crime. Tudor towns were full of every type of trickster, from 'Abraham-men' who pretended to be mad to get money, and 'hookers' who stole clothes and linen out of windows with poles, to 'clappendogens' who made out they were crippled and 'prygmen' who stole poultry: And since there was no police force, such underworld characters stood a good chance of escape.

The frightened authorities hit back with grim punishments for those who were caught. Death was a common end for lawbreakers; in Devon alone seventy-four people were hanged from the dreaded 'gallows tree' in one year of Elizabeth's reign. Men and women were hanged, drawn and quartered for treason, and hanged for a number of smaller crimes. When found begging they had holes bored in their ears. If caught a second time they were whipped 'until their backs be bloody'. Other punishments included having one's ear nailed to the pillory, noses slit or hands chopped off at the wrist. Prisons were terrible places whose inmates often died of disease or starvation.

Fortunately certain town councils, Ipswich, Norwich and London in particular, tried a different approach. Even before Elizabeth's time London had four hospitals and an empty royal palace for the poor to live in. Later Ipswich and Norwich made their richer citizens pay a special 'poor rate'. With this money hospitals were provided for the sick and work for the healthy.

Such a system was finally applied to the entire country. The Great

Grim Tudor punishment
This man is being stretched
on the rack

Poor Law (1601) allowed parish overseers to be appointed to administer the poor rate in each village or town. Workhouses and hospitals were built, poor children and orphans apprenticed to worthwhile jobs and most begging made illegal. Small parishes unable to support their own poor were helped by larger ones, or allowed to license their paupers as 'official' beggars. Not all these rules were enforced and many paupers continued to rely on private charity. Nevertheless, the principle that each parish was responsible for its own paupers lasted well into the nineteenth century and the 'poor rate' became the basis of all local taxation.

Elizabeth and her Parliaments

Elizabeth ruled chiefly through a royal Council. Parliament's total sessions amounted to a mere thirty-five months in a reign of forty-five years! Nevertheless, ever since Henry VIII summoned the 'Reformation' Parliament, its powers and influence had been increasing. This process was accelerated between 1588 and 1603 when wars and rebellions forced the Queen to ask for extra taxes. Because of this a new type of 'parliament' man emerged, able to use Commons' privileges to the full. For the first time it became possible to speak against royal policies without dying a traitor's death.

Not that members of Parliament enjoyed our modern freedom of speech. From the beginning of her reign, Elizabeth censored all printed material. After 1586 no book could be published without permission of the Archbishop of Canterbury or Bishop of London. Inside Parliament, the Queen disliked discussion of a number of subjects, including the succession to the throne, religion, foreign affairs, trade and her marriage. Such restrictions annoyed some M.P.'s, particularly those who were Puritan merchants interested in both trade and religion.

In 1572, one Puritan member, Peter Wentworth, complained about what he called 'rumours'. 'The one is a rumour which runneth about the House, and it is this, "take heed what you do; the Queen's Majesty liketh not such a matter; whosoever preferreth it, she will be offended" . . . or the contrary "Her Majesty liketh of such a matter; whosoever speaketh against it, she will be much offended with him".' This complaint about her attempts to influence parliamentary decisions angered the Queen who sent Wentworth to the Tower for a time. It was, she said, 'monstrous that the feet should direct the head'. Fifteen years later she was just as sensitive. When Sir John Cope proposed that the Church of England form of prayer should be abolished in favour of a Calvinistic one he, too, ended up in the Tower.

Yet Elizabeth knew she could not do without Parliament. For the normal running expenses of the country she received about £140,000 annually from various sources. This was not enough even for a ruler as thrifty as Elizabeth. When money did run out, the Queen frequently sold Crown property rather than call a Parliament. But as the war with Spain dragged on large sums were needed which only the Commons could supply. These were not always easy to obtain. In

1597, for example, it took twenty-four days of debate to obtain a war tax.

Fortunately, the Queen's personality charmed even Puritans. In her last speech to Parliament she remarked: 'Though God hath raised me high yet this I count the glory of my crown, that I have reigned with your loves.' She was by then old and wrinkled, with blackened teeth and a red wig, so weak that she nearly fainted under the weight of her grand clothes. Yet an eyewitness wrote: 'Her apt and refined words, so learnedly composed, did ravish (delight) the sense of the hearers with . . . admiration.'

Education

Most of the men who listened to the Queen that day were well educated and knew a good speech when they heard one. An Elizabethan gentleman's desire to 'get on' showed clearly in his attitude to schooling. Before Henry VIII's time most boys of well-to-do families had received their education in the household of a great lord or at a monastic school. After the dissolution of the monasteries some of the latter carried on as grammar or cathedral schools. In Edward VI's reign, as we have seen, chantry money was used to found 'Edward VI grammar schools', which in some cases survive to the present day.

By Elizabeth's time the growing demand for education had led to the foundation of famous public schools such as Repton (1553), Rugby (1567), Uppingham (1584) and Harrow (1590). Few were large by modern standards. John Roysse of Abingdon, Berks, for example, founded his 'grammar' school for sixty-three boys because he was sixty-three years old! None was a boarding school in the modern sense, for boys who could not travel home each night usually lived with local families.

A typical school of the period was said to have been established 'for the instruction of boys as well in the rudiments as in all the art of grammar'. The word 'grammar' refers to the teaching of Latin and possibly Greek. Lessons were learnt by heart in a dull and uninteresting way, although young children seem to have been taught the alphabet in the modern manner; one Elizabethan textbook begins with 'A for Apple' but cheats with 'X for Xpensive'! The alphabet and the Lord's Prayer were generally printed on a hornbook—a piece of wood shaped like a bat whose lettering was protected by a sheet of transparent horn. Writing was done with a goose quill (feather) which needed constant scraping to stop the ink sticking.

School hours were long. It has been worked out that an Elizabethan pupil spent 1,826 hours at lessons each year compared with roughly 1,080 today. Most boys worked six days a week with ten hours of lessons each day. Discipline was severe and vicious flogging occurred daily. An old man recalled that in his youth he had once received fifty-three strokes of the cane at one time. Boys had to be held down to endure such punishments which were often inflicted for trivial reasons. Some Tudor school badges show pupils being caned and one had a design of birches. Nevertheless, naughty boys seem to have

Tudor school scene. Magdalen Grammar School, Oxford—the teacher, his birch near at hand, is lecturing the pupils

been as common then as now. At St Albans School during Elizabeth's reign there were complaints of pupils swearing and 'drinking tobacco'.

Poor children rarely had much schooling, apart from odd lessons with a village schoolmaster or clergyman. As one sixteenth-century countryman remarked: 'This is all we go to school for—to read Common Prayers at Church and to set down common prices at markets.' Yet even this small amount of learning was rare for his class.

Universities

There were only two English universities, Oxford and Cambridge. Each consisted of a number of semi-independent colleges which had developed from 'halls' or 'hostels' which were designed originally to house and feed students. Oxford was the oldest for its first college had been founded in 1249. Cambridge's earliest 'hostel', Peterhouse, dates from 1284. In Scotland four universities, St Andrews, Aberdeen, Edinburgh and Glasgow, had been set up in the fifteenth and sixteenth centuries.

An English undergraduate studied four years for the degree of Bachelor of Arts, and a further three to become a Master. The chief subjects were religion, law, Greek philosophy, medicine, dialectic (debating), geometry, astronomy, Greek and Hebrew. Law

The life story of an Elizabethan gentleman—Sir Henry Unton. Various scenes depict: 1 his birth 2 at Oxford University 3 travelling in Italy 4 soldiering in the Low Countries 5 as Ambassador to France 6 on his deathbed 7 feasting with his family 8 watching a masque (a play with music and dancing) 9 his funeral procession

students went to special colleges in London, Grays Inn, Lincoln's Inn, the Inner Temple and the Middle Temple. Examinations took the form of a disputation (debate) in Latin between the candidate and his teachers. The final disputation after seven years' work was the scholar's 'masterpiece' which, if accepted, gave him his master's degree.

Rich men's sons tended to waste their time at university, feasting and drinking. For the poorer students, struggling to gain qualifications for a career, living conditions were hard. A student's room at Oxford or Cambridge cost about £1 a year, and he had to supply his own tables, chairs, rushes for the floor and, occasionally, glass for the windows. Since breakfast was not provided many undergraduates became expert beggars.

Elizabeth had been educated privately by some of the finest English scholars. She took a keen interest in university education and gave her support though not her money, to the founding of Jesus College, Oxford (1571). Her visits to Oxford or Cambridge were great occasions, with feasting, plays, speeches and music in her honour.

Doctors and surgeons

The best Tudor physicians were university trained men who had to cure three people before gaining a medical degree. They treated most of the diseases known today, except cancer. Unlike modern doctors, however, they also dealt with bubonic plague, and a deadly fever called the 'sweating' sickness. Plague is carried by fleas on the back of black rats. It can affect the lungs, bloodstream and various parts of the body, where it causes swellings called buboes (hence bubonic). Although the cure was not discovered until 1894, a few sixteenth-century doctors suspected that rats were in some way responsible.

Treatments for illnesses were very different from those available today. Whereas a modern medical man will prescribe one or two medicines, a Tudor doctor might suggest as many as a hundred. To relieve pain old Egyptian remedies, mandrake root or opium, were used. For other ailments there were extraordinary 'cures' involving eating crabs' eyes, partridge feathers, buttered live spiders, ants' eggs and even powdered human skull! And whereas dieting today means cutting down on certain foods, in Tudor times it usually meant the patient had to eat and drink too much.

Another medical practitioner, the surgeon, was also becoming important. Surgeons were rarely well educated; since the Middle Ages they had been barbers whose occasional operations were in fact forbidden by the Church authorities. By the mid-sixteenth century the value of such work was beginning to be appreciated, particularly in warfare where gunpowder was causing dreadful burns and injuries. In 1543 Andreas Vesalius had published, *On the Structure of the Human Body*. Illustrated with 277 woodcut drawings, this book showed the true course of the veins and the make-up of the heart. This became the guide for future generations of surgeons.

Above: Witches, standing in a circle marked on the ground, swear allegiance to the Devil

Right: Witches bringing down rain

Below: Witches being burned to death

Another pioneer, Ambroise Paré, travelled with the French army and discovered that a mixture of egg-yolk and oil of roses was better for burns than scalding with hot oils.

Witchcraft and sorcery

Whilst some struggled to increase the boundaries of knowledge, the majority remained superstitious and ignorant. One man described how as a child he had been frightened by tales of 'an ugly devil having horns on his head, fire in his mouth and a tail, eyes like a basin, fangs like a dog, claws like a bear and a voice roaring like a lion'. He was also taught to fear witches, urchins, elves, hags, fairies, satyrs, dwarfs, giants, and imps. Neither were such beliefs just for children. Grown-ups 'saw' elves, goblins, and mischievous spirits like 'Robin Goodfellow' and 'Tom Thumb' in fields and woods. They thought that ravens croaked to warn of death and sea voyages should only be started on 'lucky' days. Accidents, illness, floods and storms were seen as the work of the Devil.

Nothing was believed to show the Devil's power more clearly than the work of witches. Most witches were women; according to a German writer this was because they were the more wicked sex. Witches were thought to cause storms and lightning, to kill or injure man or beast, even to turn night into day. Many misfortunes (the loss of a ship, failure of a crop, or even the death of a cow) were blamed on them. If caught and convicted they were tortured, imprisoned, hanged or burned.

Two signs were thought to prove their guilt. First, the Devil had left a mark on their bodies; hence any sort of birthmark or deformity was suspicious. If this was pierced with a dagger or pin the witch was said to feel no pain. Second, every witch had a 'familiar', usually a cat or toad, which could turn into a devil and do her work. Consequently any old lady living alone and talking to her pet was in danger.

It was not difficult to catch witches because most boasted of their powers. One Tudor witch, Ursley Kemp, had four cats called Tyffin, Tittey, Piggen and Jacket. Two she claimed to use for injuring people and two for killing. If a witch did not confess she was tied hand and foot and thrown into a pond or river. Should she float she was guilty, and if she was 'innocent' it was usually too late to save her! Occasionally male witches called warlocks, were punished. The Earl of Bothwell was suspected of witchcraft and in 1590 did public penance to wash away his 'guilt'. The same year in Scotland a Doctor Fian was burned to death for having tried to raise a storm to sink a ship in which King James was travelling to Denmark.

Sorcery, a more 'respectable' kind of magic, was studied by scholars. The 'black art' as it was called enabled men to call up devils from hell. A clever sorcerer was thought to command seventy-nine of these spirits, ranging from Marbas, who could cure all diseases, to Asmodai, who revealed hidden treasure and made men invisible. Some sorcerers were thought to serve the Devil. Others were regarded as learned men who used their magic for good.

Church Year

Opposed to such weird beliefs was the Church, whose teachings and customs influenced the lives of rich and poor alike.

Each year was marked by various happy or solemn festivals. Christmas was celebrated for twelve days. During this period rich men entertained servants and friends in their mansions, where jesters told jokes and posed riddles, jugglers and acrobats gave displays and minstrels played or sang. Children enjoyed 'blind-man's buff' or 'Kiss in the ring' and each year a 'Boy bishop' was chosen. He played practical jokes and actually preached a sermon in church on Holy Innocent's Day (28 December).

Candlemas (2 February) was the date to start spring sowing. On that day churches and houses were decorated with extra candles. Preparations for Easter were long and serious. On Shrove Tuesday men and women confessed their sins and were shriven (forgiven). Next day, Ash Wednesday, priests drew a black cross on each person's forehead to remind them that one day they would die and turn

An Elizabethan surgeon demonstrating how to dissect a body

to dust. During the forty days of Lent leading up to Easter, Christians made some small sacrifices in memory of Christ's own sufferings in the wilderness. In particular, they were supposed to give up meat, which was not difficult as there was little remaining from the slaughter of cattle the previous autumn!

On Maunday Thursday, the day before Good Friday, the Queen and her bishops washed the feet of a few poor people, thus imitating Christ's washing of his disciples' feet at the Last Supper. The Queen did this to as many men and women as the years of her age. Afterwards food, clothing and money were shared amongst them. A similar ceremony takes place today when special Maundy money is distributed, although the monarch no longer washes anyone's feet.

On Good Friday all church statues were covered with black cloths —a way of mourning Christ's death on the Cross. A solemn service and perhaps a play about the Crucifixion was performed. Easter Day, the most important festival of the Church Year, was spent rejoicing at Christ's Resurrection. Then, seven Sundays after Easter, the descent of the Holy Spirit to the disciples at Pentecost was celebrated on White (now Whit) Sunday. This was an important holiday with feasting and plays. In medieval times it had been one of the three occasions (Christmas and Easter were the others) when the king 'wore his crown', that is, received his nobles at court.

Such religious holidays were mixed up in people's minds with pagan ideas about the 'rebirth' of the earth at spring time; the word Easter comes from 'Eostre', the name of the Saxon Goddess of Dawn. The most popular non-religious festival was May Day (1 May). On the previous evening young people would leave their homes and search nearby woods for a tree-trunk suitable for a maypole. When cut down and trimmed it was carried to the village or town green so that it could be a centre for dancing. Next day a pretty girl was crowned 'May Queen' and a young man became 'Lord of Misrule'. He spent the day frightening people with bells and rattles, chasing girls for kisses and riding a wooden hobby horse.

In later years Puritans did their best to wipe out many of these customs. They were never completely successful. Consequently,

Spring scene in the Tudor countryside. An illustration from the *Shepherd's Calendar* 1597

although Elizabeth's parliaments and fleets, her beggars and witches, are no more, it is sometimes possible to celebrate Easter, Whitsun or May Day in a way she would have recognised.

More about Elizabeth's England

Books

A. H. Dodd, *Life in Elizabethan England* (Batsford)

R. Goyder, *A Reformation Family* (Longman: Then and There)

I. Doncaster, *Elizabethan and Jacobean Home Life* (Longman: Evidence in Pictures)

A. Fletcher, *Elizabethan Village* (Longman: Then and There)

E. and G. Lay, *Tudor and Stuart Times* (Macmillan: History Picture Books)

M. Reeves, *Elizabethan Citizen* (Longman: Then and There)

M. Reeves, *Elizabethan Court* (Longman: Then and There)

H. R. Trevor-Roper, *The European Witch-craze of the 16th and 17th Centuries* (Penguin)

G. Wills, *English Life Series* (Pergamon), vol. 1

Visual aids

The Elizabethan Dream *(two filmstrips with record)* (Visual Publications)

Tudor Life (Common Ground)

Elizabethan England *(film)* (Gateway)

Elizabethan People and Houses *(film)* (Gateway)

Surgery (Hulton)

Visits

Houses of Parliament

Palace of Westminster

St Stephen's Chapel

Many English towns contain buildings dating from Tudor times.

Three famous 'great houses' are Little Moreton Hall, Cheshire, Woolaton Hall, Nottinghamshire and Hardwick House, Derbyshire.

To write and find out

1 It will probably be possible to compile a booklet of information, drawings, photographs, etc. concerned with the Tudor buildings in your own neighbourhood.

2 Make your own 'Statutes of Artificers' for the modern world, grading work in order of importance. How far does it differ from that of Elizabethan times?

3 Make a list of Elizabethan 'underworld' nicknames—see E. V. Milliken's *Lancastrian and Tudor* (Harrap). Compare it with those given to certain types of criminal today.

4 Imagine you are an Elizabethan doctor treating a patient. Prescribe a few Tudor 'remedies' to help the cure!

5 Find out how many old Church festivals are still celebrated in your neighbourhood.

14 The Upstart Crow
Elizabeth I 1588-1603

Although picnics were not 'invented' until the eighteenth century, Queen Elizabeth and her courtiers are shown here enjoying a similar recreation—a pause for refreshment during a hunt

In 1586 a young man travelled from Warwickshire to the dangerous, exciting world of England's capital. Elizabethan London was one of Europe's great cities. It was governed by twelve companies of merchants—mercers, grocers, drapers, fishmongers, goldsmiths, skinners, merchant taylors, cloth workers, haberdashers, salters, ironmongers and vintners. However ordinary these trades sound, their leaders were enormously powerful, engaged in banking, foreign trade and insurance. Even the Queen's ministers treated them with respect.

Some 200,000 inhabitants were crowded inside London's long wall with its seven gates. In tiny houses set along narrow, winding alleys they worked, played and fought in busy confusion. The clatter of tools, rumbling of wagons, shouts of street sellers and frequent clanging of bells made London a noisy place. Two unmistakable landmarks dominated the scene as they had in Henry VII's time. London Bridge almost dammed the river with its narrow arches, one of which was blocked by water mills used for grinding corn. Great skill was needed to steer a boat through these gaps, where tumbling water resembled small waterfalls. In the heart of the City St Paul's Cathedral stood as proud as ever, a meeting place for Londoners which was half church, half market place. Labourers were hired and girls picked up inside the walls; booksellers and even fishmongers traded there. Sermons and executions took place in the churchyard.

Outside the City boundaries lay Moorfields and Spitalfields, open fields which Londoners used for sport and recreation. To the west stood the Palace and Abbey of Westminster, centre of the Queen's government. To the east the grim outline of the Tower of London reminded men of royal power. Here traitors waited for the punishment which would set their heads on poles at the entrance to London Bridge, making the gate resemble a grim and ghastly pin-cushion.

Across the Thames to the south little wooden theatres, the Curtain, Rose, Swan and Globe, stood among houses and fields. Forbidden to entertain within the city walls, companies of players gave shows on the South Bank each afternoon. Of all London's attractions it was these which had brought our young man up from Warwickshire. For William Shakespeare wanted to be an actor.

'This wooden O'

The renewed interest in the Ancient World had led to productions of Greek and Roman plays, with scenery, music and dancing. These were first popular in Italy, where rich patrons had permanent theatres built in the Roman style, and they were copied by Oxford and Cambridge Universities in England. Unlike medieval plays, these

Scapino.   Cap. Zerbino.

Pulliciniello.   Sig.ᵃ L

Scaramucia

S. PAULES CHURCH

LONDON

AMESIS   FLUVIUS

South   Warke

Vischer's panoramic view
of London, 1601, with
old St Paul's in the
centre

Street players

Fricasso.

works were not Christian. They did not tell Bible stories or deal with Church teaching.

Alongside such Renaissance art, a 'drama of the streets' developed. At first, this *Commedia Dell' Arte* was mainly comic. Words were improvised by the actors during the performance but the characters remained the same. Some are still popular today, Columbine and Harlequin in pantomime, for example, and Punchinello who is known to every young child as 'Punch'. In England in the mid-sixteenth century, many groups of travelling players, usually four men and a boy, were formed under the protection of a lord. They gave shows in inn yards, town halls or large houses. In 1576 James Burbage, an actor, built the 'Theatre' at Shoreditch; the name indicates that it was the only permanent one in the country. His productions made a profit, so other theatres, the Curtain, Rose and Swan, were built. The famous 'Globe' was founded by Burbage's son, Richard, in 1599.

Elizabethan playhouses resembled a medieval inn-yard; 'boxes' in a modern theatre grew out of the balconies still visible on some hotels. Usually such theatres were round or rectangular, with the centre open to the sky, to give good lighting. Shakespeare in his play *Henry V* refers to one as 'This wooden O'. A trestle stage (the

FLUVIUS

South Warke

Scaffold) jutted out in the middle, partly covered by a roof called either the Shadow, or the Heavens (because it was sometimes painted with the sun, moon and stars). The stage was high enough for actors to be hidden underneath, or to disappear suddenly through a trapdoor.

Poorer members of the audience were called groundlings. They stood in the middle of the theatre, open to wind and weather. Well-to-do people used the galleries lining the sides, whilst the most important theatregoers occupied a private area behind the stage (the Lord's Room). Because audiences were noisy and rough few ladies ever attended. If they did they hid their identity behind masks called vizards. There were no actresses so boys played women's parts. Performances were announced by flying a flag, blowing a trumpet or even firing a cannon. Spectators did not stand for 'God Save the Queen' as we do. Instead they listened to 'A Prayer for the Queen's Majesty'.

'Tudor rant'

Shakespeare was born in 1564 in Stratford-upon-Avon, Warwickshire. He attended the local grammar school where, according to

The continuation of Vischer's view of London

Shakespeare's signature on his will

another writer, Ben Jonson, he learnt 'small Latin and less Greek'. In 1582 he married Anne Hathaway, a girl eight years older than himself. Such an early marriage seems to have made him restless and dissatisfied because three years afterwards he went to London. Here he joined the Lord Chamberlain's Company (the King's Men) led by Richard Burbage. It was a busy, hard life, performing daily before an audience 'capable of nothing but inexplicable dumb-shows and noise'.

Shakespeare arrived when new 'English' productions were challenging Greek and Roman works. Hitherto most written drama had catered for educated people. The earliest English comedy, *Ralph Roister Doister* (1553) was probably written for a school performance; the second, *Gammer Gurton's Needle* (1566), was first performed at Christ's College, Cambridge. Very few plays for the 'man in the street' existed.

In the 1580s, however, Christopher Marlowe (1564–93) burst upon the scene. Although a university man, Marlowe wrote exciting popular dramas. *Tamburlaine the Great* tells the story of an Asiatic conqueror. *Dr Faustus* describes the adventures of a man who sells his soul to the Devil, *The Jew of Malta* has a villainous 'hero' who betrays Malta to the Turks. Marlowe's characters spoke thrilling blank (non-rhyming) verse which the actors often shouted at the audience. Such speech, when delivered with special gestures to show anger, fear and other emotions, is known as 'Tudor rant'.

Marlowe lived a wild life and was killed in a tavern fight. After his death Edward Alleyn made the largest theatrical fortune of the time producing the dramatist's works. With it he founded Dulwich College in London. Shakespeare knew Marlowe and admired his work. By 1592, at latest, he had taken the unusual step for an actor of writing a play of his own, probably *Comedy of Errors* or *Love's Labours Lost*. This roused the jealousy of professional playwrights. One unsuccessful dramatist, Robert Greene, wrote bitterly, 'there is an upstart crow, beautified with our feathers, that . . . supposes he is well able to bombast out a blank verse . . . and in his own conceit (opinion) the only Shake-scene in the country'. Greene's feelings are understandable but his judgement of Shakespeare was wrong. The 'upstart crow' proved to be England's greatest dramatist.

William Shakespeare

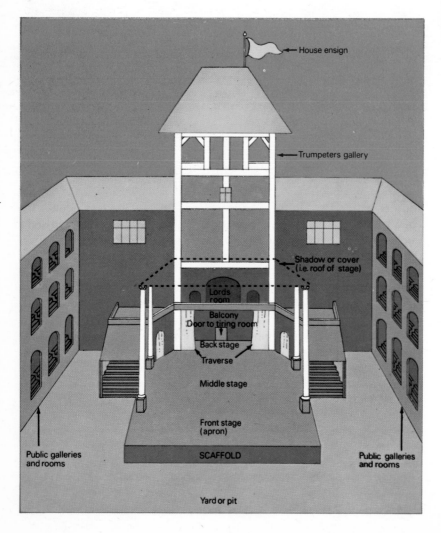

Elizabethan theatre

Shakespeare's plays

Shakespeare wrote tragedies, (plays with unhappy endings) such as *Hamlet, King Lear, Othello* and *Macbeth* which are still performed in many countries. Some have particular themes running through them. *Othello,* for example, deals with jealousy, *Macbeth* with ambition and *King Lear* with family relationships. His most famous comedies, *Twelfth Night, The Merry Wives of Windsor* and *The Taming of the Shrew* are equally popular; the last named was the basis of a recent musical called *Kiss Me Kate.*

Shakespeare's plays are full of exciting action and memorable verse. A disillusioned Macbeth, speaking of man's life on earth, says:

It is a tale.
Told by an idiot, full of sound and fury, signifying nothing. . . .

And children are not forgotten for Shakespeare describes:
the whining schoolboy, with his satchel,
And shining morning face, creeping like snail unwillingly to school.

Whether king or rebel, rich man or beggar, Shakespeare's creations are real and lifelike. Many of his phrases have become famous.

Of England he wrote:
This happy breed of men, this little world,
This precious stone set in a silver sea. . . .
This blessed plot, this earth, this realm, this England.
Of mercy:

The quality of mercy is not strained,
It droppeth as the gentle rain from heaven
Upon the place beneath; it is twice bless'd;
It blesseth him that gives and him that takes.

Of opportunity:
There is a tide in the affairs of men
Which, taken at the flood, leads on to fortune;
Omitted, all the voyages of their life
Is bound in shallows and in misery.

Apart from plays, Shakespeare wrote a number of poems, including 154 sonnets. Some of these are addressed to a man; others to an unknown woman who has been called 'the Dark Lady of the Sonnets'. They contain some of his best poetry. In one a young man measures the time he has been in love, as follows:

Three winters cold
Have from the forests shook three summers' pride
Three beauteous springs to yellow autumn turned
In process of the seasons have I seen,
Three April perfumes in three hot Junes burned
Since first I saw you fresh.
In another an old man says:
When to the sessions of sweet silent thought
I summon up remembrance of things past
I sigh the lack of many a thing I sought.

Not surprisingly, many of Shakespeare's phrases have been used by other writers as titles for their novels, plays or essays.

The 'Bard of Avon' rarely invented a story, preferring instead to borrow his tales. Of his thirty-seven plays, a considerable number are historical. Three, *Henry IV, Henry V,* and *Richard III* deal with the Wars of the Roses. Details were taken from two chronicles, those of Hall and Holinshed, and all three emphasise the need for strong government. The same theme runs through two plays about weak or unsuccessful kings, *Edward II* and *Richard II*. No Tudor was likely to disagree with such propaganda. Elizabeth, in fact, liked Shakespeare's work. Several of his plays received their first performances in her presence and she was particularly fond of Sir John Falstaff, the fat knight who appears in *Henry IV* and *The Merry Wives of Windsor*. Another play, *Midsummer Night's Dream* is supposed to have been written in her honour. Certainly one of its chief characters is a majestic fairy queen!

Shakespeare's last play, *The Tempest*, appeared in 1611. Then he retired a rich man to his home town where he built himself a house called New Place. When he died, on 23 April 1616, Ben Jonson wrote: 'I loved the man and do honour him.' He also predicted correctly, 'He was not of an age but for all time.'

The Globe Theatre, London

Tudor sunset.

Elizabeth's last years were not all glory; the 'fairy queen' lived in a real and hard world. The war with Spain dragged on, becoming a battle for profit rather than the fight for survival it had been in 1588. Treasure fleets were captured less often because the Spanish had learnt from their mistakes. Even a successful attack on Cadiz in 1596 did not produce as much plunder as expected.

At home Puritanism continued to spread. During 1588–89 pamphlets written by a man calling himself 'Martin Marprelate' appeared in London. All criticised the Church of England; in one bishops were referred to as 'petty antichrists', proud prelates, intolerable withstanders of reformation, enemies of the gospel'. Such strong language indicated that the old desire to reform the Church was being replaced in many cases by a demand for something entirely different. Separatists, or Independents, rejected the Prayer Book altogether. Presbyterians wanted a Calvinist system without any bishops.

Elizabeth detested such ideas. In her view any criticism of the Church was an attack on royal authority. In 1583 she had appointed as Archbishop of Canterbury John Whitgift, a priest who hated Puritanism as much as she did. Whitgift forced clergymen to agree to the Royal Supremacy (accept that the monarch was head of the Church), the Prayer Book and the Thirty-nine Articles of belief. His methods of fighting Puritanism were secretive and unfair. A special High Commission spent its time collecting evidence from spies. Suspects, when summoned before it, were punished by Star Chamber if they refused to answer questions, and usually fined or imprisoned if they did!

Wales gradually became more peaceful, possibly because the Tudors were a Welsh family. Catholic Ireland, on the other hand, remained bitter and discontented and from 1595 it was the scene of the most serious rebellion of Tudor times. Irish chieftains had long resented the English settlers who came to 'colonise' their country. Led by two important lords, O'Neill and O'Donnell, they now started to attack and burn the homes of English Protestants. Elizabeth did not take the threat seriously until O'Neill appealed for Spanish aid and demanded self rule for the Irish. Then she sent the largest army ever to leave England in the sixteenth century, 17,000 men commanded by the Earl of Essex.

Essex had been Elizabeth's chief favourite since the death of Leicester in 1588. He was an ambitious, spoilt young man who took full advantage of his high position as a sort of adopted 'son' of the Queen. By the time he left for Ireland his arrogance had annoyed Elizabeth; once when he dared to turn his back on her she boxed his ears! When he failed to defeat O'Neill and signed a truce with the rebel instead, she had him arrested. Released after a short while, he staged a crazy rebellion and was beheaded (February 1601).

Lord Mountjoy, his successor in Ireland, was an unusual general. He wrapped himself in three waistcoats against the Irish cold, slept in the afternoons and dined for hours on end. But he stood bravely with his common soldiers when the enemy appeared and marched his men through winter snows to surprise rebel strongholds. At Kinsale (December 1601) he severely defeated the Irish and their Spanish allies. By 1603 the Spaniards had returned home and

O'Neill was glad to come to terms. For the first time in its history, Ireland was controlled by the English.

The death of Essex made the Queen more lonely than ever. Burghley had passed away in 1598, nursed at the last by Elizabeth herself. Drake and Hawkins had both died at sea. Strange faces appeared at the palace. As her end approached Elizabeth still refused to name her successor, although everyone knew it must be James VI of Scotland, son of Mary Queen of Scots. She also refused to take any medicine or go to bed 'because she had a persuasion that if she once lay down she would never rise'. When her new minister Sir Robert Cecil (1563–1612) Lord Burghley's son, tried to insist she do so, the old Queen murmered: 'The word "must" is not to be used to princes.'

In the end Elizabeth could not speak. A messenger stood at the gates of Richmond Palace, Surrey, waiting to gallop to Scotland with the news of her death. Between two and three o'clock on the morning of 24 March 1603 lights flickered at a window as a signal. The horseman rode away as the last Tudor monarch lay dead.

More about Shakespeare's England
Books
H. M. Burton, *Shakespeare and His Plays* (Methuen: Outlines)
The City of London (Pitkin Pictorials)
J. Hayes, *London: a pictorial history* (Batsford)
C. and M. Lamb, *Lamb's Tales from Shakespeare*
H. and R. Leacroft, *The Theatre* (Methuen: Outlines)

Visual aids
Films of Shakespeare's life have been made by Rank and BBC TV
Filmstrips have been made by Visual Information Services, Education
    Productions, Rank, Hulton and EAV
Shakespeare's London (EAV). Audio Visual Ltd
Shakespeare's Avon (Carwal). Educational

Visits
Performances of Shakespeare's plays, particularly those staged by the National Theatre and at Stratford-upon-Avon, Warwickshire.

To write and find out
1 Find out more about other Elizabethan and Jacobean (living during the reign of James I) playwrights: Marlowe, Jonson, Beaumont and Fletcher.
2 See how many books and plays you can find which have as titles quotations from Shakespeare's plays. Which of Shakespeare's plays forms the basic story of the modern musical *West Side Story* ? Try and see the films, *Henry V, Richard III* and *Hamlet* made in recent years by Lord Olivier.
3 Build your own Globe Theatre.
4 Find out more about the Baconians—those who believe that Shakespeare's plays were written by Francis Bacon.

15 The Wisest Fool
James I 1603-1625

James I

Robert Carey, the messenger who left Richmond to tell King James of Scotland the news, rode the 397 miles to Edinburgh, the Scottish capital, in sixty hours. He arrived 'tired and sore, be-blooded with great falls and bruises'. James was delighted at becoming King of England at last. He asked if there were letters from the royal Council. Carey had none but he brought a ring James had once given Elizabeth as proof that she was dead.

The first Stuart was neither heroic nor attractive. Small and plump, with thin legs, rolling eyes and over-large tongue, he seemed older than his thirty-seven years. Probably this was due to illness for he suffered from piles, catarrh and diarrhoea. His personal habits were revolting. He dribbled, picked his nose and was often sick through over-eating. He was also a coward who wore extra padding in his clothes in case anyone tried to attack him. It was hard to believe his mother had been so beautiful and his father, Lord Darnley, so strong and handsome.

Fortunately there was more to the new King than ugly looks and dirty habits. Owing to his mother's flight and imprisonment, James had been King of Scotland for most of his life. His childhood had been lonely and unhappy—left without parents, beaten by his teachers, bullied by lords who struggled for power. Slowly, more by cunning than force, he overcame both murderous nobles and intolerant priests. It was centuries since Scotland had been as well governed as it was by James.

In other ways he was a suitable successor to Elizabeth. Like the Tudor Queen, he was very well educated. James was a biblical expert and the author of books on monarchy, witchcraft, sport and smoking. Only his fear of black magic was unworthy of a learned man. Of course, it was easy to laugh at him and many did so. He was called the 'Wisest Fool in Christendom', meaning that he was cunning only in trivial not important matters. This was not fair. James had many faults. He was conceited as well as being a bore and a drunkard. But he was generally kind, often witty, sometimes tolerant and always peace-loving. His best side was shown by keeping England out of war for many years; his worst in his treatment of Sir Walter Raleigh.

Raleigh was in many ways the typical Elizabethan. Besides fighting on sea and land, he was a poet, writer, merchant and courtier. Elizabeth had rewarded him with her favour. James took away all his official posts (1603). Soon afterwards Raleigh was arrested on a charge of plotting to kill the King and put James's cousin, Arabella Stuart, on the throne. The Main Plot (so called because there was a smaller, 'bye' plot) was a strange business. Raleigh was probably innocent; some historians have even wondered whether there was a plot at all.

There was little hope for a seadog who had made his name killing Spaniards and seizing their treasure. Personally James hated and feared such a brave, brilliant and boastful man. He was also about to end the long war with Spain. Raleigh was condemned to death at a trial dominated by his personal enemy, Sir Edward Coke. He was then reprieved and imprisoned in the Tower for thirteen years. Here he whiled away the time conducting chemical experiments and writing the first volume of a history of the world. In 1616 the King allowed him to search for a gold-mine in South America providing he did not attack Spanish possessions. The gold was never found and the promise proved impossible to keep; while Raleigh lay ill some of his men burned a Spanish settlement. Worse still, his own son was killed in the fight. The old adventurer returned home to die by the original sentence. Seeing the headsman's axe he remarked: 'This is a sharp medicine, but it is a sound one for all diseases.'

The last great Elizabethan went to the scaffold in 1618. The Elizabethan spirit died much earlier. Soon after arriving in London James was surrounded by an admiring crowd. Instead of making a gracious speech, he was frightened and hurried away. The 'magic touch' of the Tudors had gone forever.

Conference at Hampton

Puritans felt hopeful when James became King. Elizabeth as we have seen, had refused to alter Church of England beliefs and ceremonies. Perhaps a more truly 'Protestant monarch' would do so?

Such continual demands for change, so strange to us today, were understandable at the time. The Church was the most important influence in the lives of seventeenth century Englishmen. All persons had to attend Sunday services or be fined. A tithe (one-tenth) of every man's yearly profits or produce had to be given to his vicar. Church courts could punish men and women for heresy or immorality. Furthermore, when Puritans asked for an end to bishops or the election of clergymen they were talking politics as well as religion. In effect, they were saying that control of the Church should be taken from those ruling classes who upheld the Prayer Book and appointed bishops and priests. It was this non-religious side to the quarrel which was highlighted when James met a large number of important clergymen at Hampton Court Palace in 1604.

In his opening speech James amazed those present by the extent of his religious knowledge. They felt encouraged to remind their 'Most gracious and dread sovereign' of the Millenary Petition, (so called because it was said to have been signed by a thousand priests) presented to him soon after he became King. In it they had asked that the marriage of priests should be made lawful. They also wanted minor changes in church ritual such as an end to the use of a ring in the marriage ceremony, and a ban on making the sign of the cross.

During the debates which followed it became clear that James disliked Presbyterian church organisation. Of the election of ministers

Frontispiece of the Authorised Version of the Bible, 1611

by the congregation, he remarked: 'If you aim at a Scottish presbytery it agreeth as well with monarchy as God and the devil. Then Jack and Tom and Will and Dick shall meet and censure (criticise) me and my council.' At another point he announced, 'No bishops, no king', by which he meant that the next step after abolishing bishops would be to get rid of the king. James's attitude was due, he claimed, to the way Scottish priests had treated 'that poor lady my mother', whose supremacy over the Church had been ignored. Whether true or not, it showed that Puritans could expect no major change of policy from their new King. Mixed committees of bishops and puritans were appointed to consider changes but these failed because the bishops refused to co-operate.

A more lasting outcome of the Conference was a new English translation of the Bible. Six groups of scholars were appointed for this task. Each team studied a separate section, occasionally meeting to correct the others' translations. After six years work the famous 'Authorised Version of the Bible' was issued with James's approval (1611). No book printed in English has been more influential or popular.

Treason and plot

Puritans were not the only Christians disappointed by the new King. At first James promised to abolish the heavy fines paid by Catholics for not attending church. When told the money was used to reward important courtiers he changed his mind. His chief minister Sir Robert Cecil, Earl of Salisbury, went further, for he persuaded the King to banish Catholic priests from England. Most 'old believers' accepted the situation, knowing that to fight back would only make matters worse. Then, in November 1605, the country was horrified to learn of a Catholic plot to kill both King and Parliament.

The full story of the 'Gunpowder treason and plot' will never be known, although the main details revealed by Cecil were probably correct. In 1604 a desperate group, led by Robert Catesby, Thomas Percy and Francis Tresham, decided to blow up King and lords when they assembled for the state opening of Parliament. After this it seems likely they planned to seize the royal children, make James's younger son king, and overthrow the government with Spanish help. It was a crazy scheme, worked out by men already known to the authorities as troublemakers.

According to Cecil, the conspirators at first tried to tunnel under the House of Lords from a house just outside the walls of Westminster Palace. The going was slow and difficult, and came to a stop when they reached the nine-feet thick foundations of the building itself. By February 1605 this plan had been abandoned. Instead Percy rented a cellar under the House of Lords, and hid thirty-six barrels of gunpowder there. The plotters then dispersed to various parts of the country and waited for the opening of Parliament in November. For seven months the gunpowder lay undiscovered under piles of firewood.

In October Francis Tresham decided to warn his brother-in-law,

Lord Monteagle, not to go to Parliament on the day. He wrote a warning letter which was handed to Monteagle as he sat at dinner with friends in London. Rather strangely, his lordship permitted a servant to read it aloud. Among several sinister sentences was the following: 'I say they shall receive a terrible blow this Parliament and yet they shall not see who hurts them.' A puzzled Lord Monteagle passed the letter to Cecil who showed it to James. The King, with God's help so he claimed, realised the words meant Commons and Lords would be destroyed by an explosion.

Although nothing could now save the plotters except flight, they foolishly carried on with their preparations. Just before midnight on 4 November 1605 guards arrested Guy Fawkes, one of the conspirators, as he came to hide in the cellar. Fawkes, a Yorkshire Catholic who had served with the Spanish army, said he was 'Johnson', a servant of Mr Percy. Under torture he admitted his real identity.

Most of the plotters were tracked down and surrounded at Holbeache House in Staffordshire. Catesby and Percy were killed by the same bullet; the man who fired the shot received a pension of two shillings a day for life. Two others died in the struggle and the remainder were arrested and brought to London. A special committee was set up to suggest a suitable punishment for such a crime. Eventually it decided that hanging, drawing and quartering was fearful enough. Nearly all those involved were executed in this way in January 1606.

Robert Winter

Bates

CONCILIVM SE

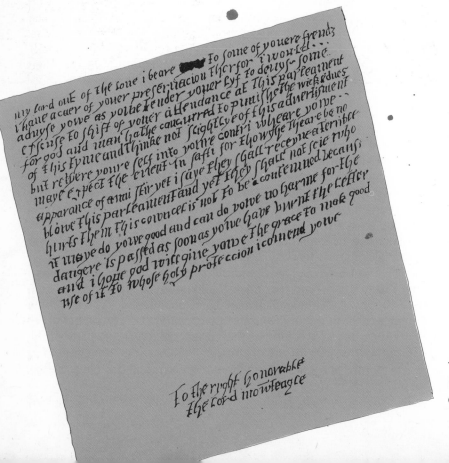

Tresham's letter to Lord Monteagle. Some experts consider it a forgery

er
John Wright
Thomas Percy
Guido Fawkes
Robert Catesby
Thomas Winter

A NOBILIVM ANGLORVM CONIVRANTIVM IN NECEM IACOBI ·I·

The Gunpowder
conspirators

Many questions remain unanswered about the Gunpowder Plot.
If a tunnel was dug, why was it never shown to anybody afterwards?
How did the conspirators obtain such a vast store of gunpowder,
bearing in mind that only the Government was allowed to make it?
Why was the cellar rented by Percy, a discontented Catholic known
to Cecil's spies? Were Catesby and Percy shot so that they could not
talk?

Most mysterious of all is Tresham's letter. Did he really write it, or
was it forged by Cecil to give him an excuse to 'find out' about a plot
he had already discovered? Some handwriting experts think the
letter is Cecil's. Almost all agree that the writing is disguised. On the
other hand, Tresham may have meant to force his friends to abandon
a hopeless plan. There is also a possibility that Tresham was a government spy. Certainly he was never brought to trial, though he died
soon afterwards.

Such doubts have never stopped Englishmen celebrating Guy

The plotters are hanged, drawn and quartered 1606

Fawkes's capture with bonfires and fireworks. It was 1859 before the special 'Gunpowder Treason Service', thanking God for James's deliverance from death, was removed from the English Prayer Book. It took almost as long for the hatred of Catholics inspired by such an event to die in Protestant England. If Cecil did plan the whole affair to make Catholics unpopular, as some historians think, he was very successful!

Divine Right

James I's reign witnessed a growing quarrel between King and Parliament. This was not entirely his fault; most of the differences had existed in Elizabeth's time. Unfortunately James was not as popular as the old Queen, nor was there a war to unite the country. Furthermore his M.P.'s were richer and more powerful. The first Tudor (Henry VII) faced Parliaments in which the Lords were wealthier than the Commons. The first Stuart inherited a Commons rich enough to buy the Lords two or three times over!

It was a difficult situation, made worse by a tactless King. James not only chose ministers whom the Commons disliked. He was also a poor judge of men. His first 'favourite', Robert Carr (or Ker), Earl of Somerset, had to retire when convicted of murder. His second, George Villiers, Duke of Buckingham (1592–1628), attracted the King because his fine features, dark hair and blue eyes reminded James of a painting of St Stephen. Called 'Steenie' for this reason, Buckingham was loaded with honours and wealth. His relations were also given good jobs. Such a swift rise made old established families jealous.

To pick such a man as his chief minister showed how little James cared for his people's opinions. Most seventeenth-century men and women believed a king was chosen, or at least favoured by God. They also thought rule by one person the only proper way to govern a country. Even so, a monarch was expected to take the advice of his more important subjects. This James rarely did, probably because his long rule in Scotland had made him conceited. In his book, *True Law of Free Monarchies* (1598), and in speeches, he made remarkable claims. 'The state of monarchy', he said once, 'is the supreme thing upon earth. . . . As to dispute what God may do is blasphemy, so it is treason in subjects to dispute what a King may do . . .' This theory became known as the Divine Right of Kings.

In years to come many were to suffer and die for such a belief. Others were not so sure. Although they thought a king was God's choice, they were worried at the idea that he was above the laws of the land. 'A good King will frame his actions according to the law, yet he is not bound thereto but of his own goodwill', James had written. This privilege, the Royal Prerogative, had never been openly claimed by the Tudors, however much they may have used it in practice.

After a time James's critics began to speak of 'the common laws of the realm' as though these, too, had been chosen by God. Nobody knew exactly what was meant by such a vague phrase but the first step had been taken towards crushing a 'divine' king with 'divine' laws!

Taxes and trade

If James had merely talked about Royal Prerogative all might have been well. It was when he used this privilege to impose taxes and regulate trade that he annoyed his richer subjects. There was no doubt James needed more money than Elizabeth to run the country. Royal income was actually less than in Tudor times, prices were rising and large debts remained due to the old Queen's wars. It was clear, too, that the 'Parliament-men' were keeping the King short of money. In 1610, for example, they refused him extra income because they said it was too much. Two years before they had objected when the King tried to raise customs charges.

James's reaction was to sell not only titles and peerages, but also more monopolies. A monopoly allowed certain men, usually royal favourites or courtiers, to buy the right to profit exclusively from trade in certain commodities. The Earl of Salisbury, for instance, received £7,000 from his silk monopoly and the Earl of Suffolk £5,000 from control of the trade in currants. Other traders disliked this system which naturally raised the price of goods in the shops and markets.

Monopolies had been granted in Elizabeth's time and had caused clashes between the Queen and her Commons. But James made matters worse by selling them in such large numbers that most well-to-do people were affected. Englishmen lived in houses built of monopoly bricks and heated by monopoly coal. They ate monopoly butter, currants and herrings, smoked monopoly tobacco and played with monopoly dice. Ladies travelled in monopoly coaches pulled by horses fed on monopoly hay; men's breeches were held up by monopoly belts and buttons. Even mice were caught in monopoly mousetraps. By 1621 the prices of at least 700 articles were higher because of monopolies.

Neither was this the only example of government interference with trade. In 1614 James tried to help English clothiers by insisting that all cloth bound for the Netherlands should be dyed before it left the country. A new company, the King's Merchant Adventurers, was formed with Sir William Cokayne as its chairman. The scheme failed completely. First, the Dutch hit back by refusing to carry English cloth in their ships. Then it became obvious there were not enough English ships to carry it direct to the Baltic countries. Finally there was insufficient equipment to dye large amounts of untreated cloth. The Cokayne Project ruined many English merchants. It was twenty-five years before cloth exports again reached the 1614 level.

James was a good-natured man who usually meant well. His government tried to ban enclosures. Furthermore it sometimes ordered J.P.s to sell corn below cost price in times of shortage, or stopped employers sacking workmen when trade was bad. Nevertheless, the first Stuart king was tampering with a 'machine' he did not understand, as well as annoying those classes on which the Tudors had relied for support.

James the peaceful

James was a peace-loving monarch. He stopped the war with Spain and refused to join in continental religious struggles. Even when Frederick of Bohemia, husband of his daughter Elizabeth, was deprived of his crown by Catholic armies (see Chapter 17) he ignored Parliament's demand for a Protestant 'crusade'. His usual excuse was lack of money. 'A King of England has no reason but to decline a war,' he once said, 'The sword is in his hand; the purse is his subjects.' In fact, his Puritan Parliaments might have granted a war tax. The real reason for the King's inaction was his love of peace.

When James died on 27 March 1625 he had been pushed into war with Spain by Buckingham and his son, Charles. Even so it was true to say of the 'Wisest Fool', that 'he lived in peace . . . and left all his kingdom in a peaceable condition'.

More about James I's reign

Books

R. Ashton, ed. *James I by his Contemporaries* (Hutchinson)
The Gunpowder Plot (Cape: Jackdaw)
W. McElwee, *The Wisest Fool in Christendom: James I and VI* (Faber)
P. Magnus, *Sir Walter Raleigh* (Collins)
D. Mathew, *James I* (Eyre & Spottiswoode)
E. K. Milliken *The Stuarts* (Harrap)

Visual aids

Sir Walter Raleigh (Visual Publications)
Sir Walter Raleigh *(film)* (Wills & Hepworth)
The Story of Guy Fawkes (Hulton)
James I (Visual Publications)
Life in Early Stuart Times (Common Ground)

Visits

Houses of Parliament, London
Holyrood Palace and Castle, Edinburgh

To write and find out

1 Write your own account of the Gunpowder Plot, explaining what *you* think happened.
2 Find out more about James's early life as King of Scotland. It is an exciting story and contains one famous mystery, the Gowrie Conspiracy.
3 James was the 'Wisest Fool'. Think of a single phrase to describe Raleigh and Buckingham.
4 Try and find extracts from James I's famous book against smoking. Then write your own attack upon the habit, preferably in James's own style of English.

16 Companies and Colonies
Beginnings of Empire 1600-1630

On 15 December 1620 the *Mayflower* dropped anchor off Cape Cod in North America with 100 passengers. Next day an advance party landed and by Christmas the first house had been built 'for common use to receive them and their goods'. The settlement thus founded, New Plymouth, was not inhabited entirely by Puritans discontented with the English Church. A minority, it was true, had fled from England to Holland in 1608 for that reason. With a twelve-year truce between the Spanish and Dutch due to expire in 1621 they were ready to face Indians rather than Catholics. But many came to a new land for a new start in life. Today these 'Pilgrim Fathers' are honoured as some of the earliest Americans.

Their journey from England had been grim and uncomfortable. A wit of that time summed up such a voyage in the form of a mock recipe: 'Take the ship, add one hundred assorted Pilgrims and a crew of twenty-five; place in the hold all necessary goods for founding a colony; clutter up the space between decks with a shallop (small boat); add cold weather, cold water dripping everywhere through leaking decks and toss liberally around the North Atlantic for two months'.

Actually the pilgrims' experiences had been far from funny. Crowded in a ship only 90 feet long and 20 feet wide, they had rolled through storms which cracked timbers and tore sails. The space between decks was a mere four feet; the ship had no portholes and only seawater was available for washing. To walk on deck was risky. One man who did so was washed overboard and only saved himself by grabbing a trailing rope. Another person died, although a mother managed to give birth to a child which was christened 'Oceanus'.

Soon after landing the Pilgrims organised their government by the terms of the 'Mayflower Compact', signed earlier in November. 'We whose names are underwritten,' declared the forty-one heads of families on board, 'the loyal subjects of our dread sovereign Lord, King James . . . do combine ourselves together into a civil body politick (government) for our better ordering and preservation.' It was agreed that they should elect a Governor and admit one extra man to their Court each year. Governor and Court together would then make laws for the infant colony.

After a miserable winter during which fifty-one of the colonists died, twenty acres of corn were grown successfully. The grateful survivors celebrated this first harvest by solemnly thanking God and entertaining local Indians to a feast of turkey and goose. Modern Americans commemorate the event with a special holiday on 'Thanksgiving Day'. Schools and factories close and families gather for the traditional meal of turkey, cranberry sauce and pumpkin pie.

A modern replica of the
Mayflower which was
sailed to America in 1957.
In the background is the
aircraft-carrier *Ark Royal*

New France

North America was first explored by the French in the sixteenth
century. In 1535 two sixty-ton ships commanded by Jacques
Cartier sailed from St Malo in France. After a seven-week crossing
of the Atlantic, they entered the mouth of a large river which was
christened 'St Lawrence'. Moving upstream, Cartier discovered
an Indian village near the tall rock on which Quebec now stands.
Further on, roaring rapids and waterfalls led to a mountain he called
'Mont Real' (Mount Royal), the site of modern Montreal. 'We beheld
a beautiful country, with the finest forests in the world', he recorded.
Unhappily, his men went down with scurvy and many died.

Cartier is honoured as the founder of French Canada. His trails
were followed by fur traders and fishermen whose roving life made
large permanent settlements unnecessary. Not until 1604 did the
French government start colonisation. In that year a number of settlers
landed at the mouth of the St Croix river, between what is now
New Brunswick and the American state of Maine. Their experiences
were awful. Food and fresh water ran out; cider froze solid and was
measured by the pound! When, after three years, the French King
cancelled their fur-trading monopoly these pioneers gave up and
returned home.

One settler decided to try again. In 1608 Samuel de Champlain
took a handful of men to Quebec where they built a fort, 'and had
some garden plots made'. During the freezing winter which followed
twenty of the twenty-eight colonists died. When summer came
Champlain's tiny party set out in canoes to explore the regions south
of Montreal. Here he discovered and named the Richelieu river, and
helped to end an Indian war by killing two redskin chiefs with one
shot! Because of this lucky chance Champlain was befriended by the
Algonkin tribe. The settlement prospered and between 1615–17 he
and Etienne Brûle explored Lakes Ontario and Huron with Indian
help.

Cartier and Champlain had helped to establish 'New France' in the St Lawrence Valley. Before the end of the century other French travellers passed through the Great Lakes and reached the Gulf of Mexico via the Mississippi. St Louis, founded in 1682, was the final link in a long, delicate French 'chain' crossing North America from Canada to the Caribbean.

Virginia

French colonies were small and scattered; usually a few wooden cabins set beside a track, lake or river. Wandering fur trappers do not need large settlements and Canada, with its cold winters was in many ways hostile to seventeenth-century communities. English colonies on the other hand were developed in areas suitable for towns and ports.

For many years experts favoured emigration which 'skimmed the milk of bitterness in England' because they believed there were too many people living in the country. Better to remove unemployed troublemakers to a distance. Consequently most organisers of expeditions thought in terms of permanent settlement. Merchants investing money also took a long view. They realised that future American farming communities would buy English manufactured goods as well as send much needed timber to the home country.

Nobody expected quick results. One writer compared the development of colonies to the growth of trees. 'You must take account to lose about twenty years' profit, and expect your recompense (reward) in the end', he noted. He was not far out in his calculations. One company spent £100,000 in fourteen years and, in fact, never did pay a dividend to its shareholders. Neither did the colonists themselves expect to return. 'We hope to plant a nation, where none before hath stood,' remarked one proud Virginian in 1610.

Since English monarchs claimed to own large areas of North America, individuals or companies bought royal charters, which allowed them to found colonies. The first was Sir Walter Raleigh who in 1584 was given permission to colonise territory which Elizabeth agreed should be called 'Virginia' because she was known as the Virgin Queen. A party of 107 men led by Ralph Lane tried to settle on Roanoke Island, which is part of present-day North Carolina. It was not an ideal choice for there was no good harbour and the natives were hostile. After being unnerved by a tornado the settlers were glad to sail home with one of Drake's fleets when it appeared offshore.

Not long afterwards another ship, commanded by Sir Richard Grenville, arrived at the abandoned settlement. In order not to disappoint his cousin Raleigh, Grenville allowed fifteen volunteers to land and hold the post until a fresh expedition could return. Next year these reinforcements found only one skeleton; there was no sign of the other fourteen men. This disheartened them so much they stayed only a month. During this time the first European baby was born on the American continent and christened Virginia Dare.

In 1587 Raleigh financed yet another attempt to found a colony. One hundred and seventeen men, women and children landed on an

Spanish

French

English

Towns MARKED * were settled before 1640

American settlement up to 1700

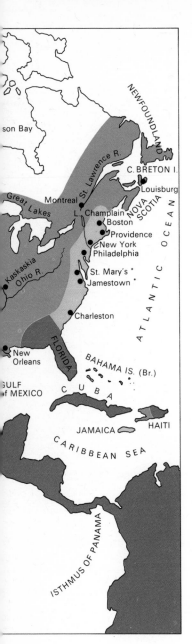

island about 100 miles south-west of Roanoke. Owing to the battle with the Armada, it was two years before anybody sailed back to see how they were getting on. Then a ship's captain reported: 'We let fall our grapnel near the shore and sounded with a trumpet a call.' There was no answer. A little later a landing party found only empty chests, rusty armour, rickety fences and rotting maps. On a tree was carved the word CROATOAN, the Indian name for the island. No trace of settlers was ever found and it will never be known whether they were killed by Indians or died in the forests.

Raleigh had spent large sums of money for nothing. Even so, he never gave up hope of a successful English colony in America. 'I shall yet live to see it an English nation', he wrote in 1602. His prediction was correct. Within six years other men founded the modern state of Virginia.

Jamestown

North America was too strange and exciting a continent to be left alone for long. Like India and China two centuries before, men told tales and dreamed about it. Gold was plentiful, it was said. Wild boar and venison (deer meat) were as common as pork and mutton in England. It was reported that rubies and diamonds lay like pebbles on the beach. Men said it was worth the risk of being eaten by large fish, or killed by men with heads below their shoulders, dog's teeth and eyes in their chests. More realistic were the reports of abundant fish and furs brought back by a captain who visited what are now New England and Massachusetts between 1602 and 1605. The following year a company of London merchants decided to finance another expedition.

Three ships, the *Discovery, Susan Constant* and *God Speed,* carried these pioneers. Their commander was instructed to establish a colony south of Long Island and to explore the river known to be there in case it led to the Pacific. The party reached Chesapeake Bay in April 1607 to see 'fair meadows, and goodly tall trees, with fresh waters'. Ashore they found friendly Indians who gave them corn bread, pipes of tobacco and strawberries four times bigger than those in England. Supplies were landed and a fort named Jamestown erected. Today nothing remains of this early settlement because the land on which it stood has been washed away.

Before leaving England the names of those chosen by the Company to rule the new community had been placed in a locked box. When opened, the list was found to number seven, including two soldiers, Edward Wingfield and John Smith. Unfortunately, most of the party had quarrelled with the boastful and arrogant Smith, so he was not made a Council member. Later, however, when the Redskins became unfriendly, 'creeping upon all fours, from the hills, like bears, with their bows in their mouths', Smith proved to be a good leader. According to his own stories, he was an experienced soldier who had fought against the Turks, killing one of their champions in single combat. Now he took charge of the defences and speeded up work with the simple rule, 'If you do not work you shall not eat'.

A strong hand was certainly needed. Food was scarce, log cabins few, tents rotten and Indian raids frequent. Moreover, by September half the original 104 colonists had died of malaria or typhoid. Yet Smith did not give up. Week by week he led food-gathering parties out of the fort, chasing and killing hostile Indians and returning with meat, turkeys, wild fowl and bread. On one trip Smith was wounded and captured. The Indian braves led him to their village where he was surrounded by men painted red and making 'hellish notes and screeches'.

Powhattan, their chief, ordered Smith to be beaten to death. Warriors seized the Englishman and held him over a stone. Suddenly Pocohontas, the chief's young daughter, rushed out of the crowd and put her arms around the victim's head. According to Smith the chief then spared him. Whether this story is true or not, Smith did manage to escape what seemed like certain death. He also survived plots by his English enemies and lived to become President of the colony in later years.

Pocohontas seems to have liked Englishmen for when she grew up she fell in love with John Rolfe, a settler who founded the Virginia tobacco industry. Under Rolfe's influence she was taught English and was baptised a Christian, with the name Rebecca. In 1614 she married him, with the Governor and her uncle Opachisco present. Rolfe brought his wife to England, attended by twelve Indian servants. One of these had been told to count the number of Englishmen by making a notch in a stick every time he saw a new face! Since the party travelled to London to meet the King and Queen the poor man must have used up quite a few sticks. Pocohontas did not like the English climate. She persuaded her husband to let her return to America but died of smallpox on board ship near Gravesend (1617).

Jamestown prospered as the years passed, in spite of fierce Indian attacks which on two occasions nearly wiped it out. Forty years after the first landing the citizens rebuilt the town further inland, away from the unhealthy swamps of the original site. They also extended their tobacco-growing with the help of Negro slaves. A nation was being planted where none before had stood.

The Emperor Akbar

Whilst 'pilgrims' were founding colonies in the west, trading links were giving birth to a different sort of empire in the east. Here, instead of lonely forests and a wilderness inhabited by a few savages, travellers encountered large cities and ancient empires.

For years Englishmen had argued about the best way to reach the wealth of the East first discovered by Spain and Portugal. Some felt it would be best not to annoy the Portuguese. They suggested sailing west via the Straits of Magellan and the Pacific. Others were inclined to defy the Portuguese monopoly and fight their way round Africa to India by the 'Vasco da Gama' route. It was the second plan which eventually proved most popular. On 31 December 1600 Queen Elizabeth granted a charter to 'the governor and company of mer-

Akbar shown hunting on an elephant

chants trading to the East Indies'. This new East India Company at first intended to trade with the Middle and Far East. In fact it was the Dutch, not the English, who seized Portugal's possessions in Ceylon, Mauritius, South Africa and Indonesia. Faced with hostile Dutch warships, the English turned their attention to the Indian mainland.

Late sixteenth-century India was ruled by the Mogul (or Mongol) Emperor Akbar (meaning 'the great'), a descendant of Muslim conquerors who had entered the subcontinent from Central Asia. Years of fighting had given him control of most of northern India and towards the end of his reign he was treated as almost super-human. His coins, for example, were stamped with the words ALLAM I AKBAR—'Akbar he is God'.

From his newly built capital, Fatepur Sikri, Akbar controlled the thousands of paymasters, high stewards, justices, police officers and tax inspectors who helped to make him the richest ruler on earth. Below these officials were the source of all Akbar's greatness—the millions of hard-working peasants who gave him the best of their crops annually, and paid taxes on everything from grass to earthen pots, fish to cowdung. Even so, Akbar was a good prince by Eastern standards. He built roads, established a national coinage and brought peace to the many races and religions living in India.

In 1580 two Catholic priests visited the Indian Emperor, hoping to make him a Christian. Akbar was known to be tolerant of other religions. Although a Muslim he had married a Hindu. He had also built

The entrance to Akbar's tomb at Sikandra, near Agra, India

a special Hall of Worship where men of different faiths were encouraged to meet for discussion. Sure enough, the missionaries were made welcome, and Akbar asked many questions, particularly about 'the heavenly Jesus'. He even permitted the priests to accompany his army on a campaign. In the end, however, the Emperor disappointed them by founding his own Din Ilahi (new religion), a weird mixture of various beliefs and ceremonies.

Such an unsuccessful mission might have been forgotten had not one priest, Father Monsarratte, written a *Journal* which contains a vivid description of India during one of its golden ages. Akbar himself was a strongly built man of medium height, with bandy legs, skin the colour of wheat and a 'lucky' wart on his nose. He laughed often and his eyes sparkled 'like the points of light on little waves when they catch the sun'. He received visitors in the marble halls of his palace, seated on couch of scarlet rugs and dressed in a white silk suit whose trousers were tucked in at the ankles with strings of pearls.

When he rode to war he was surrounded by cavalry squadrons formed in a crescent formation. Behind the royal party stretched miles of foot soldiers, horsemen and elephants. Akbar's troops marched to the rhythm of slow drumbeats, destroying every crop, killing every bird and animal in their way. In times of peace at his palace Akbar would listen politely to the missionaries' sermons, sometimes falling asleep, but occasionally asking so many questions that the priests did not know which one to answer next. The picture which emerges is of a prince who would have been at home in Renaissance Europe.

It was to this monarch that a representative of the East India Company went in 1601 to suggest trade with England.

Ambassador Roe

Akbar died before suitable arrangements could be made. Company fleets made the long voyage around the Cape without a single friendly port or a secure base when they arrived. It was 1610 before Jehangir, the new Emperor, ignored Dutch and Portuguese pressure and reluctantly allowed the Company a 'factory' (trading base) at Surat, north of Bombay.

In 1615 the Company sent Sir Thomas Roe (1581–1644) as their ambassador to the Mogul Court. It was probably fortunate that Roe was an experienced explorer who had travelled up the Amazon in South America. Leaving Surat, it took the English party five months to reach Jehangir in his capital at Ajmer. The Indian ruler received him with typical eastern politeness and did not insist that Roe should bang his head six times on the floor as was the usual custom when meeting the Emperor. Actually Jehangir was less powerful than his father. Parts of his empire had already revolted, whilst at court he was bullied by his chief wife, Nur Jahan. Jehangir's son, in particular, did not disguise his dislike of Christians. Only gradually did the annual arrival of a Company fleet loaded with fine quality goods, make the Englishman more popular.

Roe persuaded his masters in England to increase their trade with India by peaceful means. 'A war and traffic (trade) are incompatible', he wrote. 'Let this be received as a rule that if you will profit, seek it at sea, and in a quiet trade; . . . it is an error to affect land wars in India.' More and more gold was sent to buy Indian indigo, spices and cotton goods. Within ten years the Company had a settled base at Surat, and peace had been reached with the Portuguese at Goa. As the Mogul empire grew weaker and India split into separate states, the English were able to negotiate with other princes and to set up 'factories' at Madras, Bombay and Calcutta.

Roe found life in India unhealthy and boring. To make matters worse, his work at Court involved frequent insults and disappointments. 'I was not born to a life smooth and easy,' he grumbled, 'all my actions have been mingled with crosses and rubs.' He need not have been so dissatisfied. Without knowing it, Thomas Roe had laid the foundations of a British Empire in India.

More about early colonisation
Books
K. N. Chaudhuri, *The English East India Company 1600-40* (Cass)
M. Gibson, *Voyages of Discovery* (Oxford University Press)
W. Gill, *Captain John Smith and Virginia* (Longman: Then and There)
W. Gill, *The Pilgrim Fathers* (Longman: Then and There)
J. G. Gittings, *Pocohontas* (Hulton)
L. Hobley, *Exploring the Americas* (Methuen: Outlines)
Mayflower and Pilgrim Fathers (Cape: Jackdaw)
A. Villiers, *The New Mayflower* (Brockhampton Press) — (an account of the building and sailing of the *New Mayflower* to America in 1957)

Visual aids
Champlain (Encyclopaedia Britannica)
Cartier (Encyclopaedia Britannica)
The Pilgrim Fathers (Notts Rural Studies Association)
The Pilgrims *(film)* (Rank)
The Mayflower (Visual Publications)
Pocohontas (Hulton)
Early Exploration of USA (VIS)
Puritan Family in New England *(film)* (Gateway)
Foundation of Empire 1588–1688 (Visual Publications)

To write and find out
1 Write your own recipe, similar to the one quoted in this chapter, but illustrating the bad side of modern travel by road.
2 Imagine you are Pocohontas visiting England for the first time. Try to display both knowledge of seventeenth-century England and North America.
3 Find out as much as you can about the history of the English East India Company.
4 Get a map of modern Canada and list as many French-type names as you can find. Notice the areas where they tend to be more numerous and find out why.

Elizabeth I and James 'the Peaceful' had ruled England and Scotland at a time of mounting tension in Europe. During these years the Counter-Reformation (counter-attack) against Protestantism begun in the sixteenth century developed on many fronts. First, there was a move to reform the Catholic Church from within. Paul III (Pope 1534–49) chose outstanding men as cardinals and appointed a commission to investigate the working of the Church. The Catholic Council of Trent, sitting from 1545 to 1563, carried out many of the reforms they suggested. It also restated Catholic beliefs clearly in the face of Protestant attacks. After Trent no Catholic could doubt what he was expected to believe or do.

Externally, as we have seen, the movement took a more warlike turn as Catholic Habsburg armies and fleets fought those of Protestant states. Philip II of Spain sent the Armada against England, as well as fighting the Dutch. His cousins, the Holy Roman Emperors, strove to wipe out Protestantism in Germany. But thoughtful people realised the battle could not be won entirely by armies or reforms. From the early fifteenth century onwards various orders of monks and nuns were formed to preach against heresy. The most important of these was the Society of Jesus, whose members (called Jesuits) became the advance guard in this contest for men's souls. Jesuits were true 'warriors of the faith' who obeyed a General and answered only to the Pope. Their founder, Ignatius Loyola (1491–1556) had been a soldier until a severe leg wound ended his military career. During a long convalescence he read lives of Christ and the saints. This inspired him to become a pilgrim and visit the Holy Land.

At first the Society intended to convert Muslims. When this proved impossible, Loyola's men joined in the Counter-Reformation. Thanks to their efforts, many people in Poland, Bavaria, southern Netherlands, Austria and Ireland returned to Catholic beliefs.

A Crown in Bohemia

Neither the Peace of Augsburg (which stated that subjects were to take the religion of their rulers) nor later agreements could bring permanent peace to a Europe divided by religious differences. In France the series of sixteenth-century civil wars between Catholics and Protestants did not end until a strong king, Henry IV (1589–1610), restored order and issued the so-called Edict of Nantes, which granted Huguenots (French Protestants) the right to practise their religion without interference. In Germany the Habsburg rulers of the Holy Roman Empire looked with horror on the spread of Protestant ideas.

A particular difficulty arose from the fact that by the terms agreed at

St Ignatius Loyola—founder of the Society of Jesus

Augsburg only Lutheran and Catholic Churches were recognised as state religions. The influential and powerful Calvinists were not mentioned. In such a situation religious divisions could be used as an excuse for power struggles between states. It is not surprising therefore that a minor incident sparked off a European war.

In 1618 certain Bohemian (Czechoslovakian) Protestant nobles threw three Imperial (Catholic) officials out of a window of Prague's royal castle. The victims landed unhurt on a pile of manure. This insult might have been forgiven had not the Bohemians then

The Council of Trent in session. It reformed the Catholic Church and led the battle against Protestant ideas

proposed to make a Protestant prince, Frederick, King of Bohemia. Manhandling civil servants was one thing. The crown of Bohemia was another. Catholic Habsburg princes had occupied this throne for a century. It was a key position in their domination of the Holy Roman Empire.

The Habsburg Ferdinand II, who became Emperor in 1619, was a devout Catholic, educated by Jesuits. The growing independence of German Protestant princes dismayed him. His reaction to the popular rising in Bohemia was to send an army to crush it. In November 1620 the Protestant Czechs were defeated by the Catholics at the Battle of White Hill, near Prague. Frederick was driven from his country and Protestantism outlawed throughout Bohemia.

White Hill was a beginning, not an end. The war which followed lasted thirty years, and devastated large parts of Germany. This was not because of the battles which were, in fact, few. It was the march of hostile soldiers which spread ruin. Troops who besieged castles and towns, whether friend or foe, 'lived off the land', taking food and fuel from the inhabitants. Towns and villages were wrecked. Disease spread with the speed of a forest fire. Herds of cattle, flocks of sheep, livestock and crops were stolen, leaving the peasants to starve. Year by year the armies moved across the land like locusts, creating a a desert wherever they went.

Such a war made it impossible to use short-service troops. Consequently mercenaries (soldiers fighting for money) were recruited in large numbers by both sides. Their commanders were really employers who supplied a certain number of soldiers at a fixed price. The greatest 'warlord' of this type was Albrecht von Wallenstein (1583–1634), a Czech who organised Catholic armies to fight for Ferdinand. Wallenstein was a clever businessman as well as a fine general. He had already made a fortune by marrying a rich widow, producing a new Bohemian currency and buying lands taken from Protestants. In war he found an even better opportunity to become rich. Certainly religion was unimportant as far as he was concerned for he had been born into a Lutheran family and had merely turned Catholic to help his career.

By 1630 Wallenstein had a private army and his estates in Bohemia were an almost independent kingdom.

Gustavus Adolphus

At first the Protestants did badly. Armies led by Wallenstein and the Count of Tilly, defeated all comers. A tide of Catholic-Habsburg power rolled across Germany until it reached the shores of the Baltic Sea. This area, vital for supplies of timber, iron and rope, Ferdinand intended to control with a fleet.

Such plans brought the Catholics face to face with Gustavus Adolphus, King of Protestant Sweden. Seventeenth-century Sweden was a major European power. Swedish territory included what is now Finland and Estonia; Swedish troops and fleets had fought and defeated at various times, Russia, Denmark and Poland. The country was at its most powerful in 1630, for Gustavus was a master of war and his chief minister, Axel Oxenstierna (1583–1654) was a brilliant organiser.

Sweden's well-trained soldiers served for twenty years or until they reached fifty years of age, whichever was the sooner. Its rich iron-fields meant guns and ammunition were cheap, and Gustavus's men had the most modern weapons of the age. In particular, the artillery possessed light guns, called 'regiment pieces', which could be pulled by one horse. This was a big advantage at a time when bad roads made the transportation of heavy guns a major problem.

There were many reasons why Sweden entered the war against the Catholics. For Gustavus Adolphus religion and politics could not be separated. He saw no hope of religious freedom for Protestants unless they controlled their territory. Wars of conquest against Catholic powers were therefore unavoidable. He saw also the threat of Habsburg interference in the North. With Wallenstein's soldiers stationed in Jutland in Denmark, it was clear that Sweden's survival as a leading Baltic power was at stake. Thus the 'Protestant Hero' was able to mix a religious crusade with the occupation of lands vital for Sweden's safety. The Swedish troops who landed at Peenemünde, Germany, in June 1630 came to fight for their country as well as its faith.

Defeat of the tercios

Gustavus's entry into Europe coincided with Wallenstein's dismissal by the Emperor for unfair tax-collecting. Consequently it was Tilly who eventually faced the Swedes at Breitenfeld, near Leipzig, in September 1631.

Tilly was a Flemish soldier who had learnt his job with Parma in the Netherlands. Spanish armies of those days owed much of their success to the use of a formation called the *tercio* (regiment) which had been copied by other Catholic infantry. The *tercio* consisted of a square formation about 3,000 strong, half pikemen and half musketeers. The pikemen formed a dense, hedgehog-like inner square which pointed in all directions. Musketeers surrounded them at first, but retired inside their ranks when the enemy closed in. At best the *tercio* was a slow moving, defensive formation. Nevertheless, its tough centre and heavy fire power usually gave it victory.

The day of the battle dawned warm and sunny, with dust blowing from fields dry through lack of rain. One Protestant survivor remembered: 'As the lark began to peep, having stood all night in battle a mile from Tilly's army, the Trumpets sound to horse, the Drums calling to march . . . we marched forward in God's name.' Tilly had eighteen *tercios*, plus cavalry, well placed in open, rolling country, which gave plenty of room for manoeuvre.

The Habsburg army of 35,000 was an impressive sight with its massed pikes, armoured horsemen, and fluttering flags. Magnificently equipped commanders, their plumed hats trembling in the breeze, rode in front. By contrast Gustavus's army appeared ragged and caked with dust. 'Our peasant lads,' a Swede remarked, 'made no brave show upon the field, when set against the hawk nosed and

Gustavus Adolphus, the 'Protestant hero' and leader of the Swedes in the Thirty Years War

mustachio'd veterans of Tilly.' Even their horses were smaller than the fine German chargers.

An army of those days usually lined up for battle with its infantry in the centre and cavalry on either wing. Gustavus Adolphus preferred to put small squares of cavalry at intervals among his foot soldiers. This new technique proved the undoing of the Emperor's forces. During hours of fierce fighting, salvos of shot from regiment pieces and sudden charges by these small groups drove the harassed *tercios* backwards and forwards.

Worse still were the clouds of dust blown into their faces by a change of wind. Choked, blinded and constantly under pressure, the *tercios* suffered severe losses. Only night saved them from massacre. Next morning the Swedes were amazed at what they had done—13,600 enemy dead or captured, all their guns taken and 120 battle-flags left on the field. Even Tilly was wounded before he fled.

The news of this great victory was received with joy by Ferdinand's enemies. English Puritans rejoiced, German Protestants added verses celebrating the battle to one of Luther's hymns. Their delight was understandable. Breitenfeld turned back the Catholic tide and gave Gustavus Adolphus control of North Germany. It seemed that the heart of the Habsburg lands, perhaps Vienna (the Habsburg capital) itself, would soon fall to Protestant troops.

The Battle of Breitenfeld 1631

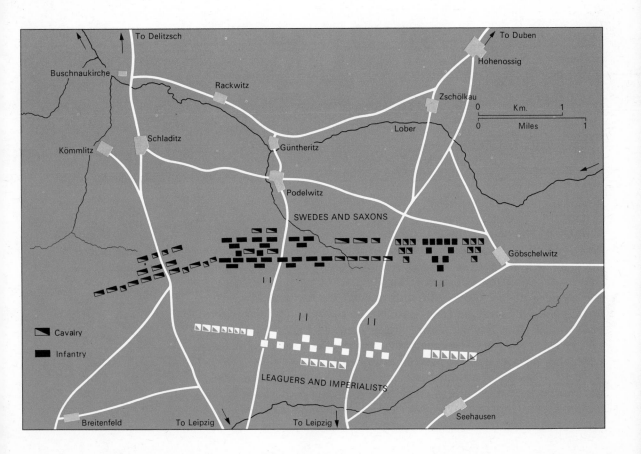

Death at the windmills

Next year Wallenstein was recalled to stop Gustavus Adolphus's advance on Vienna. After months of campaigning he faced his great opponent, at Lutzen (November 1632). On a day of swirling mist the Swedes at first drove all before them. The imperial (Catholic) cavalry were crushed and Wallenstein's left wing and centre were soon in danger. Only his right, strongly entrenched around some windmills, stood firm. Then the mist grew thicker. Many troops lost contact in a gloom made worse by gunsmoke.

As the Swedish advance slowed down, Gustavus Adolphus decided to lead a charge to spur them on. Galloping towards the windmills, his left arm was shattered by a cannon shot. He was swept helplessly amongst a crowd of enemy horsemen and shot

Gustavus Adolphus commands troops at Breitenfeld

several times. Finally as he lay in the mud an enemy soldier ended his life with a bullet through the head.

News that their King had fallen drove the Swedes into a frenzy. They broke through Wallenstein's line in several places, capturing the windmills after a desperate fight. The warlord was forced to retreat, leaving all his guns and at least half his army dead or wounded on the battlefield. It was another Swedish victory though at too great a cost. An Englishman serving with the Swedish army summed up his comrades feelings when he wrote of the dead King: 'O would to God I had once such a leader again to fight such another day, in the old quarrel.' In fact the death of the 'Lion of the North' did not end the run of Protestant successes. Axel Oxenstierna carried on Gustavus's work, using generals trained by the King. Nevertheless, without Gustavus Adolphus as its chief enemy the Holy Roman Empire was saved from complete collapse.

Wallenstein, meanwhile, lived like a prince in Prague, attended by over a thousand servants. He even tried to become King of Bohemia. This was too much for his enemies at the Habsburg court who feared he might march his men against the Emperor. In February 1634 he was murdered in his lodgings at the Czech town of Cheb. There followed a dreadful purge. Hundreds of Wallenstein's officers were executed and his enemies took over their lands. Descendants of these families dominated Czechoslovakia until the Communist takeover in 1947.

Balance of power

By 1635 nobody could pretend it was a religious struggle any more. Neither was Germany the main battleground, for the fighting had spread to Spain, Italy and the Netherlands. Typical of this new approach to the war was the attitude of Cardinal Richelieu (1585–1642), minister to the French King Louis XIII. Although a Catholic priest, Richelieu put politics before religion. It was true he attacked the Huguenot base at La Rochelle in 1628. But he also signed an

The murder of Wallenstein in his lodgings, 1634

alliance with Protestant England whereby Charles I married a French
princess. Above all, he refused to help the Catholic Habsburgs, for he
was determined that France, not Austria, should dominate Germany.

As part of Richelieu's plan, French armies marched into Italy to
attack countries allied with the Habsburgs. At the same time French
troops slowly drove the Spanish from the Netherlands, while at sea
a Spanish fleet was completely destroyed by the Dutch. Behind the
scenes French money went secretly to Protestants fighting Ferdinand.
Success finally crowned the Cardinal's policies a year after his death
when the Spanish army was crushed at Rocroi (May 1643).

Most of those involved in the war, except possibly the French,
were now exhausted. Even so, it was five years before peace came to

Europe after the Treaty of
Westphalia, 1648

Germany mainly because France and Sweden were determined to gain rewards for their sacrifices. Old religious hatreds lingered too; it took months to persuade the Papal legate (Pope's special representative) to sit in the same room with Protestant leaders.

Eventually, by the terms of the Peace of Westphalia (1648) Sweden gained parts of North Germany and so kept its commanding position astride the Baltic Sea. France received certain border towns (Metz, Toul, Verdun) which could be fortified and used to influence its German neighbours. Spain was abandoned by its allies, and left to fight France alone until 1659. As a result it lost the Dutch provinces at last. Most important, although not mentioned in the treaty, was the fact that the larger German states were freed from Habsburg interference. They could appoint their own ambassadors and negotiate directly with other states. The Holy Roman Empire, as the French writer Voltaire remarked years later, became 'neither holy, nor Roman, nor an Empire'.

The Treaty of Westphalia did not bring peace to Europe as a whole. But it did mark the end of a German war so terrible that many ordinary people came to believe that God had deserted them and the end of the world was near. It was also the first attempt by the new European nation states to arrange a 'balance of power' now that the old international forces of Empire and Papacy had ceased to matter. For the next two hundred years wars were fought, treaties signed and territories occupied to stop any one state dominating its neighbours.

More about the Thirty Years War

Books

J. Brodrick, *Origin of Jesuits* (Longman)

J. Brodrick, *St Ignatius Loyola* (Burns Oates)

D. Pennington, *Seventeenth-century Europe* (Longman's General History of Europe)

M. Roberts, *Gustavus Adolphus* (Longman), 2 vols

S. Steinberg, *Thirty Years War* (Arnold)

C. V. Wedgwood, *Richelieu and the French Monarchy* (English Universities Press: Teach Yourself)

C. V. Wedgwood, *The Thirty Years War* (Cape)

Visual aids

Germany——Feudal States to Unification *(film)* (Gateway)

To write and find out

1 Find out as much as you can about the Society of Jesus.

2 Compile a booklet of information about the arms, equipment and tactics of seventeenth century armies.

3 Gustavus Adolphus had a fine warship called the *Vasa*. Find out what happened to it.

4 A later Swedish King was killed at a masked ball. See if you can find out his name and also the name of the opera by Verdi which deals with his murder.

18 Parliaments and Prayer Books
Charles I 1625-1642

Charles I

Charles I, who succeeded to the English and Scottish thrones, was the youngest son of James I; his elder brother Henry had died in 1612. At the time of his accession he was rather immature for his age, a quiet, shy young man who stuttered if he grew excited. Although no scholar, he was a far more refined man than his father. The behaviour at James's court had been undignified and disgusting. Women as well as men lay sick and drunk; food was thrown at meals; silly practical jokes, such as putting frogs in beds, were popular. During a visit to Madrid in 1623 Charles had admired the strict rules, exact timetables and elaborate ceremony of the Spanish Court. The solemn, rather humourless young King decided to copy such customs.

The Court was typical of the man. Charles made few friends and surrounded himself with a web of etiquette (manners) which kept courtiers as well as crowds at a distance. No other European monarch of the time was served food by kneeling servants. On the other hand, the Caroline Court (from Carolus, the Latin for Charles), became a meeting place for artists, poets, painters and musicians. Charles founded the Royal Art Collection, buying nearly 1,000 pictures during his reign, and encouraging famous artists like Rubens and Van Dyck to work in England. He employed skilled architects, encouraged writers to produce plays for his court and hired a private orchestra. The second Stuart was a cultured man who presided over a civilised court.

Admirable though it was in many ways, the court at Whitehall had one big disadvantage—it cut the King off from his people. Unlike his father, Charles had a sheltered and pleasant upbringing; he had never been beaten, insulted or threatened. Charles rarely travelled and was unaware of many changes which were taking place in England. For most of his reign he lived in a dream world—a fairy prince in a fairy palace.

The Petition of Right

Charles's reign began badly for several reasons. One of his father's last acts had been to marry him to Henrietta Maria, daughter of Henry IV of France. This, 'youngest flower of the Bourbon (the name of the French royal family) . . . with eyes that sparkle like stars' certainly brought elegance and beauty to the English court. Unfortunately, she spoke very little English and refused to attend Charles's coronation because she was a Catholic.

An unpopular Queen was only one of Charles's problems. His close friendship with the Duke of Buckingham disappointed those who had hoped to be rid of James's hated favourite. When Charles suggested an expedition against Cadiz in Spain, they showed little enthusiasm once Buckingham was appointed to command it. When the attack failed the Commons blamed him for the disaster, even though he had actually taken no part in it. In Charles's second parliament a leading member, Sir John Eliot, remarked: 'Our honour is ruined, our ships are sunk, our men perished, not by an enemy . . . but by those we trust.' Charles, who usually tried to ignore Parliament, was furious. Eliot was arrested, only to be released because M.P.s refused to carry on their work without him. In the Lords matters went no better. One peer announced grimly, 'I accuse that man, the Duke of Buckingham, of high treason and I will prove it.'

Since it seemed that Buckingham might suffer the fate of some of Henry VIII's ministers, the King hurriedly dissolved Parliament to save his friend. Later he raised money for an expedition to help the Huguenots of La Rochelle (1627–28) without its permission. This time Buckingham took command in person and landed his men on the island of Rhé, opposite La Rochelle. He led an assault on the chief town on the island, but the scaling ladders for climbing the walls were too short and it failed. Consequently his men were forced to give up the siege.

Returning to England, Buckingham persuaded Charles that he could charm the Commons into financing yet another expedition to save the French Protestants. This time his luck ran out. The new Parliament's first action was to refuse any money until their complaints had been heard. To show they meant business, Eliot and another parliamentarian, Sir Thomas Wentworth, produced the Petition of Right (1628). This famous document contained demands that taxes collected without Parliament's permission and imprisonment without trial should be illegal. Other clauses condemned the custom of lodging troops in private houses and forcing civilians to obey military law. Charles accepted the Petition reluctantly, probably for Buckingham's sake. It made little difference. Although Wentworth was satisfied Eliot continued to attack the King's favourite.

The murdered Buckingham. This picture is said to have been painted by Van Dyck

The problem of Buckingham was solved in a tragic way. In August 1628, John Felton, an army officer, stabbed and killed the Duke as he sat in his lodgings in Portsmouth. Charles was horrified at the death of his only friend. His Lords and Commons were delighted. In London joyful citizens celebrated the event openly and blessed Felton as he went to his execution. As the gulf between monarch and people widened, the lonely King turned to his French Catholic wife for comfort and advice.

Laud and the Puritans

A defiant Commons now started to criticise the King's Church policy. Charles was the first English King to be brought up in the Church of England. Whereas previous monarchs had upheld the Anglican faith for political reasons, he loved it as the one true way to salvation. Consequently he could never understand or tolerate any who wanted it changed. In his opinion all complaints about the Prayer Book, all moves towards Calvinist or Lutheran organisation, had to be crushed.

Like Mary Tudor, it was his misfortune to rule many deeply religious men and women who disagreed with him.

After Buckingham's death, Eliot's chief grumble concerned the activities of William Laud, an important priest who later became Archbishop of Canterbury. Laud, 'a little, low, red-faced man' loved Church of England ceremonies as much as his master. Puritanism in his view was 'the root of all rebellion . . . and sauciness in the country'. Laud had an almost Catholic attitude towards churchmen. Bishops he believed to be chosen by God. Even lesser clergy were a superior breed of person whose services were essential for salvation. His opponents replied by accusing Laud and the King of being secret Catholics. Was not the Queen herself a Catholic and much of the Archbishop's ritual just disguised 'Popery'? they asked.

Like Elizabeth before him, Charles told the Commons that religion was none of its business. As a sincere believer in Divine Right, he saw himself as the 'father' of his people and guardian of their Church. But Eliot and his colleagues were not prepared to give way. They refused to grant the King any customs duties until he considered their criticisms. A Commons Resolution was passed, stating: 'The affairs of the King of Earth must give way to the King of Heaven.'

Charles decided to dismiss such a troublesome Parliament. But when the King's messenger arrived he was greeted with shouts of 'No! No!' As the Speaker rose to leave the Chamber, he was held in his chair by several members. Another M.P. locked the door and put the key in his pocket. During the tense debate which followed, illegal taxation, imprisonment without trial and Church policy were again attacked and anybody who disagreed was condemned as 'a betrayer of the liberties of England'. Only after such open defiance, did the members unlock the door and go home.

Eliot was put in prison where he died in 1632. No Parliament met in England for the next eleven years.

The Prayer Book riot in St Giles Cathedral, Edinburgh

Eleven years' tyranny

The years 1629–40 were generally prosperous and peaceful. Charles had promised every man 'great peace and quietness', and to a certain extent he kept his word. His enemies, however later called this period the 'Eleven years' tyranny'.

There were many reasons for their dissatisfaction. Charles ruled without consulting his wealthy subjects. His government interfered with trade, starting new companies, disbanding old ones, seizing investors' savings, ordering merchants to do this and that. Besides raising most of the unpopular taxes used by his father, the second Stuart solved his financial problems by extending Ship Money (a tax paid by ports for the upkeep of the navy) to inland towns (1635). What followed was typical of the relations between Charles and his well-to-do subjects.

The judges consulted by Charles thought the tax legal, mainly because they believed the King when he said it was essential to build ships for defence against pirates. Many of the landowners affected by the new rule disagreed. John Hampden from Buckinghamshire,

rewes in Scotland
ke in his pontificalibus
with Cricketts stooles
Stickes and Stones.

for example, refused to pay the 20s demanded of him. A long court action followed. Arguments raged amongst educated men throughout the country. Lawyers made speeches lasting three and four days. At last, by the narrow vote of 7 to 5, the Judges declared Ship Money legal. The King had won but his opponents had been able to use the trial as propaganda against him.

Meanwhile, Laud continued his reorganisation of the Church. Much of his work was beneficial. Dirty, neglected churches without windows and doors were common in those days. So were clergymen who avoided their duties, cut up clerical robes for towels, allowed parishioners to use gravestones for walls or even, as in one case, as a cheese press. Laud stopped such behaviour when he could, insisting on conscientious priests, reverent services and well ordered churches. At the same time, however, he punished Puritans who wore the 'wrong' robes, or altered the wording of the Prayer Book. He also censored the press and tried to restrict the sermons so popular with Puritans.

More irritating still were the severe punishments imposed for offences against the Church. A famous case occurred in 1637. Three Puritans, William Prynne, Henry Burton and John Bastwicke, were convicted before Star Chamber of publicly criticising Church policy. They were each sentenced to life imprisonment, a heavy fine and loss of their ears. Savage sentences of this sort merely created sympathy for the victims. When the time came for them to suffer the penalty Londoners laid sweet herbs in their path and gave them cups of wine. It was an impressive demonstration of how unpopular Laud's Church had become.

Revolt in Scotland

Prynne, Burton and Bastwicke were punished in June 1637. A month later an event took place which made it unlikely they would be in prison for long. On 28 July English-style Prayer Books were issued to worshippers in St Giles's Cathedral, Edinburgh. The Presbyterian congregation rioted. Bibles and folding stools were thrown at the Bishop and his clergy. Crowds outside pelted the windows with stones and rubbish. The Prayer Book Revolt had begun.

Making the Scots use the English Prayer Book arose from Charles's belief that all his subjects should enjoy the same religion. Unfortunately, such an action ignored the strong Presbyterian feelings of many Scots. The St Giles's riot was the signal for similar uproar in many Scottish towns and villages. All over the Lowlands men rushed to sign a National Covenant, promising to defend their Calvinist faith 'against contrary errors and corruption'. Quite soon they numbered a large army, with Alexander Leslie, a veteran who had served with the Swedes in the Thirty Years War, as their commander. As happy preachers called this revolt 'the great marriage day of this nation with God' an expert told the King he would need 40,000 men to force the Prayer Book on a Presbyterian people.

When the King decided to fight he found that English Puritans were unwilling to crush Puritanism in Scotland. A few lords, it was

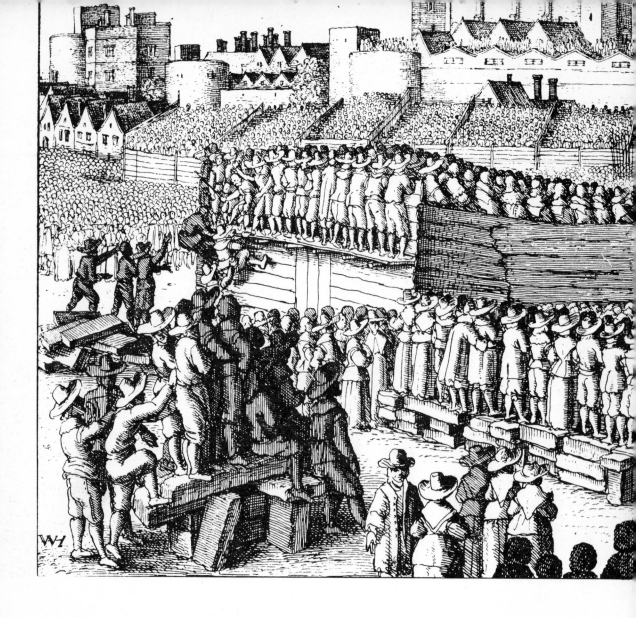

The end of 'Black Tom'. The Earl of Strafford is executed on Tower Hill, London, 1641

true, gave money or volunteered for service. Most merely made excuses, saying they were too poor, too young or too old for the expense and danger of a campaign! It was hardly surprising that soldiers recruited during 1638 were badly equipped and untrained. 'Our army is but weak', wrote an officer, '. . . if we fight with these forces . . . we shall have our throats cut'.

After some fighting, Charles was forced to sign a truce to prevent the Scots crossing the border. Then came another surprise. When he called Parliament in April 1640 he expected they would raise money to fight the Scots. Instead they listened to John Pym (1584–1643) a lawyer who 'broke the ice by a two hours' discourse'. Pym cleverly attacked the King's government, persuading the members to refuse to grant a war tax until Charles had listened to their grievances. Faced by Puritan M.P.s in London and Puritan enemies on the Border the

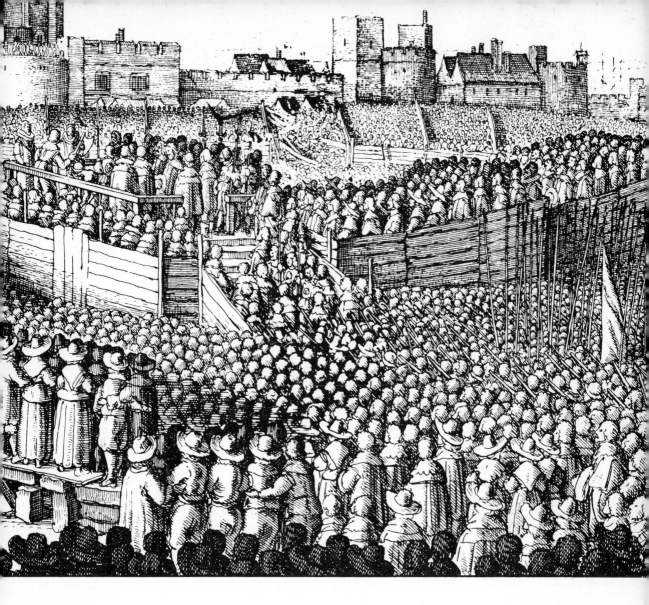

King dismissed the first and paid the second £850 a day not to invade England. The result was bankruptcy. In November 1640 Charles summoned the so-called Long Parliament, which was to sit for nearly thirteen years and destroy his life's work.

The Fall of 'Black Tom'

The new Commons showed no interest in the Scottish menace; indeed many of its members, including Pym, were on friendly terms with the Presbyterian leaders in Scotland. It preferred to turn upon Charles's two chief ministers, William Laud and Thomas Wentworth, Earl of Strafford. Of the two, Strafford was the more feared. By joining the King's service after 1629, the man who had helped frame the Petition of Right was regarded as a traitor to the Commons' cause. Furthermore, 'Black Tom Tyrant', as M.P.s called him, had great ability. As Lord Deputy of Ireland, he had ruled with efficiency and an iron hand. Seventeenth-century Ireland never knew such peace as Strafford gave it.

There now began a deadly game. Strafford hoped to force Pym to put him on trial so that he could defend royal policies and win a resounding victory. Pym, for his part, was afraid Strafford might reveal his own secret negotiations with the Scots. What if the Lord Deputy charged him with treason? What if he brought Irish troops to help Charles? There could be no mercy in such a struggle, for both men's lives were at stake.

Pym decided to prove Strafford was guilty of treason. Evidence was not easy to find. The best he could do was to quote a remark said to have been made by Strafford to the King—that he had an Irish army 'here to reduce (conquer) this Kingdom'. Such a phrase could have two meanings. When Strafford's impeachment (a trial in which the Commons act as accusers and the Lords as judges) opened in March 1641, the Lord Deputy naturally claimed that 'this Kingdom' meant Scotland. His enemies said it referred to England. After three weeks trial there was still no verdict and it was obvious Strafford would not be found guilty.

Now a desperate Pym decided to switch to a Bill of Attainder which needed no proof but simply declared a man guilty of treason. Charles promised Strafford he would save his life. For a time he seems to have considered some sort of military action to save his minister. Wild rumours of an army plot helped turn some moderate M.P.s against the King. In the streets of London angry mobs rioted. Inside Parliament, members became so frightened that once when a floor-board creaked, someone shouted 'gunpowder' and they all rushed out.

In such a mood the Commons began to hint at charges against the Queen herself. From the Tower a sick and weary Strafford advised the King to let him die. 'I am not guilty of treason', he wrote, but added 'To set your Majesty's conscience at liberty, I do most humbly beseech Your Majesty . . . to pass this bill.' Charles decided to sacrifice his minister, 'If my own person only were in danger', he explained, 'I would gladly venture it to save Lord Strafford's life; but seeing my wife, children and all my kingdom are concerned in it I am forced to give way.' In May 1641 Strafford went bravely to his death, blessed by the imprisoned Laud as he passed.

Soon afterwards Parliament set about reducing royal power. A Triennial Act allowed regular meetings of Parliament with or without Charles's permission. Ship Money and other 'illegal' taxes were abolished. So were Royal Courts such as Star Chamber and the Church Courts. It was clear that effective government would now be in the hands of the English gentry acting through Parliament.

Charles was soon to regret his weakness. He had lost his best man. Parliament still had John Pym!

Rebellion and Remonstrance

Few people mourned 'Black Tom'. Spectators at his execution rode home, waving their hats and shouting 'His head is off. His head is off!'

Some examples of the tortures which, it was rumoured, Catholics inflicted on Protestants during the 1641 rebellion

In Ireland far worse happened. No sooner was the Lord Deputy dead than the Irish broke into savage and disorganised rebellion.

The causes of this outburst went back many years, although fear of what Pym's puritan parliament might do to Catholics helped to light the flame. Ever since O'Neill's uprising in 1595 (see Chapter 13) English and Scottish Protestant settlers had been encouraged to 'colonise' Ireland. Such men took the best land and treated the inhabitants very badly, occasionally even hunting and killing them like wild animals. The native Irish saw their religion despised and their country occupied by enemies. Strafford had tried to protect the people as well as keep strict order. With his strong hand gone there was nothing to stop a national rising against the English 'master race'.

Beacons soon spread the news of rebellion to wild clansmen who promptly attacked Protestants. Farms were burned and their owners murdered or driven out. Hundreds, perhaps thousands, died. The grim story was exaggerated by the time it reached England. Puritan writers maintained it was a plot by the Queen and the Irish to destroy Parliament's power. Their pamphlets contained tales of raped women and children roasted by Catholic priests!

It was now that Charles's lack of contact with his people proved his downfall. The King was in Scotland when he heard the news. Instead of confronting his enemies as soon as possible, he travelled south in a leisurely fashion. By the time he did ask Parliament for an army to crush the rebellion, Pym was ready. No one knew better than the parliamentary leader that his success, possibly his life, depended on the King having no armed forces. To allow Charles to raise an army now would be madness from his point of view, for it would be used to crush Parliament, not reconquer Ireland. Pym decided his best plan was to remind men what an untrustworthy King they had. A document called the Grand Remonstrance was prepared, describing every royal act of which Parliament disapproved and proposing reforms in the Church.

By now moderates in the Commons were becoming alarmed by Pym. To object to illegal taxes and imprisonment without trial was one thing. To destroy both Church and royal authority was another. The danger of a too powerful King seemed to them to have been replaced by that of a too powerful Parliament. In the furious debate on the Remonstrance swords were rattled and members tore each other's clothes.

Those against the Remonstrance complained that no good could come from dragging up the past. They realised that the Bill, although addressed to the King, was in fact a direct appeal to the English people to support Parliament against Charles. Pym's defence was that Parliament was threatened by certain hotheads friendly with the King and Queen. Liberty and religion were in danger and strong measures were needed. In the early hours of 22 November 1641 the votes were counted by candlelight. It was a close victory for Pym— 159 members for and 148 against.

The result of this famous debate was encouraging for Charles because it showed that he had some parliamentary supporters at last. He indignantly rejected a proposal by Oliver Cromwell, M.P. for Huntingdon, that any force assembled for the reconquest of Ireland should be commanded by the Earl of Essex, one of Pym's supporters. Consequently, no army was recruited and the Irish revolt continued. For the second time in two years the King had been refused the means to crush a rebellion.

The five members

London was in a violent and angry mood that Christmas. Armed bands roamed the streets, often with drawn swords. Mobs ran wild and rumours spread like forest fire. For the first time two abusive nick-names were heard. Royalists called their opponents 'roundheads' because so many were short-haired apprentices. Parliamentary mobs shouted 'cavalier', comparing their opponents to the brutal Spanish *cabbaleros* who had slaughtered the Protestant Dutch in the days of Alva.

Charles felt the time was ripe to hit back. On recent journeys in England he had seen plenty of evidence of loyalty and affection for himself. The Grand Remonstrance vote had shown he could count on many members of Parliament. He must act quickly, because rumours were reaching him of a possible trial of his Queen. In January 1642 he gave orders for the arrest of five parliamentary leaders, Pym, Hampden, Holles, Strode and Haselrig. When the Commons refused to surrender them he took the advice of Henrietta Maria. 'Go and pull those rogues out by the ears, or never see my face again,' she is supposed to have said. Certainly the Queen suggested he should use force to capture them.

It was essential for Charles that the plan should succeed. If the five men were locked up opposition would collapse and the King would be supreme. If they escaped, he would have struck what might well turn out to be the first blow of a civil war. Had Pym been less clever the King might have succeeded. But the parliamentary leader knew from his spies exactly what Charles intended and to make sure the King and his soldiers *did* break into Parliament he stayed in the Commons Chamber until the very last moment! Then he and his four friends fled down river to the City (4 January 1642). Charles entered the Commons, leaving his soldiers at the door. In utter silence he asked for each of the five members by name. The Speaker refused to tell him whether they were present. Charles looked around. Significant empty spaces told him all he needed to know. 'I see all my birds have flown,' he remarked and walked out. The master stroke had failed.

London went mad that night. To the citizens Charles's action seemed to prove that Pym was right. The King *did* intend to destroy parliamentary liberties! Barricades were set up, cannon were dragged into firing positions and water boiled ready for throwing on the heads of royal soldiers. Houses of Catholics were attacked and several Catholic priests murdered. When the King himself ventured out his coach was surrounded by an angry mob shouting 'Privilege!

Charles I raises his standard as a sign of war, August 1642

Privilege!', meaning the privileges and liberties of parliament. As one man remembered years afterwards, 'the war began in our streets before the King and Parliament had any armies'.

War is declared

In January the King left London with his family to seek armed support for his cause. Finally on 22 August 1642 he raised his standard in a field near Nottingham as a sign of war.

It was a strange setting for so important an act. Pouring rain reduced the number of spectators. The heavy flagpole needed twenty men to heave it upright. A gloomy Charles seemed more worried about the exact wording of his proclamation than anything else. The standard itself was decorated with the royal coat of arms, a crown and a hand pointing towards it with the words, 'Give Caesar his due'. By this Charles meant that he was entitled to the powers Parliament denied him. A roll of drums and the blaring of trumpets marked the end of the ceremony. Men cheered and hurried to shelter out of the rain. Later that week a strong wind blew the flagpole down.

More about Charles I's reign

Books

I. H. Hexter, *The Reign of King Pym* (Oxford University Press)

C. Hibbert, *Charles I* (Weidenfeld & Nicolson)

H. F. Kearney, *Strafford in Ireland* (Manchester University Press)

K. Moore, *Richard Baxter, Toleration and Tyranny* (Longman: Then and There)

E. Murphy, *Cavaliers and Roundheads* (Longman: Then and There)

R. R. Sellman, *Civil War and Commonwealth* (Methuen: Outlines)

H. R. Trevor-Roper, *Archbishop Laud 1573-1645* (Macmillan)

Visual aids

Royalist and Puritan (Visual Publications)

Charles I (Visual Publications)

Charles I *(record)* (Fontana)

Visits

Houses of Parliament, London

The Queen's House, Greenwich

National Portrait Gallery, London

To write and find out

1 Had you lived in seventeenth-century England whom would you have supported, the King or Parliament? State what your own status is (whether a rich or poor man, merchant or lord) and give reasons for your choice.

2 Do you think Hampden was right to refuse to pay Ship Money?

3 Why is Charles sometimes known as 'the White King'?

From Edgehill to Naseby
The English Civil War 1642-1646

The King's announcement alerted a country which had seen no serious fighting since the Wars of the Roses. An island state like England had no need of large armies. Charles, when he declared war, had 300 infantry. In addition, his nephew, Prince Rupert, son of Frederick of Bohemia, commanded 800 cavalry. The men of the Parliamentary militia which assembled at Coventry and Northampton were badly equipped and untrained. Few officers on either side were experienced soldiers, although some had seen service on the continent in the Thirty Years War.

Not that the organisation and tactics of European armies were unknown in England. English foot soldiers, like those on the continent, consisted of pikemen and musketeers. Since fighting with a pike required greater strength it was considered more honourable. Pikes were about 16 feet long and made of wood with a metal point. Pikemen were taught to form rings when attacked. Muskets were of two types, matchlocks and firelocks. Matchlocks took some time to load as these firing orders indicate:

Try your match
Draw forth your scouring stick
Put in your bullet and ram home
Guard your pan
Blow off your loose powder
Come up to your musket
Return your match
Give fire!

Later in the war, firelocks, in which the bullet was fired by a 'flash pan' of powder ignited by a flint, became more common.

Horsemen carried pistols as well as swords. Swedish tactics in the Thirty Years War had made charging straight into the enemy popular, except with those horse regiments known as dragoons (they carried a pistol called a 'dragon') who were really mobile infantry in that they rode to battle but fought on foot. Much cavalry work involved being the 'eyes' of the army — spying on the enemy, attacking supply routes, seizing bridges and other strong points, even capturing enemy soldiers to obtain information. The artillery had a less important role. Most field guns were old and out of date. They were difficult to move, often needing eight horses to pull them and a crew of three to load and fire. Consequently, their main use was for sieges.

A continual problem for both sides was food supplies. The relatively few villages and towns of those days could not feed an army for long. Only biscuits and cheese were ever issued as rations; troops had to find other food and drink for themselves. Fodder for horses was also a difficult problem. Good grass was available in

Try your Match.

Draw forth your scouring Stick.

Put in your Bullet & Ram hom

spring and summer but there was little at other times. This fact, added to the bad state of roads in winter, meant that all major campaigns were fought in the summer.

The country divides

The King needed to win quickly if he was to win at all. London was the basis of Parliament's power and wealth and it also controlled the richest parts of the country, southern England and East Anglia. Another Parliamentary advantage was the support of the navy. This made it difficult for the Royalists to get help from abroad, besides giving the Roundheads customs' duties from the ports. Areas loyal to the King, Wales, the western counties and the North, tended to be poorer. Such regions supplied good soldiers but little money. Many Roundheads were rich merchants. Like John Hampden they could equip complete regiments out of their own pocket. If wealth had been all that mattered, the King would have stood no chance.

Each side claimed it was fighting for the King. Early in the war, it was Parliament's intention to destroy Charles's army, and, once the King had agreed to their terms, leave him on the throne. For Royalists the matter was simple. They fought for Charles the king even if they disapproved of Charles the man. Both Roundheads and Cavaliers believed God was on their side. The King went to war to defend the 'true Protestant faith'. Yet one Puritan soldier was typical of thousands when he wrote: 'When I put my hand to the Lord's work . . .I did not do it rashly . . . but had many an hour and night to seek God to know my way.'

The majority of ordinary folk were not interested in the dispute. For them it was a quarrel between their masters and its causes, religious, political or financial, were understood only by educated men. Indeed, as in the Thirty Years War, civilians grew to hate all soldiers. In Devon and Cornwall they even formed armed bands of 'clubmen' to protect themselves against either army.

Approximate division of England on the outbreak of the civil war 1642

for parliament

The division of England at the start of the Civil War, 1642

Guard your pan.   *Blow of your loose powder.*   *Return your match*   *Give Fire.*

154

Edgehill

In the autumn of 1642 the King's army began to march towards London. Its cavalry was commanded by the twenty-three-year-old Prince Rupert. This young man had already fought on the continent, where he had been taken prisoner by the Catholics. In the first charge of the war, his men so terrified the enemy that they ran for nine miles! At that moment the 'legend' of Rupert was born. Tales of his deeds were exaggerated until he was supposed to be able to move faster than the wind, to be unhurt by bullets and to be a friend of the Devil. Even his little white dog, Boy, which ran beside his horse, was said to be a familiar!

The Earl of Essex, the Parliamentary commander, decided to get behind Charles and so cut off his retreat. The King halted and offered battle at Edgehill, near Birmingham. About 14,000 men faced each other on 23 October 1642, in the first major engagement of the war. Before the battle Charles rode along his lines and told his men, 'come life or death, your King will bear you company'. Sir Jacob Astley one of his generals, prayed, 'Lord, Thou knowest how busy I must be this day; if I forget Thee, do not forget Thou me.'

Rupert began the battle with an assault which broke Essex's left wing. He then led his men in joyful and disorganised pursuit. Whilst they were away, the Roundhead cavalry smashed the squadrons facing them, leaving Royalist infantry to fight both foot-soldiers and horsemen. In a desperate skirmish Sir Edmund Verney, the King's standard bearer, was cut down with sixty of the royal bodyguard. His severed hand was found still fixed to the captured staff. Eventually Rupert's cavalry drifted back in time to prevent a Parliamentary victory.

Next day Essex marched his men off towards London. Neither side had won but the King's losses were heavier. A few weeks later Rupert, moving towards the capital, found 24,000 apprentices barring his way at Brentford. He retreated to the Royalist base at Oxford for the winter. No royal army ever got as near London again.

Newbury

In 1643 Charles decided to attack London with three armies. When this plan failed because both his western forces and those in the North could not fight their way through in time, the King decided to march his own army west from its base at Oxford and take Gloucester. This town was being heroically defended by the Puritan townsfolk. The task proved impossible. When its walls were broken by cannon balls, Gloucester's women and children filled the holes with earth and bedding. The Royalists then tried cutting off the town's water supply. Its inhabitants replied by pumping water from the river Severn. Finally, when the Cavaliers dug explosive mines under the defences, heavy rain flooded their tunnels.

The cautious Essex waited until he was sure London was safe before moving to save Gloucester. His troops, mostly Londoners, were issued with bread and cheese for a week. Beer was supplied by the countryfolk. It was a cold, dangerous march. Twice they drove off

Prince Rupert of the Rhine

Royalist cavalry which attacked them on the bare Cotswold Hills. On 5 September Royalist lookouts saw Essex's watchfires burning on the hills behind them. They promptly abandoned the siege and themselves set off towards London. The apprentices turned back, only to find the King's army blocking their way at Newbury. If Essex's men could be beaten the capital would be in real danger.

The Parliamentarians had been living for days on nuts, blackberries and apples. They were tired, hungry and wet from frequent rain. The King, meanwhile, had been joined by fresh cavalry from Oxford. A confused fight followed in countryside divided by narrow lanes and tall hedges. Apprentices and farm labourers, gentlemen and shop-keepers, ambushed each other, fighting hand to hand without formation or planning. Rupert's cavalry drove the London trained bands back but suffered heavy losses from well aimed musket fire from cover. Late that evening the Prince rode to and fro trying to locate his scattered Royalist horsemen. Essex's men continued their weary march towards the capital. When they reached London cheering crowds put flowers in their hats.

It was obvious it was not going to be a short war. Both King and Parliament spent the winter looking for allies.

Oliver Cromwell

The obvious ally for Parliament was the Scots, who had done little to help their Puritan friends since 1641. This was because Scottish clergymen, besides hating the Church of England and 'the great Idol . . ., the Service Book', also disliked those Puritans who demanded religious toleration (freedom of religious belief). Not until the Commons agreed to establish an English Presbyterian Church after the war did they send aid. In November 1643 a Scottish army of 20,000 arrived to fight the King. Charles, meanwhile, did not do so well in his negotiations. Although he signed a truce with the Irish rebels and brought home English reinforcements, they were beaten by General Fairfax at Nantwich, Cheshire (January 1644).

The Scottish alliance was John Pym's last masterstroke before he died in December 1643. Royalists claimed he had been 'eaten by worms'; his supporters said he had died of overwork. Whatever the cause of death, his achievements while alive had been impressive. In three years he had destroyed much of the royal power established by the Tudors, making Parliament stronger than ever before. But he left England in the middle of a war, knowing his work would only be permanent if Parliament won.

As one great Roundhead leader passed from the scene, a greater one arrived. Oliver Cromwell (1599–1658) was distantly related to Henry VIII's minister, Thomas. At first he lived the usual life of a gentleman, hunting, hawking and gambling whenever he could. But his days at Cambridge University laid the foundation of a Puritanism which grew deeper and stricter with every year that passed. Until the war he farmed his lands in Huntingdonshire, besides serving as a J.P. and a member of Charles's second Parliament. In that troubled assembly he became known as a rather uncouth critic of the King

Battle of Edgehill, October 1642

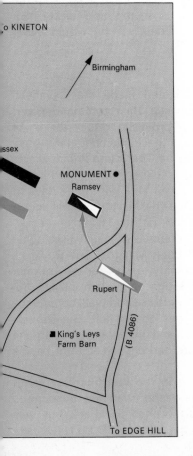

o KINETON

Birmingham

ssex

MONUMENT ●
Ramsey

Rupert

(B 4086)

■ King's Leys
Farm Barn

To EDGE HILL

Oliver Cromwell

who stood up to speak in a 'plain cloth suit, which seemed to have been made by an ill country tailor'.

During the Eleven Years Tyranny he supported his cousin, Hampden, in the Ship Money case, opposed a royal plan to drain the Fenlands near his home, and frequently demanded freedom of worship. He took this line where religion was concerned because he was an Independent, that is, one who disliked both Presbyterian and Church of England discipline. In 1642 Cromwell joined the Parliamentary army as a captain of cavalry. From the start he showed great ability. He disciplined his men firmly, teaching them to advance to the attack knee to knee at a 'pretty round trot'. Such a charge was slower than Rupert's but easier to control.

Above all, Cromwell liked Independents as soldiers, believing that in battle their love of God would make them fight as well as the Cavaliers. At Grantham in 1643 both the 'new men' and new tactics worked. As Cromwell reported afterwards, 'our men charging fiercely upon them, by God's providence they were immediately routed, and ran all away'. It was a story to be repeated many times in the years which followed.

By the time of Pym's death Cromwell was a lieutenant-general in Lord Manchester's Army of the Eastern Association. Essex and Sir Thomas Fairfax were then the most famous Roundhead generals. Yet one who had seen Cromwell's Ironside cavalry in action told the King that Oliver was 'the most dangerous enemy his Majesty had. For tho' he were at that time of mean rank . . . he would climb higher.'

The 'Whitecoats' last stand

The Scottish invasion of northern England made the Cavaliers' position desperate. The Duke of Newcastle, their commander, put his army behind the defences of York and promised to surrender if not relieved by 4 July 1644. The King kept the Parliamentarians busy around Oxford and sent Rupert to the rescue. The young Prince was at his best on such a mission. He stormed Stockport, Bolton and Liverpool, crossed the Pennine Hills, and entered York with three days to spare. Then, although outnumbered two to one, he proudly challenged the Roundheads to battle on Marston Moor (2 July 1644).

All through a hot summer day the two armies gradually assembled between the villages of Tockwith and Long Marston. The Royalists were on the moor and the Parliamentarians on higher but rougher ground. A ditch separated them although in certain places the cavalry of either side were uncomfortably close. Cromwell, commanding the Eastern Association cavalry, was on the left; Sir Thomas Fairfax had his horsemen on the right and his infantrymen in the centre. Leslie, the Scottish Commander, had chosen to fight beside Cromwell's men.

As evening came the psalm singing in the Parliamentary camp died away. Silence fell on a strange scene, watched by curious villagers from a safe distance. Rupert wished to attack but was persuaded by Newcastle to wait until the next day. Both Newcastle

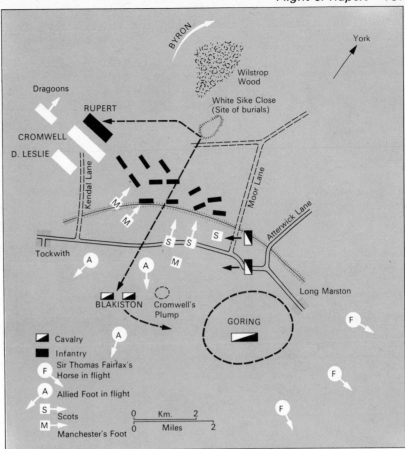

The deciding battle of the war—Marston Moor, 1644

and Rupert went to their coaches. Their men broke ranks and began to prepare supper. Suddenly, at 7.30 pm, Cromwell's horsemen crossed the ditch in the light of the setting sun and cut up Rupert's unprepared cavalry. This surprise action brought on a full scale battle.

Galloping horses and shouting men destroyed the peace of a summer evening. Musket fire lit the countryside with flame and sent clouds of smoke drifting over friend and foe. The Royalist centre, mostly recruits in their first battle, quickly gave way. Only on the left, where the Royalist Lord Goring drove Fairfax's regiments from the field, did the King's men do well. As night fell Rupert tried to rally his scattered horsemen but it was no use. During a fierce charge his dog Boy was killed, much to the delight of the superstitious Puritan soldiers. Meanwhile, Cromwell was temporarily blinded by a powder flash during hand-to-hand fighting and had to retire from the field.

When he returned it was all over. Goring's victorious cavalry had been swept away by the Eastern Association cavalry who had turned a full circle behind the enemy front. Thousands of Royalists were dead or wounded. The Prince himself had fled, leaving his battle flag. Alone in the moonlight one regiment remained firm. Newcastle's

Whitecoats had sworn to stain their tunics red with Roundhead blood. Refusing Fairfax's offer of surrender, they fought on for hours in Wilstrop Wood. By midnight only thirty were left alive to lay down their arms.

Battle of Naseby

Marston Moor shattered the legend of Rupert's superiority and gave Parliament control of the North. It was the turning point of the war. After such a defeat the King was in the same position as his Whitecoats. He could fight on but he could not expect to win.

The 'New Noddle'

Back in the south Cromwell and other Independent generals were disgusted to find that Essex and Manchester had been beaten during the summer. They therefore suggested that no member of the Lords or Commons should be an army officer. This Bill, the Self-Denying Ordinance, seemed a fair way to weed out inefficient officers. It was, after all, most difficult to make a man obey military rules if he enjoyed parliamentary privilieges. But behind the proposal lay an attempt by the Independents to gain control of the Army because any M.P. could stay in the army by resigning whereas a lord could not give up his title! Consequently, when it became law, the Roundhead army lost Essex and Manchester, the two generals Cromwell suspected of not fighting hard enough.

In religious matters there were similar sweeping changes. In January 1645 a Calvinist Directory of Worship replaced the Prayer Book, whose services were described as 'unprofitable and burdensome'. On the same day Archbishop Laud was condemned to death at a trial in which the prosecution was led by William Prynne. The fact that the King had demanded Laud should be pardoned was ignored. On the scaffold the Archbishop denied that he was a Catholic and claimed also that the King was 'as sound a Protestant . . . as any man in the Kingdom'. Such a dignified end did not satisfy one minister who said the Archbishop should have been put in a sack and thrown in the Thames. Laud was the fifth and last Archbishop of Canterbury to suffer a violent death.

Even as he was executed a new armed force was recruited to destroy his master. The New Model army was the first truly professional army in English history. Initially it consisted of 22,000 men, well supplied with guns and other equipment. Infantry regiments were dressed in scarlet tunics; the cavalry wore brown leather coats. Unlike the King's forces, the New Model was well paid. Colonels received £1 a day, troopers 2s 6d and privates 10d. It was also well disciplined. Death was the penalty for several offences, including threatening an officer and hitting a civilian. Tongues were bored through for blasphemy and men were whipped for swearing. An entire army was influenced by Independent religious ideas and taught it was fighting God's battle.

Royalists sneeringly called it the 'New Noddle' yet Charles's badly equipped troops stood little chance against it when the two sides met at Naseby near Market Harborough in Leicestershire on 14 June 1645. Rupert charged first, determined not to be surprised as he was at Marston Moor. His men did well until the Royalist infantry were overcome by superior numbers. Wave after wave of Cromwell's Ironsides completed the rout. With his enemies closing in, Charles decided to gallop into the fray. A cavalier seized his bridle and persuaded him to turn back. By early afternoon there was 'not a horse or man of the King's army to be seen except the prisoners'.

The battle of Naseby was the final disaster for the cavalier cause. That evening Cromwell wrote to the Speaker of the Commons. 'Sir, this is none other but the hand of God; and to Him alone belongs the

Equipment of a New
Model Trooper

glory', adding, when speaking of his Independents: 'Honest men served you faithfully in this action. Sir, they are trusty; I beseech you . . . not to discourage them.' It was a clear warning that the New Model had not fought for a Presbyterian Church. Significantly, this part of the letter was not published in London.

Fighting continued until March 1646 when Sir Jacob Astley was defeated at Stow-on-the-Wold. Two months later the King gave himself up to the Scots. When he refused to help them establish Presbyterianism in England they handed him over to Parliament. The war was over.

More about the English Civil War
Books
Some of those listed for Chapter 18, also:
M. Ashley, *Cromwell* (Prentice-Hall)
R. Atkyns and J. Gwynn, *The Civil War,* ed. P. Young and N. Tucker (Longman: Military Memoirs)
The English Civil War (Cape: Jackdaw)
J. Kinross, *Discovering Battlefields in Northern England and Scotland* and *Discovering Battlefields in Southern England* (Shire Publications)
B. Martin, *Our Chief of Men* (Life of Cromwell) (Longman)
E. K. Milliken, *The Stuarts* (Harrap)

Visual aids
The English Civil War *(two films)* (Rank)
The Civil War (Educational Productions)
Oliver Cromwell *(record)* (HMV)
Oliver Cromwell *(film)* (BBC TV)
Oliver Cromwell (Hulton)

Visits
Many of the towns etc., mentioned in this chapter will preserve signs, monuments and relics connected with Civil War battles and sieges. The major battlefields can in most cases still be examined but an expert guide or a detailed guidebook is almost essential to make such a visit worthwhile. The Society of the Sealed Knot is a group of enthusiasts who occasionally 'stage' Civil War battles on the original site. Their activities are well worth viewing.

To write and find out
1 Go to your local library or the County Record Office and examine the *County History.* This will almost certainly contain accounts of what happened in your area during the Civil War.
2 Scale models of battles can be made as a class or group project.

20　Charles the Martyr
Charles I 1646-1649

Sitting wearily on a drum after his final battle, Sir Jacob Astley, the old Cavalier, told his victorious enemies: 'You have done your work and may go and play, unless you fall out among yourselves.' His words were very true. Parliament seemed to have won a great victory. But two questions remained unanswered. First, would the Independents who dominated the army allow a Presbyterian system to be forced upon the country? Second, what if the King still refused to give way to Parliament's demands? If the answer to either of these questions was 'No', Parliament would have lost the Civil War as surely as the King.

Of the two problems, that of the army was to prove the most dangerous. Within its ranks were men of unusual religious and political opinions. A minority were 'wild men' who believed Christ was about to return to earth. They called themselves 'Saints' and dreamed of building a 'New Jerusalem' in England. Others demanded far more political freedom than mere 'parliamentary liberties'. 'Honest' John Lilburne thought the 'ancient laws of England', for which the war had been started, 'mumbo jumbo'. He was afraid that his comrades had defeated one set of tyrants only to be crushed by another.

Lilburne was a Leveller. This group demanded something quite extraordinary for those days—a vote for most males over twenty-one years of age. 'The poorest that lives hath as true a right to give a vote as well as the richest', they claimed, although in fact they would have left out servants, paupers and Cavaliers. Cromwell did not see eye to eye with them. His religious ideas were revolutionary by seventeenth-century standards. His political opinions were not. Cromwell was a landowner and gentleman whose grandfather had been a baronet and whose mother's family had shared some of the spoils when the monasteries were dissolved. Like most of his class, he believed that only those who owned property should run the country.

'Honest' John Lilburne behind bars

Crisis at Putney

Early in 1647 Parliament and its army prepared for a showdown. Parliament made the first move by ordering part of the New Model Army to disband and the rest to go to Ireland. For those to be demobilised its terms were harsh. Pensions would not be paid to the wounded or to widows. No trooper could keep his horse even if it was his own. The question of overdue pay—eighteen weeks for the infantry and forty-three weeks for the cavalry—would be settled after the men had gone home.

The army saw all it had fought for in danger. It refused to obey and

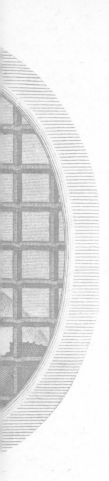

elected agitators (agents) to carry its grievances to London. At first Cromwell stayed out of the quarrel. Then, when it became clear there would be a serious clash, he sided with his men. This set the pattern for the rest of his career. However much he disliked its political ideas, Cromwell needed the army. Without such armed support, religious freedom and possibly Cromwell himself would be destroyed. The army, in turn, would probably have been lost without his firm leadership and great reputation.

It was clear that possession of the King in the coming negotiations would be a trump card. Since his surrender Parliament had confined him at Holmby House in Northamptonshire. Following secret meetings at Cromwell's house in Drury Lane, London, a force of 500 troopers seized Charles and carried him off to Newmarket (June 1647). The Commons tried to arrest Cromwell as a traitor but he escaped. Soon afterwards the army occupied London, and expelled eleven leading Presbyterians from Parliament. The victors had fallen out among themselves, as Astley predicted.

The New Model generals now offered the King very fair terms. Their Heads of Proposals (July 1647) suggested religious freedom for all except Catholics, parliamentary elections every two years and a return to both bishops and Prayer Book. A Council of State appointed by the army was to rule the country for seven years; ministers chosen by Parliament for ten. Certain of Charles's friends advised acceptance. 'A crown so near lost was never recovered so easily as this would be,' commented one.

Charles rejected the offer for several reasons. First, he disliked Cromwell as a religious extremist whose soldiers had damaged cathedrals. Second, knowing his enemies had quarrelled, he hoped to play one against the other. Indeed, even as the negotiations seemed about to succeed a spy reported to Cromwell that Charles planned to destroy them all. Such dishonesty on the King's part was fatal. The army represented the only effective power left in the land. No agreement the King might reach with Scots or Parliament could succeed unless the army was beaten, and this was unlikely.

Meanwhile many troopers were dissatisfied by the behaviour of the 'grandees', as they called Cromwell and his generals. The Heads of Proposals in their opinion, were too moderate for a defeated King. At Putney, near London, they debated an alternative solution, the Agreement of the People, put forward by prominent Leveller leaders. This demanded complete religious toleration, no bishops, biennial elections (every two years) and absolute power for Parliament. More important, votes would be given to all 'freeborn Englishmen', which meant heads of families and their servants. Cromwell was horrified and General Ireton, his son-in-law, asked whether, since one man was the equal of another 'he hath an equal right to any goods he sees'?

Disagreements among the Roundheads soon became serious. At Ware, Hertfordshire, two cavalry regiments drove off their officers and paraded with copies of the Agreement of the People in their hat-bands (November 1647). Cromwell is said to have drawn his sword

Gateway of Carisbrooke
Castle, Isle of Wight,
where Charles I was held
prisoner in 1647

and ordered them to throw down their papers. The sight of their Lieutenant-General so angry made the troopers obey. Afterwards one of the ringleaders was court-martialled and shot.

At this critical moment the King made the wrong move and united his enemies. In the same month as the Ware mutiny Charles escaped to the Isle of Wight, where he was well treated by the Governor. Within weeks of his arrival he signed an alliance with the Scots by which, in return for military aid, he agreed to establish Presbyterianism in England for three years. At the same time he promised to put down 'the opinions and practices of Independents'. A copy of this 'Engagement' was wrapped in lead and buried in the garden of Carisbrooke Castle where Charles was staying.

Faced by another war, the New Model Army forgot its differences, appealing once more to the God of battles.

War and purge

Nothing showed more clearly the power of the New Model Army than the speed with which it ended the second Civil War. The Scottish troops who marched south were not the disciplined army of the Covenant which had fought for Parliament but Royalists and Catholics. Although they outnumbered Cromwell's force by two to one they were crushed in a three-day battle around Preston (August 1648). Other Royalist risings in Kent, Essex and Wales were equally unsuccessful. In Essex Fairfax took Colchester after a siege; bullets remain embedded in some of its houses to the present day.

Whilst Cromwell stamped out the last flickers of rebellion in the North, other generals prepared to settle with King and Parliament once and for all. Charles Stuart 'that man of blood' was to be put on trial as 'the grand author of our troubles'. Parliament, which was found to have signed an agreement with the King, was 'purged' by soldiers led by Colonel Pride. Under the eyes of his musketeers, forty-one Presbyterian members were arrested and ninety-six expelled. Only the 'Rump' remained—a mere shadow of the Long Parliament which had executed Strafford and brought Charles to his knees seven years before.

Cromwell has said during the war, 'if the King were before me I would shoot him as another'. Afterwards he described him as 'the uprightest and most conscientious man in his three Kingdoms' (England, Scotland and Wales). Charles's dishonesty and the Scottish invasion changed his attitude. He decided the King must die. 'This is a more prodigious treason,' he remarked, 'than any that hath been perfected before; because the former quarrel was that Englishmen might rule over one another, this is to vassalise (make slaves of) us to a foreign nation.' Furthermore he believed it went against the will of God, shown by favouring the New Model Army with victory on so many battlefields.

On 20 January 1649 a court consisting of 135 commissioners assembled in the Painted Chamber of Westminster Palace to try Charles. Its President, John Bradshaw wore a special hat lined with metal in case somebody tried to murder him. When news arrived that

The Rump roasted salt it well it stinks exceedingly.

Oliver declars himself and the Re: bells to be the Gadly Party

The Rump and dregs of the house of Com: remaining after the good members were purged out.

Royalist playing-cards. The roasting of the 'stinking' Rump. Cromwell declares his supporters to be the Godly party. The 'Rump' Parliament shown as dregs left in a wine barrel

Metal hat worn by John Bradshaw, President of the court which tried Charles in Westminster Hall. He feared that he might be killed by a royalist

the King had landed from the river and was walking through the garden, Cromwell rushed to the window and turned pale. 'My masters,' he cried, 'he is come, he is come, and now we are doing that great work that the whole nation will be full of.' He and his friends were about to become regicides (king killers).

A royal trial

Charles had been a prisoner at Carisbrooke since the Governor had discovered his plot with the Scots. He was brought to London after a short stay at Hurst Castle, a lonely fortress beside the river Solent in Hampshire. As he gazed out to sea, or walked along the beach, he must have known his end was near.

In this grim situation a mysterious change came over the King. The shy hesitant man became bold and determined; even his stutter left him. Perhaps the simplicity of the task before him helped. There were now no awkward decisions or problems. All he had to do was die bravely. For a man of courage like Charles this was perhaps not difficult. Whatever his past sins or mistakes, it was his enemies who now had made a wrong move. Some army leaders were against putting Charles to death. It was, they thought, an illegal act by men who claimed to have been fighting to defend ancient laws. It would replace a King who was a prisoner with one who would surely try to recover the throne—Charles's son in Holland. Finally, it was certain to horrify all moderate men and women and create sympathy for the victim.

Charles was charged with a 'wicked design' to be a dictator and overthrow the 'rights and liberties of the people'. He was also blamed for the war, and the deaths of innocent people. His reaction was to listen contemptuously to the indictment, refuse to remove his hat before the judges and laugh when called a 'tyrant, traitor and murderer'. In reply he ignored the charges and demanded what right the Court had to try him. 'I would know by what authority, I mean lawful?' he asked.

'By the authority of the Commons of England, assembled in Parliament,' came the answer.

'The King,' retorted Charles, 'cannot be tried.'

This, of course, was the weak point in the proceedings; as one lawyer had told Cromwell: 'The King can be tried by no court.' Then, referring to the fact that Parliament was a carefully selected assembly controlled by the army, he remarked that this particular court was not fit to try anybody. Consequently the King was able to pose as a defender of the people's liberties. 'If Power without law can make law . . . I know not what subject in England can be sure of his life or anything he calls his own,' he commented. The days when such words could have been used to describe Charles's own actions were over. Now he faced an illegal court certain to give the verdict Cromwell and the army wanted. It was, indeed, 'power without law'.

After nearly a week of argument, Bradshaw summed up. A monarch, he told Charles, must obey the law and protect, not make war on, his subjects. Then the clerk read out the sentence 'That the said Charles Stuart, as a Tyrant, Traitor, Murderer and a public enemy, shall be put to death by the severing of his head from his body'. Only now did Charles decide to defend himself. But Bradshaw replied that as the King did not recognise the court's authority he could not speak to it. '*I am not suffered to speak. Expect what justice other people will have,*' said the King. He was led away through ranks of jeering soldiers. Shouts of 'Execution, Justice' echoed round the hall.

Execution in Whitehall

On Tuesday, 30 January 1649 Charles I was brought to his own Banqueting Hall in Whitehall, London. It was a gloomy, cold day, white with frost and snow. A procession of soldiers beating drums accompanied him. Slowly they surrounded the black-draped scaffold set in front of the building. This was to keep the large crowd at a distance and prevent attempt at a rescue. Whilst the King retired to a room in the palace, officials hurried to and fro and a shivering crowd waited.

At about two in the afternoon, a Colonel Hacker tapped quietly on Charles's door. The King finished praying and walked to the place of execution. Dense crowds surged forward, stretching their necks to see him and calling out prayers and blessings. The scaffold itself was packed with officers and clergy. Charles's executioners, probably a Richard Brandon and his assistant, were disguised by cloaks, masks and obviously false hair and beards.

The execution of Charles I in Whitehall, London, on 30 January 1649

Charles decided to speak even though he knew the spectators were too far away to hear him. Briefly he summed up the principles for which he believed he was dying. As King he had desired, he said, freedom for his people as much as any man but this was possible

Frontispiece of *Eikon - Basilike*

only if they were well governed. Freedom could not be achieved by the people sharing in the government. 'A subject and a sovereign are clear different things,' he added. Of his faith he remarked, 'I die a Christian according to the profession of the Church of England. I have a good Cause and I have a gracious God. I will say no more.'

Charles then stripped off his jewels, the badge of the Order of the Garter and his outer clothing. The block was only ten inches high so he was forced to lie flat to place his head on it. After a few seconds he gave a signal to the executioner. The axe swung down, cutting off his head at one blow. An eyewitness wrote of this moment: 'There was such a groan by the thousands then present, as I never heard before and desire I may never hear again.' Cavalry quickly cleared the crowd away. Only a few managed to dip their handkerchiefs in the blood that dripped from the scaffold.

Royal image

On the day Charles was buried in St George's Chapel, Windsor, a book called *Eikon Basilike* (royal image) was published. It consisted of thoughts and prayers supposed to have been written by the King during his imprisonment. Cromwell and his supporters looked upon the King's death as a righteous judgment of God. In their opinion the land was 'cleansed' of the blood shed in the Civil War by the blood of the man who caused it. The 'King's Book', on the other hand, presents a picture of a saintly ruler forced to fight to save his people and ready to die rather than give in to unjust demands. *Eikon Basilike* was certainly not written by the King, although it contained many of his opinions. This did not stop it becoming a 'Bible' to Royalists in later years.

As a King Charles Stuart nearly ruined the English monarchy. His brave death saved it. Few English kings since 1066 have been saintly. Only one is a 'martyr'.

More about Charles the Martyr
Books
People of the Past, vol E (Purnell: Finding Out Books) —contains 'A Roundhead Soldier' and 'A Puritan Preacher'
H. Shaw, *The Levellers* (Longman: Seminar Studies in History)
The Trial and Execution of Charles I (Cape: Jackdaw)
C. V. Wedgwood, *The Trial of Charles I* (Collins)
H. R. Williamson, *Charles I and Cromwell* (Duckworth)

Visual aids
As for Chapters 18 and 19

Visits
London Museum
Banquetting Hall, Whitehall, London
Westminster Hall, London
Carisbrooke Castle, Isle of Wight

To write and find out
1 After proper preparation stage a class room debate on the question, 'Did Charles I save the English monarchy?'
2 Write an essay describing what you think would have happened if Charles I had won the war.
3 Is there a church of 'Charles the Martyr' near your home?
4 Who was the next king (not English) to be beheaded after Charles I? What were the circumstances surrounding his execution?

The Council of State set up to rule the new Commonwealth faced grave difficulties at home and abroad. Other countries treated regicide England as an outcast. The Tsar of Russia ordered its representative from his court. The Dutch government did nothing to punish those who murdered the Commonwealth's ambassador in Holland. French privateers and a Royalist fleet commanded by Prince Rupert attacked English merchant ships. The Scots recognised Charles's eldest son as King Charles II; the Irish continued to live in defiance and disorder. Even the army, real ruler of a 'headless' country, was itself disturbed by more Leveller mutinies.

The Civil War caused ordinary people's opinions to be heard. Cromwell's soldiers had experienced more in seven years than their grandparents in a lifetime. They had met and talked freely with men they would never have known, and seen parts of the country they would never have laid eyes on, in ordinary circumstances. A majority, particularly the infantry, wished for little more than good food and pay. In the ranks of the cavalry however, enough 'extreme' ideas were discussed at this time to make the ruling classes fear the 'many headed monster' (the ordinary people) for centuries to come.

Typical of such extremists were the Diggers. It was no new thing for men to complain about their land being taken by enclosure. But Gerard Winstanley, an Independent who claimed he received instructions from God while in a trance, went further. Those who owned no land were, in his opinion, entitled to 'all the commons and waste ground in England'. And, in April 1649 at St George's Hill, near Cobham in Surrey, he and a few friends actually cleared rough ground and planted parsnips, carrots and beans.

These pioneers proposed to share crops as they shared work. The local inhabitants had other ideas. Their bitter complaints rose as high as Fairfax, who sent soldiers to Cobham to disperse the community. Their commander came to the conclusion Winstanley and his friends were harmless lunatics. When the Diggers promised to take only common or park land, not private property, Fairfax decided to leave them alone. This satisfied neither rich nor poor in Cobham. Farm workers pulled up the Diggers' crops; J.P.s arrested them and confiscated their tools. A novel experiment was crushed almost before it started.

Three years later Winstanley asked Cromwell to help establish Digger communities. He reminded him that Diggers and Levellers had risked their lives fighting for the rights now refused them. Cromwell thought differently. The Civil War had never been started for such 'rights'. The privileges and rights of Parliament were far different things from land for all and votes for 'freeborn Englishmen'.

'The dreadful appearance of God'

The Commonwealth government tackled its problems quickly. In 1649 Cromwell was sent to Ireland to restore order. Leading the final assault himself, he captured Drogheda and allowed his men to slaughter both defenders and civilians. At Wexford a similar massacre took place without his permission. Cromwell was cruel partly because he was in a hurry to get back and fight the Scots and partly because he was determined to avenge the death of Protestants in Ireland in 1641. His whirlwind campaign was no worse than many in the Thirty Years War but it remains a blot on his reputation.

Arriving home in 1650 Cromwell took command of the New Model Army on the retirement of Fairfax, and led it north against the Covenanters. He found southern Scotland stripped of food and an army led by his old comrade Leslie waiting for him. Cromwell had no hatred for Presbyterians. He would have preferred to avoid bloodshed, provided the Scots allowed religious freedom and expelled Charles II from their country. In a letter to the Scottish Church he begged the elders to 'think it possible you may be mistaken'. He was wasting his time. Presbyterians, like Independents, were sure God was on their side.

Cromwell had no heavy guns to lay siege to Edinburgh, and the Scottish policy of destroying their crops left his men without sufficient food. When Leslie refused to give battle, the New Model Army 'poor, shattered, hungry, discouraged' according to Cromwell, retreated to the port of Dunbar. Immediately the Scots left their trenches near Edinburgh and occupied the pass south through the Lammermuir Hills. The English were now trapped between the sea and mountains. It was the most dangerous moment of Cromwell's military career.

So far all had gone well for Leslie. But the Scottish clergy disliked such waiting tactics, preferring that he should leave his defences and destroy the English. When the Scottish general reluctantly gave way to their demands, the move was carried out badly. As a result his battle lines were ragged, with frequent gaps and too many troops massed on the right wing. At dawn on 3 September 1650 Cromwell led his men to the attack, quoting Psalm 68, 'Now let God arise and his enemies shall be scattered'. While General Monk shattered the weak Scottish left, guns pounded the powerful right, driving it into a crush on Doon Hill. The Scots were soon utterly defeated and flying from the field. Afterwards happy New Model troopers grouped around Cromwell and sang Psalm 117—'O give praise unto the Lord, All nations that be.'

Dunbar was a shattering blow to the Covenanters who had never believed God would 'desert' them in this way. Public debates between Presbyterian ministers were arranged to consider 'the dreadful appearance of God against us at Dunbar'. The men who had once humbled Charles I were now themselves humbled. Never again would they be so confident of God's favour or so certain that England could be turned Presbyterian.

Next year the young Charles II invaded England with a mixed army of Scots and Royalists. He was trapped at Worcester and

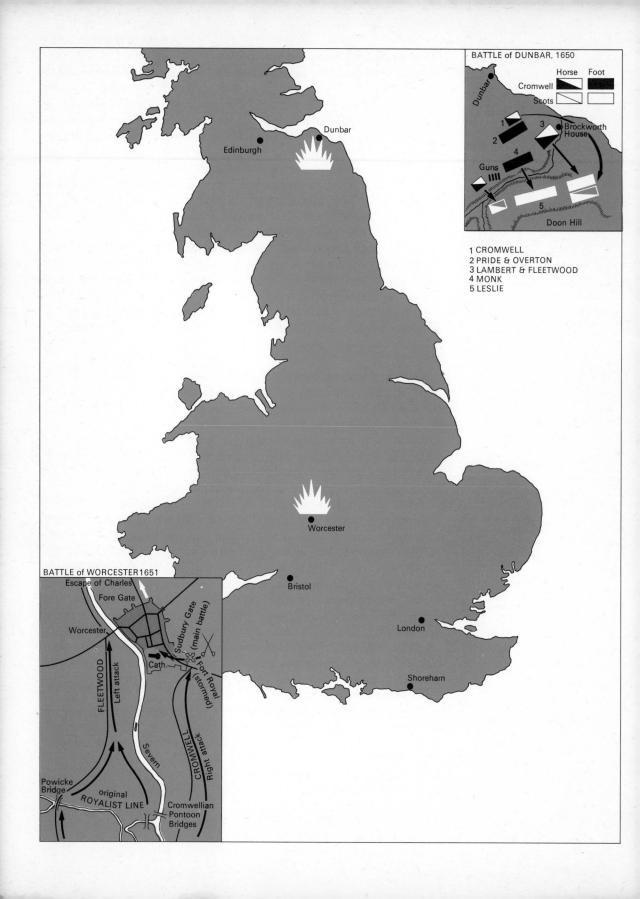

BATTLE of DUNBAR, 1650

	Horse	Foot
Cromwell		
Scots		

Dunbar

1
2
3 Brockworth House
4
Guns
5
Doon Hill

1 CROMWELL
2 PRIDE & OVERTON
3 LAMBERT & FLEETWOOD
4 MONK
5 LESLIE

Edinburgh

Dunbar

Worcester

Bristol

London

Shoreham

BATTLE of WORCESTER 1651

Escape of Charles
Fore Gate
Worcester
Sudbury Gate (main battle)
Cath.
Fort Royal (stormed)
FLEETWOOD
Left attack
Severn
CROMWELL
Right attack
Powicke Bridge
original ROYALIST LINE
Cromwellian Pontoon Bridges

Cromwell's Dunbar and
Worcester campaigns
1650–51

defeated in a fierce five-hour fight. It was, as Cromwell wrote after-wards 'a crowning mercy'. Fought on the anniversary of Dunbar, it ended both the Civil Wars and Cromwell's military career. Charles escaped abroad after many exciting adventures. Cromwell and his Independents were masters of the newly formed Commonwealth of Great Britain.

A new navy

For all practical purposes the English navy had died with Drake. No successful sea action had been fought since the attack on Cadiz in 1596. In Stuart times English ports had been raided by the French and Dutch on several occasions, and pirates operated openly in the Thames and Severn. Large warships were expensive to build and maintain; it cost twice as much to keep a seventeenth-century sailor at sea than a soldier on campaign. Consequently there was little money available for ship building during James I's peaceful reign. Charles I, as we have seen, tried to remedy this sad state of affairs by raising Ship Money. With this revenue he built the world's finest warship, the *Sovereign of the Seas* between 1635 and 1639. Yet even as the *Sovereign* was launched the Dutch ignored the English navy and destroyed a Spanish armada within sight of Dover. In America the Dutch defiantly founded 'New Holland' in the heart of the English colonies. It was clear that Holland now had the best navy in the world.

The Commonwealth government was prepared to contest such supremacy. Instead of abolishing Ship Money, they used it to build forty ships purely for war. The days of the armed merchantmen were over. Their crews were well fed and well paid by seventeenth-century standards. Seamen received a regular ration of meat and biscuits, plus seven gallons of beer a week. They were also offered prize money for success in battle. In the case of captured ships, half their sale price was divided between captain and crew. If a ship was sunk a sum reckoned at £20 for each of its guns was shared out. Although the Tudors founded an English navy, it was during the Commonwealth period that it became a government-controlled fighting force.

The Government's choice of commander was Colonel Robert Blake (1599–1657). This appointment of a soldier for a sea-commander was not as unusual as it would be today. Rich Stuart courtiers often went to sea as officers, crowding the admiral's quarterdeck during the summer cruise like holidaymakers. The Commonwealth also picked landsmen for naval posts but instead of playful sons of the rich they chose soldiers. Blake had worked and played hard at Oxford University. 'He was an early riser and studied well', wrote the diarist John Aubrey, 'but also took his robust pleasures of fishing, fowling etc. He would steal swans.' At first he thought of becoming a professor but in 1626 returned home to Bridgwater, Somerset, to help run the family shipping business when his father died. Thus it is possible he had some knowledge of ships and the sea.

The new 'General-at-sea' was a strong Puritan, fond of quoting the Old Testament and a hater of monarchy. During the war he fought for Parliament and made his name defending Taunton, in Somerset, for nearly a year. He brought the same fighting spirit to his naval duties. Soon after his appointment he chased Prince Rupert from his Irish bases and finally drove his fleet on to the rocks off Carthagena in the Mediterranean. The spirit of Drake was alive again.

'Butterbox' battles

The Commonwealth's first foreign war was with the United Provinces (Holland). Englishmen had grievances against the Dutch going back many years. 'Butterboxes', as they called the Netherlanders, had driven them from the Spice Islands (East Indies), destroying an English settlement (1623). The Dutch East India Company was the wealthiest corporation in the world, with a monopoly of many commodities reaching Europe from the Far East. Indeed its ships carried so much foreign cargo that the Dutch were nicknamed 'the wagoners of the seas'.

The fleet which had destroyed Rupert was now free to humble the Dutch. In 1651 an English Navigation Act ruled that no goods could enter England except in English ships or ships of the country which produced the goods. To deny the Dutch trading monopoly in such a way meant war. When a Dutch fleet of forty-two ships commanded by Maarten Tromp (1597–1653) started manoeuvres off the south coast of England Blake ordered the Dutch admiral to lower his flag in salute. Tromp was an arrogant and brave fighter who had wiped out the Spanish fleet in 1639. He refused, and a fierce battle continued until nightfall (May 1652). So began a large scale sea war, fought, as one English M.P. remarked, 'for the fairest mistress in the world—trade'.

For all their aggressive behaviour, the Dutch were at a disadvantage now that England had a fleet at last. Since all trade routes to the East involved passing through the Channel they were forced to protect every merchant ship which left their ports. Escorting convoys of such 'lame ducks' was a handicap when faced by a powerful force with nothing to do except fight. Moreover English warships were bigger, because Dutch harbours were too shallow for large ships.

A stern Puritan— General-at-Sea Robert Blake

In December 1652 Tromp appeared off Margate with 400 ships. He defeated an outnumbered Blake who afterwards offered to resign. But the government had confidence in their admiral. Next spring they were proved right when the English chased Tromp for three days, nearly destroying his fleet off Cap Griz Nez. In this battle Blake was severely wounded. He was replaced by another ex-soldier, George Monk (1608–70) who beat the Dutch in a hard fought fight. Soon afterwards Tromp was killed by a stray bullet in yet another battle (July 1653). It had been a clash of naval giants but there was no doubt who had won. With its trade facing ruin, Holland was forced to make peace.

One great admiral had died but Blake's conquering career continued. In 1655 he destroyed the Algerian pirate base at Porto Farina.

Finally, when Cromwell began an Elizabethan-type war with Spain and Jamaica in the West Indies was captured from the Spanish by British forces, Blake caught a Spanish squadron at Tenerife in the Canary Islands. By clever use of the tides, he was able to sweep into the harbour, burn sixteen ships and leave the town in ruins. Nothing like it had been seen since Drake's attack on Cadiz in 1587.

A tired Blake sailed triumphantly home, only to die of fever as his ship entered Plymouth.

Rump and Barebones

Warlike victories overseas were not matched by political successes at home. By 1653 the army leadership had grown tired of the 'Rump' Parliament. Many of the reforms they desired had not been carried out. General Lambert, for example, wanted a parliamentary system modelled on the 'Heads of Proposals' scheme presented to the King six years before. General Harrison, a religious fanatic, preferred an Assembly of 'godly' men to run the country until Christ returned. The ordinary soldiers had less lofty ideas. They were concerned that many of their demobilised comrades were unemployed and that they themselves had not been paid regularly.

On all sides Cromwell found men urging him to dissolve Parliament, an action which he admitted made 'his hair stand on end'. In April he took the plunge. Entering the Commons in person, he told them, 'It is not fit that you should sit here any longer. You shall now give place to better men.' Some members, he remarked, were drunkards, some corrupt, unjust persons, some living in open contempt of God's commandments. 'In the name of God, go!' he shouted. The members, we are told, 'gloomily vanished', watched by thirty or forty musketeers with loaded weapons. That night somebody wrote on the locked door of the empty Chamber, 'This House to be let, now unfurnished'. The

Seventeenth-century painting of a sea battle during the First Dutch War 1652–54

Cromwell dismisses the 'Rump' and closes Parliament.

Long Parliament, which had fought the Civil War and beheaded a King, was no more.

Very few were sad at its passing for it had outlived its usefulness. Even so, Cromwell's violent act ended legal government in England for the next seven years. From that moment Cromwell was a reluctant dictator, disliked by many of his own social class. Parliamentarians had not gone to war with the King to increase taxes and grant religious toleration. Yet the cost of keeping a large navy and army was enormous. Furthermore, the Independents in the army insisted on a freedom of worship which many Puritans regarded as sinful.

Any Parliament elected in the old way, even without the votes of Royalists, would certainly disband the army, reduce the navy and probably imprison or execute Cromwell and his friends. In these circumstances it was easy for the 'saintly' soldiers of the New Model Army to convince themselves that they must not ignore the clear signs of God's favour shown upon the battlefield. Better to rule with God and against the people! When told that a certain policy of his would annoy nine persons out of ten, Cromwell replied grimly 'But what if I should disarm the nine, and put a sword in the tenth man's hand? Would that not do the business?'

The next five years witnessed several unsuccessful experiments in parliamentary government. After the dissolving of the Rump, Cromwell asked Puritan congregations throughout the country to nominate members of Parliament. Those suggested were then vetted by the Army Council who picked out 140 men they considered 'persons fearing God, and of approved fidelity and honesty'. Barebones' Parliament, so called because one member was named Barbon, was laughed at as a collection of tradesmen and religious cranks. Certainly it contained some eccentrics. One member, for example, hoped to reduce English laws until there were only enough to fill a pocketbook. But the Assembly also included lords, businessmen, headmasters and generals.

In spite of this Parliament's unpopularity at the time, some of its work has a modern look. It passed laws to improve prisons, take better care of lunatics and register births and deaths. Unfortunately its few cranks were peculiar enough to alarm the army leaders. Early one morning moderate members were persuaded to meet and dissolve Parliament before the others arrived. Thirty of the strangest M.P.s were furious at this and staged a 'sit-in'. When asked by a colonel what they were doing, they answered, 'seeking the Lord'. 'Come out of this place then, for to my knowledge, the Lord has not been here these twelve years past,' replied the officer.

'A good constable'

In March 1655 a small, unsuccessful Royalist rising caused Cromwell to abandon parliamentary rule altogether for a while and rely on the army alone. England and Wales were divided into eleven districts, each ruled by a Major General. The government of the Major Generals probably did more than anything else to make Cromwell's rule unpopular, chiefly because these 'saintly' soldiers saw themselves as defenders of morals. Almost overnight a pleasure-loving people discovered that most pleasures were wrong. Bear-baiting, cockfighting, and gambling were forbidden. Drunkenness was outlawed; one General closed a third of the public houses in Warwickshire. Fines for swearing were imposed according to rank. A duke, for example, paid 30 shillings whereas an ordinary person paid 3s 4d. Examples of 'swearing' were 'God is my witness' and 'Upon my life'. Even theatres were closed, in case they were used by Royalist conspirators. Within a year, some of the most loyal Parliamentary areas in England, such as the South and East, had turned against Cromwell's government.

By 1657 a change was essential so a new style of government replaced the unpopular generals. This constitution allowed for the election of two Houses of Parliament with power to control the Protector. At the same time Cromwell was offered the crown, but he refused. Many New Model officers were against these proposals; at first only those M.P.s given tickets by the army were allowed in. Later Parliament insisted on all those elected being admitted (January 1658). As a result Cromwell was faced by a hostile Commons which he was forced to dissolve.

It was a sad end for a man who had first stood up 'in a plain cloth suit' to speak against a King's tyranny. Cromwell once said he

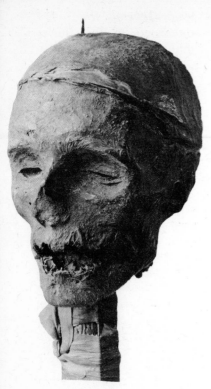

Cromwell's skull, put on a spike after he was dug up and hanged. It is now buried at Sidney Sussex College, Cambridge, where he studied as a young man

wanted to be 'a good constable . . . to keep the peace of the parish' not 'a little god to rule over men'. His fate was to be remembered as a kill-joy who ruled thanks to 'the tenth man's sword'.

'His people'

In August 1658 the Lord Protector lost his favourite daughter, Elizabeth. Heartbroken, he retired to bed at St James's Palace, London, where he died on 3 September 1658, the anniversary of Dunbar and Worcester. Within two years the ineffective rule of his son Richard had ended, and Charles II had been invited back as King. Even the famous army Oliver had led to so many victories decided to disband. Only three regiments were incorporated in the new royal army. They are now the Life Guards, Royal Horse Guards and Coldstream Guards.

On his death bed Cromwell had hoped that he had done 'his people' some good. Unfortunately the majority of the nation had not been his people.

More about the Commonwealth and Protectorate
Books
G. A. R. Callender and F. H. Hinsley, *The Naval Side of British History* (Christophers)
Cromwell's Commonwealth and Protectorate (Cape: Jackdaw)
J. Kinross, *Discovering Battlefields in Northern England and Scotland* (Shire Publications)
R. Ollard, *The Escape of Charles II after the Battle of Worcester* (Hodder & Stoughton)
A. H. Woolrych, *Oliver Cromwell* (Oxford University Press)

Visual aids
As for Chapters 18, 19 and 20, also:
Commonwealth and Protectorate (Visual Productions)
Seventeenth-century Ship *(film)* (Gateway)

Visits
Maritime Museum, Greenwich

To write and find out
1 Make a study of either the New Model Army or the Commonwealth navy.
2 Write a life of Robert Blake.
3 Write an essay assuming that Oliver Cromwell had became King and lived to be eighty-six (the year Charles II died). In what ways do you think English history would have been altered? It would be as well to read Chapters 22 and 24 before you try to answer this question.
4 Do you think God can ever be on the side of one army against another, as both Cromwell and the Covenanters believed?
5 Draw, or collect drawings of, Dutch and English warships of this period.

22 The Restoration World
Life in Charles II's England

On 29 May 1660 John Evelyn wrote in his diary: 'This day, His Majesty Charles the Second came to London, after a sad and long exile. . . . This was also his birthday.' Evelyn went on to describe how the King was greeted by the Lord Mayor in full regalia, lords in velvet and cloth of gold, and 20,000 soldiers, shouting and waving their swords. It was a day to remember, with bells ringing, streets gay with flowers, houses hung with tapestries and fountains running wine. Less than a week before, the warship *Naseby* which brought Charles to England had been hastily renamed *Royal Charles*. The rule of the Saints was over.

The thirty-year-old King, standing 'above two yards high', was a far different man from his father. Charles II loved wine, women, gambling, yachting and horseracing. He was talkative and witty, with a sense of humour which earned him the nickname 'The Merry

The warship *Naseby*, re-named the *Royal Charles*

Monarch'. On a more serious level he was interested enough in science to become the first patron of the new Royal Society (1660). Religious he may have been in an easygoing way. Nevertheless his habit of sleeping through sermons would have horrified Charles I. Indeed, the Martyr's son cared little for old beliefs or superstitions. Once when an astrologer offered to foretell the future he invited him to come to Newmarket races and spot winners!

Beneath the charm and laughter lay an experienced man of the world. Charles's early life had not been easy. As a teenager he had lived through the defeat and death of his father and had courageously tried to regain his crown, in the bloodstained streets of Worcester (1651). He had known what it was to be a hunted fugitive and an almost penniless exile. He came to the throne with no high ideas about 'divine right', knowing that if he ruled like his father he would 'go on his travels again'. Deep down he seems to have believed that his family's right to the throne must be safeguarded. Otherwise he had few principles which could not be altered to suit the occasion.

Second-class citizens

The easygoing King was prepared to forget the past. 'Mercy and indulgence is the best way to bring men to a true repentance' he told his first House of Lords. His chief minister, Edward Hyde, Earl of Clarendon, held a similar view and begged the Commons to restore 'the whole nation to its primitive temper and integrity, its old good manners, its old good humour, and its old good nature.'

The so-called 'Cavalier' Parliament which existed until 1678 felt differently about its former enemies. Soon after the Restoration (Charles's return) the bodies of Cromwell and Ireton were dug up and hanged. Cromwell's head was fixed on London Bridge and is now buried in Sidney Sussex College, Cambridge. Nine survivors of the fifty-nine who had signed Charles I's death warrant were executed. Four men closely involved in Charles's execution were also hanged, drawn and quartered. But all who had fought against the King in the wars were pardoned. Where possible dispossessed Royalists received their land back. In Ireland nearly two-thirds of the farm land was left in the hands of Protestants.

As far as religion was concerned the few Presbyterians who had supported Charles's return were soon disappointed. The Cavaliers in Parliament felt it was their duty to preserve intact the Church for which Charles I had died. Various Acts of Parliament, the so called Clarendon Code, gradually prevented all persons not members of the Church of England (called nonconformists) from sharing in the government, administration or education system of their country. A Corporation Act (1661) dismissed all town councillors who refused to take Communion according to the rites of the Church of England. The Act of Uniformity (1662) authorised a new edition of the Prayer Book. Nearly one thousand Puritan clergymen and university teachers who would not use this form of prayer were sacked; another 700 left of their own accord. Further Tests Acts in 1673 and 1678 prevented nonconformists being M.P.s or holding any government posts.

Charles II

'Sweet Nell of Old Drury'. Nell Gwynne was the actress friend of Charles II

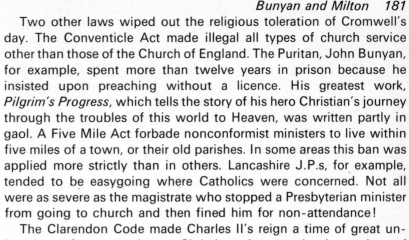

Two other laws wiped out the religious toleration of Cromwell's day. The Conventicle Act made illegal all types of church service other than those of the Church of England. The Puritan, John Bunyan, for example, spent more than twelve years in prison because he insisted upon preaching without a licence. His greatest work, *Pilgrim's Progress*, which tells the story of his hero Christian's journey through the troubles of this world to Heaven, was written partly in gaol. A Five Mile Act forbade nonconformist ministers to live within five miles of a town, or their old parishes. In some areas this ban was applied more strictly than in others. Lancashire J.P.s, for example, tended to be easygoing where Catholics were concerned. Not all were as severe as the magistrate who stopped a Presbyterian minister from going to church and then fined him for non-attendance!

The Clarendon Code made Charles II's reign a time of great unhappiness for many sincere Christians. It created a large class of second-class citizens, the Nonconformists whose distinctive way of life continued long after the Code itself was forgotten.

'Paradise Lost'

Drama, which had been banned by the Puritans, came to life again with the return of Charles II. Two companies, the King's and the Duke's, started performing in London. Later the King's Company settled at the Theatre Royal, Drury Lane. Its actors took an oath of loyalty to the King and were allowed to wear the uniform of his servants. The manager, Thomas Killigrew (1612–83), employed as his star player, Charles Hart, a great nephew of Shakespeare. An important change was the use of women to play female parts instead of boys. The first actress to appear on an English stage was Margaret Hughes but the most famous of the period was Nell Gwynne, Charles's mistress. She never acted at any other theatre and was nicknamed 'Sweet Nell of Old Drury'. By this time the older type of theatre had been replaced by an enclosed building with a 'picture frame' setting for the play. This allowed the French scheme of a drop curtain and elaborate scenery to be adopted.

In spite of royal interest, Charles's reign did not produce dramatists to match the Elizabethans. Many Restoration plays are vulgar comedies, often witty but usually far below the literary standard of Shakespeare or Marlowe. Indeed, the seventeenth century was famous for poets rather than playwrights. The greatest writer of the period was John Milton (1608–74). From his earliest days he had wanted to be a poet. 'I hardly ever left my studies or went to bed before midnight' he admitted later. Although he gained a Master's degree at Cambridge, he decided to live quietly in the country rather than find regular employment. In 1629 he proved he had not been wasting his time. *On the morning of Christ's nativity*, one of his earliest poems, is a masterpiece. It was followed by another, *Lycidas,* written in memory of a drowned friend.

The outbreak of the Civil War changed Milton from a poet to a propagandist. Being a staunch Puritan, he offered his pen to the Roundheads as eagerly as other men offered their swords. The next

John Milton

few years were spent writing pamphlets and books in support of the Parliamentary cause. In 1649, for example, he defended the execution of the King. Soon afterwards he criticised *Eikon Basilike* in a book called *Eikonoclastes* (the image breaker). But his most famous book of this period was *Areopagitica* (named after Areopagus, a hill in Athens where the city council met), a fine defence (in prose) of freedom of the press.

Such activities pleased the Commonwealth government, so in 1649 he was made Latin Secretary to the Council of State, a position he kept even after he went blind in 1651. When Charles returned, Milton's defence of the execution of Charles I was not forgiven. He was fined, imprisoned and banned from public life. Literature gained whatever politics lost by this ban, for Milton set about his greatest work. *Paradise Lost* tells the story of Adam and Eve, but it is far more than the retelling of a Bible story in verse. Milton used the theme to describe the sort of battle between good and evil he believed he had witnessed in his own lifetime. Many scholars believe that no greater poem has been written in the English language. Like another of his works, *Samson Agonistes* (Samson the Athlete) *Paradise Lost* asks a question which must have been in many puritan minds after the Restoration, 'Why had God deserted his 'saints'?'

Milton received only £10 for *Paradise Lost* and it did not become really popular until after his death. One man who admired it was John Dryden (1631–1700), who stands second only to Milton in seventeenth-century English literature. Unlike Milton, however, Dryden's poetry is not concerned with God and Man so much as with politics and great events. His *Annus Mirabilis,* for example, describes the Great Fire of London, whilst *Absalom and Achitophel* made fun of some politicians of the time. Dryden wrote in an elegant way which was copied by many writers in the eighteenth century. He became famous for using couplets, that is, verses where the lines are rhymed in twos. He also wrote plays and in 1677 produced a dramatic version of *Paradise Lost.*

Samuel Pepys

In 1664 England again went to war with Holland, after attacking the Dutch colony of New Amsterdam (now New York) in North America. Most battles took place in the Channel where the fighting was at murderously close range. Of the Four Day Battle (June 1666) a certain Samuel Pepys, recorded in his diary: 'The Earl of Falmouth, Muskerry, and Mr Richard Boyle killed on board the Duke's ship, the *Royal Charles*, with one shot; their blood and brains flying in the Duke's face.' The wounded survivor who brought the news had, he wrote, 'his face black as the chimney and covered with dirt, pitch and tar and powder, and muffled with dirty clouts (rags) and his right eye stopped with oakum'.

Pepys began his diary in 1660, writing it in a special shorthand so that it would remain secret. After his death in 1703 it was given to the library of Magdalene College, Cambridge, where it remained unread until decoded in 1822. The effect was almost miraculous—out of the

FAC SIMILE OF AN EXTRACT FROM THE SHORT-HAND M.S. DIARY.

(Vide Page 1 3rd sentence)

The condition of the State was thus - viz. The Rump after being disturbed by my Lord Lambert, was lately returned to sit again. The Officers of the Army all forced to yield — Lawson lies still in the River. & Monk is with his Army in Scotland.

An example of Pepys's shorthand from his diary

dusty sheets there emerged a vivid picture of life at that time.

Pepys's success dated from the day he sailed to Holland in the *Royal Charles* as an insignificant member of the party sent to escort Charles II to England. The diarist's friend and close relative, Lord Sandwich, introduced him to both Charles and his brother James, who promised him their favour. Within a year Pepys had risen from a penniless university graduate to an important official in the Admiralty and he was also a justice of the peace.

Pepys owed his position to having the right friends. He kept it by hard work and honesty, teaching himself the multiplication tables, studying how to tell good timber and rope from bad, even boring holes in his office walls so that he could see whether his clerks were wasting time. By 1665 he was earning £4,000 a year and buying expensive instruments to satisfy his great passion for 'music, the thing in the world I love most'.

The Great Plague

As Pepys rode through London in June 1665 his coachman complained of sickness. He was one of many being taken ill at the time, for the capital was in the grip of bubonic plague. Plague had been rife in England since the Black Death (1348–51). During Elizabeth's reign there were bad outbreaks. In 1603 over 33,000 people died in London alone and in 1625 and 1647 thousands more died. Indeed, this dreadful disease was as common in the seventeenth century as influenza is today. For centuries small children had sung:

Ring a ring of Roses
A pocketful of posies
Tishoo, tishoo, we all fall down.

The 'roses' refer to the red rash which was the first sign of the disease; 'pocketful of posies' to the herbs used to sweeten the air around a patient and 'tishoo' to the sneezing which was a symptom. 'All fall down' needs no explanation.

By August many rich people, including the King and his courtiers, had fled from the narrow infected streets of London. Pepys stayed, although he sent his family to Woolwich. On 7 June he noted: 'This day . . . I did in Drury Lane see two or three houses marked with a red cross upon the doors and ''Lord have mercy upon us'' writ there.' London became a silent, dreadful place. 'Everyday', another eye-witness wrote, 'looks with the face of a Sabbath day. Now shops are shut in, people rare and very few that walk about, in so much that the grass begins to spring in some places.' At night carts moved through

Bills of Mortality were published weekly, showing the various causes of deaths. This one records a week in London when the plague was almost at its height, during August 1665

The Diseases and Casualties this Week.

Abortive	6	Kingsevil	10
Aged	54	Lethargy	1
Apoplexie	1	Murthered at Stepney	1
Bedridden	1	Palsie	2
Cancer	2	Plague	3880
Childbed	23	Plurisie	1
Chrisomes	15	Quinsie	6
Collick	1	Rickets	23
Consumption	174	Rising of the Lights	19
Convulsion	88	Rupture	2
Dropsie	40	Sciatica	1
Drownd two, one at St. Kath. Tower, and one at Lambeth	2	Scowring	13
		Scurvy	1
Feaver	353	Sore legge	1
Fistula	1	Spotted Feaver and Purples	190
Flox and Small-pox	10	Starved at Nurse	1
Flux	2	Stilborn	8
Found dead in the Street at St. Bartholomew the Less	1	Stone	2
		Stopping of the stomach	16
Frighted	1	Strangury	1
Gangrene	1	Suddenly	1
Gowt	1	Surfeit	87
Grief	1	Teeth	113
Griping in the Guts	74	Thrush	3
Jaundies	3	Tissick	6
Imposthume	18	Ulcer	2
Infants	21	Vomiting	7
Killed by a fall down stairs at St. Thomas Apostle	1	Winde	8
		Wormes	18

Christned	Males	83		Buried	Males	2656	Plague	3880
	Females	83			Females	2663		
	In all	166			In all	5319		

Increased in the Burials this Week ———— 1289.
Parishes clear of the Plague ——— 34 Parishes Infected ——— 96

The Assize of Bread set forth by Order of the Lord Maior and Court of Aldermen.
A penny Wheaten Loaf to contain Nine Ounces and a half, and three
half-penny White Loaves the like weight.

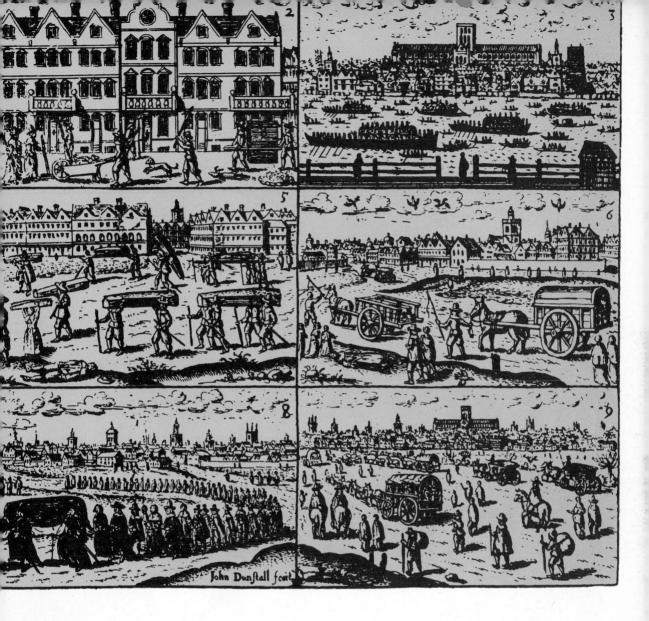

Plague scenes

the streets, pulled by men shouting 'Bring out your dead'. With people dying at such a rate there was no time for proper burial. Large pits were dug to take the dead. One in Aldgate churchyard received 1,114 corpses in two weeks.

Medical men were helpless. Some suspected that 'small worms' carried by rats or cats ate into the bodies of humans. None knew the real cause. Even if it had been known there would have been little hope of preventing the disease while men and women washed rarely and lived in filthy conditions. In the meantime the brave few who stayed to help the sick relied on remedies like poultices of yolk of egg, honey, turpentine, flour and 'London' treacle!

When the plague died down 100,000 people had lost their lives— nearly a quarter of London's population. That winter Pepys reported

Map and drawing of the Great Fire of London 1666

that many still refused to buy wigs in case they had been made from the hair of plague victims. Fortunately this epidemic was the last of its kind in England. Increased cleanliness and the extermination of the black rat by the brown rat (which does not carry the plague), meant that London's streets would never again echo to the dismal cry 'Bring out your dead'.

'London's burning'

Early next year Charles II returned to Whitehall and his people hoped for better things. Unfortunately 1666 proved nearly as bad. In January the French joined the Dutch in fighting England. Despite a naval victory in June, rumours of an invasion by '30,000 mounsieurs' (Frenchmen) caused thousands of Englishmen to join the militia. Londoners were therefore in a dangerously excited mood when early on Sunday, 2 September a fire broke out in the house of Thomas Farrinor, a baker of Pudding Lane.

At first it seemed a small incident. Farrinor and his family escaped through an upstairs window. Only his maidservant, who refused to jump on to the cobbles below, was burned to death. Then a steady east wind caused the fire to spread swiftly through the narrow alleys and overhanging houses with their 'umbrellas of tiles'. Worse still, the flames soon destroyed the lead pipes and the water-wheels at London Bridge. Thus there was little water with which to fight the blaze. As night fell, Evelyn, the diarist, wrote, 'All the sky was of a fiery aspect, like the top of a burning oven'. Smoke clouds, reckoned to be fifty-six miles long, hung over the inferno, and at Oxford the inhabitants looked towards London and saw 'a dim, reddish sunset'.

Various factors helped the fire to spread. An old London law stated that anyone who knocked a house down must rebuild it at his own expense. Consequently men were reluctant to remove houses from the fire's path. And since there was no insurance in those days, citizens stayed 'in their houses as long as till the very fire touched them', according to Pepys. Those who lived near enough to the river, threw their belongings in boats on the river. Less fortunate ones watched their homes disappear in minutes.

'A dismal desert'

London's mayor at first underestimated the danger. When he did try to fight the fire the task overwhelmed him. Pepys met him and was told, 'Lord! What can I do? I am spent; people will not obey me. I have been pulling down houses, but the fire overtakes us faster than we can do it.' Fortunately, the King and his brother, the Duke of York, took personal command of the firefighting. Sailors were brought ashore to blow up houses and so destroy fuel for the hungry flames. A circle of fire-posts, manned by soldiers and civilians, was set up around the disaster area. The old law about rebuilding houses was repeatedly ignored.

After three days the wind veered south, driving the flames back on to areas already burned. This slowed down, although it did not stop, the destruction. Old St Paul's Cathedral burned from the roof

downwards, its stones exploding with the heat, its six acres of lead roof melting like 'snow before the sun'. The City's widest street, Cheapside, was crossed by fiery sparks which fed on piles of timber left in the middle. London Bridge was saved but the Royal Exchange burned until only the statue of its founder, Sir Thomas Gresham, stood in the empty shell. When the fire died away at last the centre of one of the world's great cities was like 'some dismal desert'.

Wren's London

The Plague and the Fire crippled England's war effort. In 1667 shortage of money forced the fleet to remain in port. The Dutch sailed up the Thames and Medway, burnt Chatham and captured the *Royal Charles*. Over one hundred Dutch warships cruised menacingly at the mouth of the Thames. Even so, they were glad to end a war which, despite such victories, was ruining their trade.

At home men began to think of rebuilding London. Only a few days after the Great Fire, Sir Christopher Wren (1632–1723) placed before the Royal Society a plan for a 'new city' to replace the old. Wren was a mathematician, astronomer and scientist as well as an architect. His ambitious schemes would have made London one of the wonders of the world. But those who had lost their houses wanted them built exactly where they had been before, so Wren's wide streets and squares remained a dream. Despite this setback Wren built at least sixty churches. As an architect he was influenced by the work of Inigo Jones (1573–1652) who had designed the Banqueting Hall in Whitehall and the Queen's House at Greenwich. Jones had visited Italy as a young man where he had seen the Renaissance-style buildings of an Italian architect Andrea Palladio, with their large windows, elaborate decoration and Roman-type columns. Both he and Wren built in this Palladian style.

Wren's first task was to erect a tall column to commemorate the Fire. Called the Monument, it stands about 130 feet from the site of Farrinor's baker's shop. He also rebuilt the Royal Exchange. His most famous task began in 1673 when the King ordered him to prepare plans for a new St Paul's Cathedral. The work lasted the rest of Wren's lifetime. It was 1711 before the huge dome was in place and another five years before the cathedral was opened for public services. Year after year Wren supervised the work, travelling to the top regularly in a basket, arguing with authorities who grumbled at its cost, trying to solve the problems of placing such a vast weight on wet sand and gravel. His salary worked out at £4 a week. His reward was to be dismissed from his official posts by his enemies at the age of eighty-six.

Wren designed many buildings, including the Royal Hospital, Chelsea; Morden College, Blackheath (near London) and the naval hospital at Greenwich. The words on his tomb in St Paul's are most appropriate, *Si Monumentum Requiris Circumspice* (If you seek his monument, look around you). For hundreds of years visitors to London have done just that, admiring the many churches he built as well as his fine cathedral.

The Monument, built near the spot in London where the Fire started

New colonies

Most of England's American colonies were founded during the seventeenth century. The original settlement at Jamestown, Virginia, was followed by New Hampshire and Maine in 1622 and Massachusetts in 1629. Three years later Lord Baltimore obtained permission to establish Maryland. Because he was a Catholic he allowed freedom of worship there. A fourth colony, Carolina, was planned, but no successful landings took place until after the Restoration. In March 1663 Charles II gave eight men the right to found a colony 'west in a direct line as far as the south seas'. After several failures, Carolina was established in 1670. From the start it was troubled by Spanish attacks and pirate raids, but gradually it developed into a land of plantations worked by Negro slaves.

During the second Dutch War an English fleet arrived off New Amsterdam and offered the Dutch colonists good terms to come under English rule. In spite of a desperate defence by Peter Stuyvesant, called 'Peter Silver Leg' because he had a wooden leg studded with silver, the settlement was captured by the English and renamed New York. Finally, in 1682, Charles allowed William Penn, a Quaker, a charter to found Pennsylvania (Penn's forest). This 'Holy Experiment' grew up along the banks of the Delaware river. The capital was called Philadelphia, meaning 'brotherly love', and the Quakers made a treaty of friendship with the Indians who promised to be 'good friends with him (Penn) and his white children as long as the sun and moon give light'.

Charles's charter to Carolina brought the colonists into conflict with the Spaniards of Florida. In the North there was trouble with the French due to trade rivalry. In 1669 two French sailors who had quarrelled with their Governor led an English expedition through the ice-packs of Hudson Bay. This vast stretch of water opened a way into the heart of the Canadian fur country. Next year the King allowed the Hudson's Bay Company to trade 'over all regions whose waters empty into the Hudson Bay'. Like the wording of his Charter to the Carolinians, this vague sentence could mean a vast area, in this case the entire Canadian West! Before long the Company, whose motto *Pro pelle cutem* meant 'Skin for skin', was taking so many furs that fighting broke out with the French.

At home the attitude towards colonies was changing. The idea they were useful to drain off 'surplus' population was replaced by a theory that large numbers of people were needed in England to grow food and make goods for export. From 1660, therefore, colonists were either foreigners, or misfits and undesirables from England. Colonies came to be regarded as 'children' who existed solely to increase the power and wealth of the parent country. The King, for example, was entitled to one-fifth of any precious metal found, goods sent to colonies were charged royal customs and all colonial exports were supposed to come to England first.

According to this theory, an ideal colony would be one which supplied England with everything it produced and received everything it needed from the home country. The West Indian islands,

An example of Grinling Gibbons's wood carving on the choir stalls in St Paul's Cathedral. Gibbons's work is some of the finest ever executed in wood

supplying sugar and rum, were the most useful in this respect. The northern 'New England' colonies were the least useful to England because they made the same goods as those manufactured in the mother country. Of the mainland settlements, Virginia, Maryland and Carolina were the most popular with English governments. Virginia tobacco, in particular, was in great demand. The days when James I had described smoking as an 'ignoble habit, reducing man to the level of a chimney' were gone. Now tobacco was praised for its good qualities which included, it seemed, use as a disinfectant and the power of cheering people up. Whether this was true or not, it certainly 'cheered up' the Treasury which was receiving £100,000 from duties on tobacco imports by 1671!

More about Charles II's England
Books
M. Ashley, *Stuart England* (Batsford)
L. W. Cowie, *Plague and Fire* (Wayland) — with four tapes
E. Murphy, *Samuel Pepys in England* (Longman: Then and There)
Restoration of Charles II (Cape: Jackdaw)
St Paul's Cathedral (Cape: Jackdaw)
Samuel Pepys, *Diary of Samuel Pepys* (Dent), 3 vols
Pepys and the Development of the British Navy (Cape: Jackdaw)
Plague and Fire (Cape: Jackdaw)
Sir Christopher Wren (Pitkin Pictorials)

Visual aids
Christopher Wren (Common Ground)
Life in Restoration Times (Common Ground)
Pepys's London *(with record)* (EAV)
Samuel Pepys *(record)* (Fontana)
Social Life in the Seventeenth Century (Hulton)
Stuart Britain *(two filmstrips)* (Visual Publications)
Stuart Britain *(film)* (Gateway)
William Penn (Hulton)

Visits
St Paul's Cathedral, London
Naval College, Greenwich
The Monument, London

To write and find out
1 Write a diary of modern events in the style of Pepys. This can either be done individually or as a class project with each pupil compiling an entry.
2 Find out more about John Bunyan. Read *Pilgrim's Progress*.
3 Any school within reasonable distance of London can make a photographic record of Wren's London buildings and churches.
4 Why was a recent musical based on Pepys's diary and called *And so to bed*?

Wren's most famous achievement, St Paul's Cathedral, from the front

23 'Miracles are Past'
Science in the Early Modern Age

One of Shakespeare's characters remarks, 'They say miracles are past.' By the mid-seventeenth century there were quite a few no longer prepared to believe in miracles. Science became fashionable and more and more educated men looked for reasonable answers to their questions. Charles himself, as we have seen, took a keen interest in the Royal Society. Prince Rupert, once his fighting days were over, studied chemistry and invented both a new kind of gunpowder and an improved process for engraving. Simple folk still believed in witches and the English authorities continued to execute them until 1712. Oxford and Cambridge universities ignored much of the new science. Nevertheless the age of miracles was passing as man's knowledge of nature and the universe increased.

Aristotle's universe

Since earliest times men observed the sun and moon rising in the east and setting in the west. They noticed also that some stars appeared brighter at certain times of the year. From these facts they assumed that the sun, moon and planets were moving around the earth; the very word 'planet' is Greek and means 'wanderer'. Aristotle, the greatest of Greek philosophers, thought the earth was a solid sphere fixed in the centre of the universe. He explained the apparently 'odd' movements of the planets by suggesting that they revolved in epicycles (smaller circles) on the outer circumference of the universe. It was a brilliant theory based on the known facts. Its most complicated part, the epicycles, arose from the mistaken notion of a stationary earth and moving sun. At least one Greek, Aristarchus, claimed that the earth itself was revolving but he could produce no proof and was ignored.

Western man came to know of Aristotle's theory through the writings of Ptolemy (see Chapter 2). Just as his *Geography* guided early travellers, so another of his books, *Astronomy,* influenced fifteenth-century scientists. Ptolemy had based his scientific ideas on Aristotle's universe, but produced extra 'epicycles' to explain planetary movements. Not surprisingly, scholars who followed this system discovered that their calculations made inaccurate calendars.

One man puzzled by this problem was Niklas Koppernigk (1473–1543), a Polish scholar. Copernicus—he is usually known by the Latin form of his name—was a busy civil servant at Frauenberg on the German–Polish border. Apart from his duties as judge, tax-collector, physician and military governor, he found time to study the heavens from a small turret set in the walls of Frauenberg Cathedral. Just before his death he published *On the Revolution of the Celestial Spheres*. In it he suggested that if mathematicians

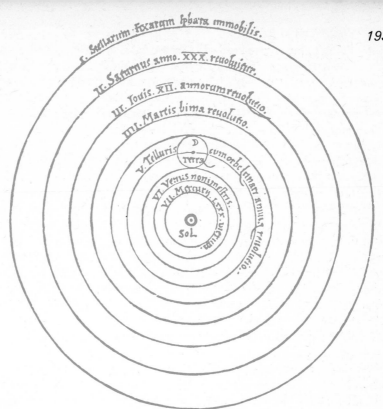

Planets in their orbits round the Sun according to Copernicus

assumed the earth moved round the sun certain problems to do with calendar-making would be solved.

Copernicus did not say Aristotle was wrong. He did not even think the sun was in the exact centre of the universe. Obviously he had no way of proving that the earth moved. The idea seemed laughable and Copernicus may have been afraid he would be thought mad. For many years his book was known to an educated few who used it to produce more accurate calendars. One day, however, his suggestion would bring the entire Aristotelean system tumbling down.

Eight minutes out

Copernicus was not an astronomer. He could not prove his theory right or wrong. The Danish astronomer Tycho Brahe (1546–1601), although he believed the earth was stationary, made the next step towards the truth by starting regular observations of the heavens. In 1572 his interest was aroused when a new star appeared amongst the fixed stars. According to Aristotle, this was impossible. Helped by the King of Denmark, Tycho established Uraniborg, an observatory on the island of Hveen. As a result of studying the sky he came to believe that the planets circled round the sun, but that the sun itself revolved around the earth. Four years before he died Tycho quarrelled with his master and fled to the Court of the Emperor in Prague. Here he employed Johannes Kepler (1571–1630), whose father had been one of Alva's soldiers.

Kepler was a clever astronomer with a fixed idea in his head, 'My aim', he wrote, 'is to show that the heavenly machine is not a kind of

divine living being, but a kind of clockwork.' Using Tycho's calculations, Kepler became convinced that Mars moved round the sun
in an ellipse (oval) not in a circle. The difficulty was to find the exact
shape of the ellipse. For nearly twenty years Kepler struggled with
the problem, frustrated and unhappy because most of his calculations
were incorrect by eight minutes. 'With those eight minutes I will yet
unlock the secrets of the heavens', he declared.

Kepler's predictions came true. In the end he found the exact path,
not only of Mars, but of all the planets. He was helped in this work
by the discoveries of William Gilbert (1540–1603), one of Queen
Elizabeth's doctors. Gilbert's interest in magnets had made him
wonder why compass needles turn roughly in the direction of the
North Pole. He concluded that the earth itself was a magnet. Kepler
went further, for he thought that magnetism was the key to movement in the universe. Each planet, in his opinion, was really a smaller
magnet reaching to a larger one, the sun. Each would speed up or
slow down according to its distance from the sun, whilst the
elliptical path was due to the varying attraction of the sun's magnetic
pull. In fact, planets are attracted to each other by their mass; it is
what scientists term a gravitational, not only a magnetic, pull.

Galileo's first telescope

The discovery of the elliptical path was Kepler's greatest contribu-
tion to man's understanding of the universe. It solved many problems
and allowed for more accurate predictions of planetary movement.
In 1627 he published his *Rudolphine Tables* (named after his
employer, the Emperor Rudolph) which remained an essential reference book for astronomers for nearly a century. Three years later the
man who had tried 'to draw the obscure facts of nature into the
bright light of knowledge' died poor as a result of the upheavals of the
Thirty Years War.

Galileo

The accurate astronomical records started by Brahe were continued
by an Italian, Galileo (1564–1642), using the telescope, newly
invented by a Dutch spectacle-maker of Middleburg. In 1610 he
made his own Occhiale (spy-glass), in which two lenses, one convex
and the other concave, placed at opposite ends of a metal tube,
caused objects to appear closer. Later models magnified up to a
thousand times. Such instruments revealed many of the secrets of
the heavens. 'The surface of the moon is not perfectly smooth,'
recorded Galileo, 'on the contrary it is full of irregularities.' He had
found the 'mountains' of the moon. The Milky Way was made up of
many fixed stars packed closely together. Venus had phases just
like the moon, during which it changed from a thin crescent to a full
orb. The moon was not the only satellite revolving around a larger
planet; Galileo counted four similar satellites associated with Jupiter.
Above all, Galileo's observations made him even more certain that
the earth moved, although he did not believe his friend Kepler's
theory that the planets travelled in an elliptical path.

Galileo wrote popular books in Italian, not Latin. Consequently
his views became famous enough to be condemned by the Catholic

Church. In 1616 the Holy Office (Inquisition) declared that the idea of the sun as centre of the universe was 'foolish and absurd'. Galileo was forbidden to 'hold, teach or defend' such views. Some years later he published his theories in open defiance of the ban. As a result the astronomer was forced to retire into the country.

The truth was that the churchmen themselves were not sure that Galileo was wrong. For many years they had found Copernicus's theory essential for astronomical calculations. It had been used, for example, to produce the Gregorian Calendar in 1582. By 1632 most scientists thought that Copernicus was right. Even a cardinal at Galileo's trial had remarked that should the theory be proved correct it might be necessary to assume that the Church had misunderstood those parts of the Bible that stated the earth stood still! The way was open for a new view of the Universe.

Sir Isaac Newton

Copernicus had suggested that the earth and other planets moved round the sun. Kepler explained their exact path. It was left to the greatest scientist of the seventeenth century, Isaac Newton, to explain why the Solar System moved in the way it did.

Newton was born in Lincolnshire in 1642 and educated at Grantham Grammar School and Cambridge University. About 1665 the fall of an apple is said to have set him wondering why some objects are pulled towards the earth and others, like the moon, are not. His answer was to suggest that the moon does fall towards the earth but because of the speed and the course of the earth the two never meet. It is really 'in orbit' in a way which no longer surprises us because of sputniks and space travel.

In 1669 Newton became Professor of Mathematics at Cambridge and two years later a Fellow of the Royal Society. Instead of working on his new theory he spent years studying other subjects. He invented the reflecting telescope, in which light is concentrated by a concave mirror, and in 1672 managed to break white light into its colours with a prism. Meanwhile, another scientist, Robert Hooke, suggested that all planets have an effect on each other. He thought they would all travel in a straight line unless deflected by a force, and that this attraction would become stronger the nearer they were to each other. At a Royal Society meeting Hooke showed that it was possible to make a pendulum move in an ellipse by exerting a constant pull towards the centre. Could not the sun be doing just that, he asked?

A boy playing on the seashore

In 1684 a young astronomer, Edmund Halley, asked Newton's help in working out the orbit of certain planets. Newton replied that he had the necessary calculations but then discovered he had mislaid them. He promised that he would write them out again. From such a trivial incident came his greatest work, for Newton's rewriting developed into the *Mathematical Principles of Natural Philosophy* (1686).

In this famous book Newton demonstrated that the planets were kept in place by two forces, their own speed and the gravitational

Sir Isaac Newton

pull of the sun upon them. Furthermore, their correct orbits and exact speed could be obtained if one assumed that all bodies are attracted by a force which depends directly on their mass and distance from each other. For this Newton produced his inverse square law, the mathematical rule for assessing the strength or weakness of such a pull. This states that if the distance between a planet and the sun is divided by three the force will be multiplied by nine (three squared); on the contrary, if the distance is multiplied four times the force will be divided by sixteen.

Newton's theory of Gravitation was truly universal for it described a universe governed by fundamental laws. It showed that moving objects will behave similarly whether they are planets, pendulums or cannon balls. It revealed that the same forces control planets, tides or falling apples. Such discoveries encouraged later scientists to look beyond the surface disorder of nature for unchangeable laws beneath. In one science, chemistry, they were successful. The atomic theory developed in the early nineteenth century, which saw all chemicals as being built up from a small number of basic particles called atoms, was as universal in its own way as Newton's.

Above all, Newton showed scientists *how* to work. His own life's work established a pattern to guide them, for he insisted that researches leading to certain conclusions in any branch of science must be followed by more and more experiments to prove or disprove the theory that resulted. This emphasis on proof is called 'scientific method', and it became the essential tool without which much of 'science' would have remained guesswork and superstition.

Newton himself never realised that he had both summed up the work of several centuries and pointed the way to the future. Near the end of his life he remarked: 'I do not know what I may appear to the world, but to myself I seem to have been only a boy playing on the seashore . . . whilst the great ocean of truth lay all undiscovered before me'. A century later another scientist made a fairer assessment when he complained that as there was only one universe to be explained, no one could repeat Newton's performance.

Aristotle's humours

Aristotle had written his own explanation of the universe. Although wrong, it was a mighty achievement based on what could be seen and understood in his day (fourth century BC). Aristotle believed the universe to be made up of four elements, fire, air, water and earth. He also maintained that each contained the qualities of two of the others. Fire was hot and dry, water moist and cold, earth dry and cold, and so on. Because of the movement of the planets there was a constant battle between these elements.

In Aristotle's opinion the human body was part of this struggle, being composed of four conflicting 'humours'—blood, which was associated with spring, yellow bile associated with summer, black bile with autumn and phlegm with winter. These four corresponded to the stages of a man's life, childhood, youth, maturity and old age. They led to four types of human personality, sanguine or high-

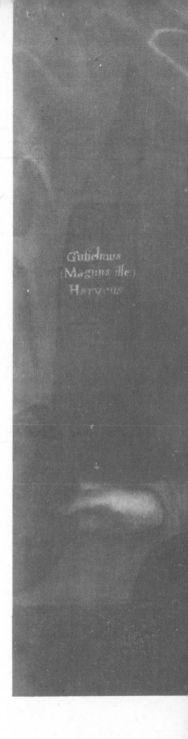

Gulielmus
Magnus ille
Harveus

William Harvey

spirited (blood), choleric or bad-tempered (yellow bile), melancholy (black bile) and phlegmatic (phlegm). Thus each human body and soul was seen as a little world (microcosm) reflecting the larger world of the universe (macrocosm).

This ingenious theory reached medieval Europe via the writings of Galen, a physician to the Roman emperors, and it was used as a basis for medical treatment. All illness was thought to be the result of a lack of balance between the humours. As a result doctors spent their time trying to counteract the too powerful effects of a particular humour. Bleeding was used for a too sanguine patient, and purging for an unfortunate who was choleric and melancholy.

During Renaissance times certain physicians questioned Aristotle's theories. Paracelsus (1493–1541) thought that the human body was composed of mercury, sulphur and salt. He did not believe in humours, and became known as the 'Luther of Chemistry' because he publicly burned the writings of Galen just as the religious reformer had burned the Papal Bull. Because he believed that disease was caused by chemicals outside the body he used medicines made from metals. Sometimes the results were beneficial although his reasons were somewhat peculiar. Anaemic patients, for example, were given iron salts because iron was associated with Mars, the Roman War God of blood and iron. Paracelsus's followers were called iatrochemists. Before long the medical schools of Europe were the scene of quarrels between iatrochemists and those who still believed in Galen's teachings.

Meanwhile the work of Vesalius had begun to show the correct structure of the body. Galen's descriptions had been the result of dissecting animals such as apes, not humans. They were therefore not strictly accurate where man was concerned. Vesalius's fine anatomical drawings (1543) represented a real 'breakthrough' in surgical knowledge.

The circulation of the blood

To dissect a body is like taking an engine to pieces—it shows the parts but not how they work. Galen taught that the heart pumped blood out along tubes and then sucked it back again, rather like the tidal movement of the sea. It was William Harvey (1578–1657), a lecturer at the Royal College of Physicians, who first discovered exactly how the heart controls the flow of blood around the body.

Harvey thought the heart was a pump. 'It is certain', he wrote, 'that the perpetual movement of the blood in a circle is caused by the heart beat.' It was known already that the heart was divided into two parts and that each part consisted of two separate chambers. Sets of tubes run from the 'left heart' to all parts of the body and a similar set run from the right section. Harvey proved that blood travels from the right heart to the lungs and so on to the left chamber through special arteries. From these it is pumped all over the body.

Harvey's explanation, *On the Motion of the Heart and Blood,* was published in Germany in 1628 after much deliberate delay. This was because he thought he would be laughed at or persecuted. 'I not

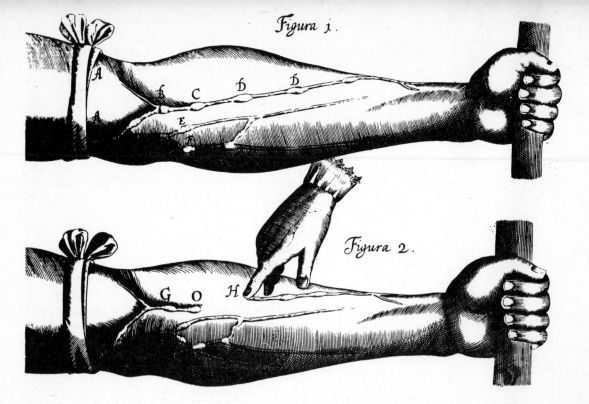

Figura 1.

Figura 2.

only fear that I may suffer from the ill will of a few,' he wrote, 'but dread lest all men turn against me.' Even the book itself was poorly printed and only fifty-five copies have survived to the present day. For some time Harvey was regarded as 'crackbrained' and his position as physician to Charles I did not help his career once Parliament won the Civil War. Many patients refused to be treated by him and it was years before his great discovery was accepted on the continent.

Drawing demonstrating the way the valves of the veins work, from William Harvey's book on the circulation of the blood, 1628

Microbes and capillaries

Harvey realised that this one-way movement could only be explained by the existence of thousands of tiny vessels at the end of the arteries and veins through which the blood flowed to complete a circle. He could not see such 'capillaries'. A Dutch scientist, Leeuwenhoek (1632–1723), first saw them using a microscope of his own invention. With this instrument he also saw the actual circulation of the blood in the tail of a tadpole and the foot of a frog. Leeuwenhoek's microscope did not consist of several lenses but was a tiny glass ball no bigger than a pinhead, fixed in a bat-shaped piece of wood. Such a ball magnifies many hundreds of times but needs to be held very close to the eye. Indeed, modern experts have failed to get a satisfactory view through those of Leeuwenhoek's instruments which survive. Yet his glass ball must have magnified at least 160 times for he was the first to see red corpuscles in the blood as well as microbes.

God and the scientists

Aristotle had tried to explain everything. In proving him wrong, the scientists of the Early Modern Age split science into different 'departments'. It soon became clear that man, nature, and the universe were too vast to be understood by one man, or studied as one subject. The old dream of finding a universal answer to the riddles of earthly life was blown away by the very men who enlarged human understanding.

After Copernicus and Newton, men and women realised that the earth could no longer be regarded as the most important part of the universe. To spin round the sun was a less significant action than to have a whole universe revolving around you. When Copernicus suggested the earth might move round the sun he was changing men's view of life as well as enlarging their knowledge. When Newton depicted the universe as a 'divine clock' he changed men's ideas of God as well as their scientific understanding. In some ways the age of miracles was replaced by the age of confusion.

More about science in the Early Modern Age
Books
G. Dawney, *Aristotle and Greek Science* (Chatto & Windus: Immortals of Science)

B. Farrington, *Aristotle* (Weidenfeld & Nicolson: Pathfinder Biographies)

D. Guerrier, *Discovering with Newton* (Blond Educational)

W. C. Harrison, *William Harvey* (Collier-Macmillan)

Harvey and the Circulation of the Blood (Cape: Jackdaw)

D. C. Knight, *Isaac Newton* (Chatto & Windus)

Newton and Gravitation (Cape: Jackdaw)

Visual aids
Aristotle and the Scientific Method *(film)* (Gateway)
Galileo *(film)* (Gateway)
Galileo (Hulton)
Isaac Newton *(film)* (Gateway)
Isaac Newton (Hulton)
History of Medicine (Hulton)

Visits
Royal Observatory, Greenwich
London Planetarium
Science Museum, London

To write and find out
1 Do you think the age of miracles is past? Give reasons for your answer.
2 Study the later history of medicine, particularly the work of Jenner, Simpson, Lister, Röntgen and Fleming.
3 Many people thought Harvey 'crackbrained' yet he was proved right. What do you think future generations will think of modern heart transplant surgery?
4 Has science helped to produce an age of confusion?

24 From Popish Plot to Revolution
Charles II and James II's Reign 1670-1689

In August 1678 Charles II heard rumours of a plot to kill him. When he asked for proof a Dr Israel Tonge was brought before his Council. Tonge confirmed that there was indeed a conspiracy by the Pope, the French King and Jesuits to murder Charles and place his Catholic brother James on the throne. After much questioning he also admitted that a certain Titus Oates had told him. The tale, like the names, was strange. Oates was a shady character whose evidence consisted of obviously forged documents. He changed his story frequently and when examined by the Privy Council contradicted himself.

The King was sure Oates was a liar, yet he did nothing about it. There were several reasons for his silence. In the first place Charles was himself a secret Catholic who regarded it as 'the only religion fit for a gentleman'. Furthermore in 1670 he had signed the Treaty of Dover with the French King Louis XIV, containing unpublished clauses in which he promised to persuade, not force, his subjects to return to the Catholic faith. But when he dared to cancel the Clarendon Code by a Declaration of Indulgence (1673) making it easier for Nonconformists to worship and get jobs, he had been attacked by an angry Parliament and compelled to give up even this small step in the direction of religious toleration.

In such circumstances Charles dare not appear friendly towards the Catholics. If men 'discovered' Popish plots it was best not to speak, for some already suspected his religious beliefs and if the Treaty of Dover's secret clauses became public he might well lose his throne. After the Privy Council had finished with Oates, Charles went off to enjoy some horse-racing at Newmarket.

A hellish plot

Protestants who discovered 'Popish' plots were fairly common in seventeenth-century England. Generally they were exposed as liars and forgotten. This time two dramatic events appeared to confirm the story. Edward Coleman, secretary to James's wife, was found to have written to foreign Catholics discussing ways of changing England's religion. Then, in October 1678, the country was alarmed by an unsolved murder.

Sir Edmund Berry Godfrey, the magistrate to whom Oates had made his first statement, disappeared. Later his body was found in a ditch on Primrose Hill near London. Nobody knows who killed Godfrey. Doctors certified that he had actually been strangled, although a sword was fixed through the body. In recent times it has been suggested that Godfrey might have committed suicide and that friends made it look like murder so that he could have a Christian burial. Whatever really happened, his death convinced every loyal

Right: The Earl of Shaftesbury, Whig leader during Charles II's reign

Below: The Secret Treaty of Dover

Protestant that Catholics had killed him to destroy evidence of their wicked schemes.

For the next two years there was panic in England as Charles's political opponents, led by Lord Shaftesbury, used the Plot as a way of attacking the King's government. Wild rumours alarmed the country. Tales of French armies landing in Kent, of Catholic troops advancing underground and of cellars full of swords, became commonplace. James, the Catholic heir to the throne, felt it safer to retire abroad for a time and his friend, honest Samuel Pepys, was put in the Tower as a suspected Papist, because he knew a Catholic musician! The Commons even set up a special committee to examine the royal fireworks maker because he had a French name. Altogether thirty-five innocent men, including a lord and an archbishop, were executed, and Oates and his friends made a comfortable living 'discovering' plotters.

Whigs and Tories

The Popish Plot panic gradually became a battle over the succession to the throne. Charles II had several children, but none by his wife, the Portuguese Catherine of Braganza, whom he had married in 1661. As a result his Catholic brother James was due to succeed him, a fact which numerous Protestants were not ready to accept. One group wanted Charles to follow Henry VIII's example and divorce his Queen Catherine. This idea did not appeal to Charles who seemed to dislike divorce more than adultery. Another suggestion was that James's Protestant daughter Mary and her husband, the Dutch King William of Orange, should rule after Charles's death.

A third, more dangerous scheme was to allow Charles's illegitimate son, James Duke of Monmouth, (whose mother, Lucy Walter, had been one of Charles's mistresses) to become king. Some wanted him proclaimed legitimate. Less honest men remembered that Charles had known Lucy before his marriage. They whispered of a mysterious 'black box' which contained the marriage certificate of Charles and Lucy. Had this been true it would have made Monmouth heir to the throne. But the King admitted that he had never married Lucy.

During the fierce war of words which followed, Shaftesbury's followers placed a Bill before Parliament proposing that James should not be allowed to become King (the Exclusion Bill). The battle which followed saw the birth of the first political parties in English history. Those who wanted to get rid of James were called Exclusionists or Petitioners. Those against interfering with the succession were referred to as Abhorrers because they abhorred (detested) the suggestion.

Such clumsy names were soon replaced by simpler ones as each side abused the other. Abhorrers called the Petitioners 'Whiggamores' or Whigs after the Presbyterian rebels still fighting against the Government in Scotland. Petitioners referred to their opponents as 'Tories', the name given to Irish Catholics battling to be free of English rule. And so it was that the two parties became known as Whigs and Tories.

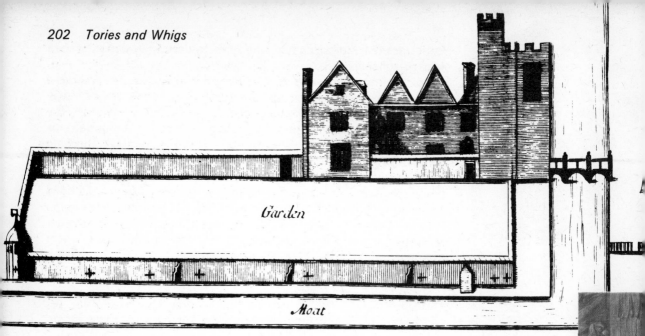

Garden

Moat

The Rye House Plot

One should not think of these rivals as political parties in the modern sense. Nobody joined them by filling up a form and paying a subscription. The present day idea of an opposition party which has a useful job to do and is really an alternative government never entered the minds of seventeenth-century men. Opposition to royal policies, however peaceful, was still seen as near to treason.

Nevertheless the two groups did have different interests and points of view. Whigs stood for many of the ideals of those who had gone to war with Charles I. Shaftesbury, for example, had fought for Parliament and served in Cromwell's government. Such men believed that royal power should be limited and Parliament powerful. They disliked a regular army, were inclined to allow religious toleration, and hated France as a threat to England's trade and colonies.

Tories stood more firmly for the Established Church and were intolerant of Nonconformists. Many still believed in divine right and the prerogative (privileges) of the Crown. They were prepared to accept James simply because he was the rightful heir, even though they disliked his faith. Both sides possessed extremists. The Whig 'Green Ribbon Club' in London, for example, contained old Republicans (against monarchy), while a few Tories were almost Catholic in their beliefs. The majority, however, were moderates who shared a love of the Church of England.

When it became clear that Charles had organised enough parliamentary support to defeat the Exclusion Bill his Whig opponents acted very differently from a modern political party. During 1682 Shaftesbury plotted an armed rebellion. This was discovered by the authorities so he fled abroad, where he died in December. Some of his disappointed followers then decided to shoot Charles and James as they rode along a narrow lane at Rye House, near Hoddesdon in

Rye House, Hoddesdon, Hertfordshire, where plotters planned to kill Charles II and his brother James

Hertfordshire, on their way home from Newmarket races. The plot misfired because the royal pair travelled to London earlier than expected. Its discovery led to investigations ending in the execution of several Whig lords. It also marked the end of the 'Popish Plot' terror. Soon afterwards Oates was flogged and imprisoned for daring to call James a traitor.

In 1685 Charles suffered a stroke. Anxious doctors gathered at the palace, bleeding him repeatedly and putting hot coals on various parts of his body. When their efforts failed the King sent for a priest who performed the last rites of the Catholic Church. Just before mid-day on 6 February Charles II died.

Years before a witty courtier had suggested Charles's epitaph:
Here lies our sovereign lord the King
Whose word no man relies on
He never said a foolish thing
And never did a wise one
This was rather unfair for, as the King had quickly pointed out, his words were his own whilst his actions were often his ministers'.

Rebellion in the West

The new King, James II, had proved himself brave in war and a capable organiser in peace. In his early years he had been a Protestant; both daughters by his first marriage were of that faith. Following the Restoration his beliefs slowly changed, especially after his second marriage to a Catholic, Mary of Modena. In 1670 he openly announced his conversion—a courageous act which Charles never dared to make.

Thanks to his brother's efforts, James II inherited the most Royalist Parliament of the century. The majority of M.P.s felt that the new King had served his country well as commander of the fleet in the Dutch Wars, and should be given a chance to prove his worth as King. Even Tories who disliked his faith accepted him because of their belief in divine right.

With such firm support, the first two rebellions against his authority were easily suppressed. Monmouth had sailed to Holland soon after the failure of the Rye House Plot, in which he had treacherously given evidence against his fellow conspirators. Here he was joined by the exiled Scottish Presbyterian leader, the Earl of Argyle. When James became King the two plotted his overthrow. In May 1685 Argyle went to Scotland and raised a rebellion. It failed and he was executed. Next month Monmouth landed at Lyme Regis in Dorset to a disappointing welcome. Local Whig gentlemen were not interested in following such a weak, unreliable leader. Those who did rally to his flag were mainly discontented Nonconformist peasants. After he had been proclaimed King at Taunton, Monmouth issued a Declaration accusing his uncle James of starting the Great Fire, conspiring in the Popish Plot and murdering his brother! He then advanced to meet the royal army encamped at Sedgemoor, three miles from Bridgwater in Somerset.

By this time he must have realised the hopelessness of his

James II

position. Recruits were few and even those he had were untrained and badly equipped; some had only scythe blades fixed on poles. Watching the enemy from the tower of Bridgwater Church, Monmouth recognised the flags of a regiment he had once commanded. 'I know those men. They will fight,' he remarked gloomily.

Monmouth decided on a surprise attack at night. Unfortunately, flooded streams slowed his advance down so much that by the time his men reached the royal camp dawn was breaking. Once the first shots had been fired, John Churchill, second in command to Lord Faversham, quickly rallied his troops. The fight which followed, although officially the last battle fought on English soil, was really a massacre (July 1685). Monmouth galloped towards the Hampshire coast, only to be captured near Ringwood. He was taken to London and beheaded.

The Bloody Assize
Monmouth's sad end was followed by the savage punishment of his followers. Lord Chief Justice Jeffreys had made his name trying the Rye House Plotters. He was a brilliant lawyer and a keen Tory who

Fierce fighting ends Monmouth's hopes at the Battle of Sedgemoor 1685

supported King and Church. During what Whig writers later called 'the Bloody Assize', he and his fellow judges toured the West Country on a special Commission sent to deal with the rebels.

The driving force behind this Commission was James himself. Instead of executing a few ringleaders, the King ordered large numbers of Monmouth's followers to be punished. Altogether about 1,300 men and women were condemned, of whom about 200 suffered hanging, drawing and quartering. Another 800 were given to the Queen and her courtiers to be sold as slaves in the West Indies. Most accounts of Jeffreys's bullying behaviour at these trials were written by Whigs after his death in 1689. They presented him as a devil in human shape, a monster who joked as he gave sentence. He was even described as having an ugly face when all portraits show him to have been handsome. Actually his behaviour was no worse than that of many judges before and since. James, rather than Jeffreys, was responsible for the Bloody Assize.

Royal Indulgences

The Monmouth Rebellion showed that James was unlikely to be deposed if he supported the Church of England. But he went too far and decided to give toleration to Catholics and other Nonconformists. During 1686–7 James's intentions became clear. Tory ministers were replaced by Catholics. Parliament was first adjourned and then dismissed. The rules of certain corporations (chartered towns) were 'regulated' to allow Catholics to be town councillors. The Test Acts were bypassed so that Catholics could become army officers. Cambridge University's Vice Chancellor was sacked for refusing to grant a degree to a Catholic priest. At Oxford, Magdalen College was forced to accept a Catholic President. Such policies frightened both rich and poor. Ordinary folk feared a return to Army rule, this time by Catholics instead of 'Saints'. Churchmen were horrified at the thought of their university training grounds coming under Catholic influence. Political leaders saw their power being taken over by representatives of a religious minority.

In April 1687 James issued a Declaration of Indulgence which cancelled the Clarendon Code. In it he admitted that he wished 'all his subjects were members of the Catholic Church'. Soon afterwards it became known that the Queen was pregnant. This was bad news for all Protestants. As matters stood the fifty-four-year-old James would be succeeded by his Protestant daughters, Mary and Anne. If a boy was born to his second wife, England would be faced with a line of Catholic monarchs. Suspicious Protestants wondered whether the Queen was really pregnant or whether the country was about to be tricked.

Events moved to a crisis in 1688. In April James published a second Declaration of Indulgence. Sancroft, the Archbishop of Canterbury, and six other bishops asked permission not to read it in their churches. James's reaction was to charge them with 'seditious libel'. Whilst the Seven Bishop's Case was proceeding in the courts, the Queen gave birth to a son, James (June 1688).

Primitive scythe weapons used by Monmouth's men

A New SONG.

made upon ye Irish upon Tyrconnels going Deputy thithr
25. Oct. 1688

Ho Brother *Teague* doft hear de Decree, Lil - li Burleró Bullen a -- la, Dat we fhall have a

new Debittie, Lil - li Bur-le-ro Bullen a-la, Le-ro, Le-ro, Le-ro Le-ro, Lil-li Bur-le-ro,

Bullen a la Le - ro, Le - ro, Le - ro, Le - ro, Lil - li Burlero Bullen a la;

Ho by my Shoul it is a *Talbot*,
Lilli Burlero, &c.

Lilli, &c.
Lero, Lero, &c.

Lilliburlero. This song was sung by the enemies of James II in 1688–89. The words are meaningless—probably a password used by Irish rebels in 1641. But the song had been composed originally to make fun of James's representative in Ireland, the Earl of Tyrconnel

The coming of William

In normal circumstances everyone would have been pleased by such an event. But the people did not want a Catholic prince and were prepared to believe all sorts of wild rumours. The baby had been born in a crowded room with the King himself present. Why then had the infant been carried instantly into the next room, they asked? Protestant writers soon supplied an answer. The real prince had died within a few seconds. A miller's son had been smuggled into St James's Palace in a warming-pan from a Catholic convent nearby. In another version the prince died a few weeks later and was replaced by a brickmaker's son. Although false, these stories were believed for many years.

Three weeks after the prince's birth Sancroft and his colleagues were found not guilty by the jury. It was the first time an English monarch had lost an important law case and a shattering blow to a King who believed, like his grandfather James I, that 'Kings are accountable to none but God alone for their actions'. That night, as Londoners lit bonfires to celebrate, the 'impossible' happened. Leading Tories and Whigs met together and wrote an 'Invitation' to William of Orange, James's son-in-law, to come to England and restore England's 'true liberties'.

A great deal now depended on affairs abroad. William was the sworn enemy of France. If he did come to England would the French King, Louis XIV, try to stop him? William found the decision easy. He cared nothing for England's parliamentary liberties or even its Protestant religion. What he did wish to prevent was a Catholic England allied with France against him. On 1 November 1688 he sailed from Holland with an army of 15,000 Dutch and English troops. Delayed at first by bad weather, the fleet soon benefited from a 'Protestant wind' which blew it swiftly down the Channel. The English navy, meanwhile, did nothing to stop it. Louis XIV half-heartedly offered James the use of the French fleet but in fact he was anxious not to do anything which would unite England and Holland against him.

William decided to land on 4 November because it was his birthday and wedding anniversary. But his English friends advised 5 November for obvious reasons. They got their way. In later years Whig writers made much of the fact that England had been twice saved from a Catholic plot on that date.

James's flight

William spent his first night in England in a fisherman's hut. Next day his troops started to advance along bad roads in pouring rain. At most places he was joined by important local gentlemen, or blessed by

Dutch William

poor folk who came to catch a glimpse of their 'Protestant saviour'. In London his 'orange' colours began to appear on men's coats and ladies' petticoats.

Since 1685 Protestants had worried about the fact that James kept a standing (regular) army. Now that it was called upon to fight these fears were found to be groundless. The royal troops were dis-spirited and mutinous. They often disobeyed their Catholic officers and had even approved of the acquittal of the seven bishops. When James joined them at Salisbury he saw at once they were not to be trusted. As he explained: 'It was on no ways advisable to venture myself at their head.' When his best general, John Churchill, deserted to William, taking with him details of the army's size and strength, he knew it was hopeless to resist. James fled towards the coast where he was captured by some fishermen at Faversham in Kent.

An ill-treated and ragged King returned to London. Here he received orders to leave his court and accept Dutch guards. James was now afraid he would suffer the fate of his father. 'If I do not retire,' he said, 'I shall certainly be sent to the Tower and no King ever went out of that place but to his grave.' Consequently he escaped again, arriving in France just before Christmas. For the second time in forty years the English had rid themselves of a Stuart king.

More about Charles II and James II's reign
Books
S. B. Baxter, *William III* (Longman)
A Bryant, *Charles II* (Collins)
H. Chapman, *Charles II* (Cape)
G. W. Keaton, *Lord Chancellor Jeffreys and the Stuart Cause* (Macdonald)
J. Kinross, *Discovering Battlefields in Southern England* (Shire Publications)
The Monmouth Rebellion and the Bloody Assize (Cape: Jackdaw)

Visual aids
Charles II (Visual Publications)
James II (Visual Publications)
Jacobean London (Educational Productions)

Visits
The County of Dorset contains many reminders of the Bloody Assize.

To write and find out
1 Write an account of the murder of Godfrey in the style of a modern newspaper account.
2 Write your own four line epitaph for Charles II.
3 Do you think James was really in favour of religious freedom, or was he trying to make England a Catholic state once more?
4 Find out more about the Bloody Assize, particularly the trial of Alice Lisle. This trial could be made the basis of a classroom play.

25   Dutch William
William and Mary 1689-1702

The events of 1688–89 were a turning point in English history. A new kind of monarchy had been established in England. Even William himself, when he first put on the crown, 'fancied he was like a king in a play'. In many ways the new ruler seemed as powerful as the old. He appointed his own cabinet, negotiated with foreign governments and saw to the day to day running of the country. The essential difference was that he had been chosen by Parliament, not born king by divine right. In effect, William signed a contract with his wealthy subjects. A Bill of Rights, modelled on the famous Petition of Rights of 1628, gave to Parliament alone the right to raise taxes, pass laws and control the army. It allowed the Commons to hold regular elections and speak freely during debates. Since 1689 many English monarchs have had influence, but none has wielded 'God-given' power.

Such a revolution suited both Whigs and Tories. England's ruling classes remembered the Levellers and the New Model Army. Better to settle their differences than to find their power again threatened by that 'many headed monster', the people! So rule passed to a Parliament controlled by a minority of rich men. The dreams of Pym, not Winstanley or Lilburne, came true.

Settlement and toleration
The question who should succeed to the throne was decided by Parliament. At first it was agreed that William and Mary should be followed by their children. If they had no children the throne would pass to Mary's sister Anne and her family. Few expected Mary to become a mother and in fact she died childless in 1694. When the last of Anne's seventeen children died in 1701 the descendants of James I's daughter Elizabeth were named as her successors. Since Elizabeth had married a German prince it was George, Elector of Hanover, who became King in 1714. Thus the Catholic line founded by James II was excluded from the throne.

Side by side with this settlement went new freedoms. A Toleration Act of 1694 cancelled many of the laws against Nonconformists. In future they could worship openly, although they were still disqualified from government jobs or university training. Soon they were able to establish their own educational academies.

The press also benefited. England's first newspaper had been published in 1622, but the Church censored what was written. During the Commonwealth there was little government interference. Journals were produced for various groups, including one for the New Model Army. After the Restoration, a Licensing Act again controlled printing, allowing only news of which the government

Numb.

The Daily Courant.

Wednesday, March 11. 1702.

From the Harlem Courant, Dated March 18. N. S.

Naples, Feb. 22.

ON Wednesday last, our New Viceroy, the Duke of Escalona, arriv'd here with a Squadron of the Galleys of Sicily. He made his Entrance dreft in a French habit ; and to give us the greater Hopes of the King's coming hither, went to Lodge in one of the little Palaces, leaving the Royal one for his Majefty. The Marquis of Grigni is alfo arriv'd here with a Regiment of French.

Rome, Feb. 25. In a Military Congregation of State that was held here, it was Refolv'd to draw a Line from Afcoli to the Borders of the Ecclefiaftical State, thereby to hinder the Incurfions of the Tranfalpine Troops. Orders are fent to Civita Vecchia to fit out the Galleys, and to ftrengthen the Garrifon of that Place. Signior Cafali is made Governor of Perugia. The Marquis del Vafto, and the Prince de Caferta continue ftill in the Imperial Embaffador's Palace ; where his Excellency has a Guard of 50 Men every Night in Arms. The King of Portugal has defir'd the Arch-Bifhoprick of Lisbon, vacant by the Death of Cardinal Soufa, for the Infante his fecond Son, who is about 11 Years old.

Vienna, Mar. 4. Orders are fent to the 4 Regiments of Foot, the 2 of Cuiraffiers, and to that of Dragoons, which are broke up from Hungary, and are on their way to Italy, and which confift of about 14 or 15000 Men, to haften their March thither with all Expedition. The 6 new Regiments of Huffars that are now raifing, are in fo great a forwardnefs, that they will be compleat, and in a Condition to march by the middle of May. Prince Lewis of Baden has written to Court, to excufe himfelf from coming thither, his Prefence being fo very neceffary, and fo much defir'd on the Upper-Rhine.

Francfort, Mar. 12. The Marquifs d' Uxelles is come to Strasburg, and is to draw together a Body of fome Regiments of Horfe and Foot from the Garifons of Alface ; but will not leffen thofe of Strasburg and Landau, which are already very weak. On the other hand, the Troops of His Imperial Majefty, and his Allies, are going to form a Body near Germefhein in the Palatinate, of which Place, as well as of the Lines at Spires, Prince Lewis of Baden is expected to take a View, in three or four days. The English and Dutch Minifters, the Count of Frife, and the Baron Vander Meer, and likewife the Imperial Envoy Count Lowenftein, are gone to Nordlingen, and it is hop'd that in a fhort time we fhall hear from thence of fome favourable Refolutions for the Security of the Empire.

Liege, Mar. 14. The French have taken the Cannon de Longie, who was Secretary to the Dean de Mean, out of our Caftle, where he has been for fome time a Prifoner, and have deliver'd him to the Provoft of Maubeuge, who has carry'd him from hence, but we do not know whither.

Paris, Mar. 13. Our Letters from Italy fay, That moft of our Reinforcements were Landed there ; that the Imperial and Ecclefiaftical Troops feem to live very peaceably with one another in the Country of Parma, and that the Duke of Vendome, as he was vifiting feveral Pofts, was within 100 Paces of falling into the Hands of the Germans. The Duke of Chartres, the Prince of Conti, and feveral other Princes of the Blood, are to make the Campaign in Flanders under the Duke of Burgundy ; and the Duke of Maine is to Command upon the Rhine.

From the Amfterdam Courant, Dated Mar. 18.

Rome, Feb. 25. We are taking here all poffible Precautions for the Security of the Ecclefiaftical State in this prefent Conjuncture, and have defir'd to raife 3000 Men in the Cantons of Switzerland. The Pope has appointed the Duke of Berwick to be his Lieutenant-General, and he is to Command 6000 Men on the Frontiers of Naples : He has alfo fettled upon him a Penfion of 6000 Crowns a year during Life.

From the Paris Gazette, Dated Mar. 18. 1702.

Naples, Febr. 17. 600 French Soldiers are arrived here, and are expected to be follow'd by 3400 more. A Courier that came hither on the 14th. has brought Letters by which we are affur'd that the King of Spain defigns to be here towards the end of March ; and accordingly Orders are given to make the neceffary Preparations againft his Arrival. The two Troops of Horfe that were Commanded to the Abruzzo are pofted at Pefcara with a Body of Spanifh Foot, and others in the Fort of Montorio.

Paris, March. 18. We have Advice from Toulon of the 5th inftant, that the Wind having long ftood favourable, 22000 Men were already fail'd for Italy, that 2500 more were Embarking, and that by the 15th it was hoped they might all get thither. The Count d' Eftrees arriv'd there on the Third inftant, and fet all hands at work to fit out the Squadron of 9 Men of War and fome Fregats, that are appointed to carry the King of Spain to Naples. His Catholick Majefty will go on Board the *Thunderer*, of 110 Guns.

We have Advice by an Exprefs from Rome of the 18th of February, That notwithftanding the preffing Inftances of the Imperial Embaffadour, the Pope had Condemn'd the Marquis del Vafto to lofe his Head and his Eftate to be confifcated, for not appearing to Anfwer the Charge againft him of Publickly Scandalizing Cardinal Janfon.

ADVERTISEMENT.

IT will be found from the Foreign Prints, which from time to time, as Occafion offers, will be mention'd in this Paper, that the Author has taken Care to be duly furnifh'd with all that comes from Abroad in any Language. And for an Affurance that he will not, under Pretence of having Private Intelligence, impofe any Additions of feign'd Circumftances to an Action, but give his Extracts fairly and Impartially ; at the beginning of each Article he will quote the Foreign Paper from whence 'tis taken, that the Publick, feeing from what Country a piece of News comes with the Allowance of that Government, may be better able to Judge of the Credibility and Fairnefs of the Relation : Nor will he take upon him to give any Comments or Conjectures of his own, but will relate only Matter of Fact ; fuppofing other People to have Senfe enough to make Reflections for themfelves.

This Courant (as the Title fhews) will be Publifh'd Daily : being defign'd to give all the Material News as foon as every Poft arrives : and is confin'd to half the Compafs, to fave the Publick at leaft half the Impertinences, of ordinary News-Papers.

LONDON. Sold by E. Mallet, next Door to the King's-Arms Tavern at Fleet-Bridge.

Front page of the world's first daily newspaper, the *Daily Courant*

A London coffee house

approved. By 1695 Parliament no longer regarded the open expression of religious ideas as a threat to law and order. The Licensing Act, due for renewal by Parliament, was conveniently dropped. By such deliberate 'forgetfulness' it became possible for authors and publishers to write and print what they liked, subject to the law of libel. The result was a flood of journals and in 1702 the world's first daily newspaper, the *Daily Courant*, began to be published in England.

Coffee houses

Newspapers could be heard read aloud in the coffee house. Coffee drinking spread from the East and the first such establishment in England was probably Jacob the Jew's 'Coffeey House' in Oxford in 1650. Despite the name it was possible to buy chocolate and tea when dining.

Coffee houses were more like clubs than restaurants. Some were used as meeting places for particular professions or groups. Whigs favoured the St James's; Tories, the Cocoa Street Chocolate House.

Scholars went to the Grecian, literary men to Wills, and ships' captains to Edward Lloyd's coffee house, to hear the latest news of shipping movements. A few were used as salerooms where bidding took place 'by candle', that is, it continued until an inch of tallow candle had melted. Today some have survived as exclusive men's clubs, whilst Lloyds is now the centre for world marine insurance.

Tea came later to England; the first consignment was sold at Garraway's Coffee House in Cornhill, London. It had originally been brought to Europe by Dutch merchants. At first it was expensive and because it was thought good for health, tea drinking became popular. Since ladies were not allowed in coffee houses they took to tea at home, where it was common to pour hot water on leaves in each cup, not to make it in a teapot. The strangest experiment occurred in Scotland in 1668 where certain ladies brewed it, threw away the liquid and tried to eat the leaves!

The Scottish rebellion

William's revolution was far from bloodless in Scotland. Since 1660 Presbyterians had been crushed and replaced by an episcopal (bishop controlled) Church. The new government changed this policy. Bishops were abolished so that the Presbyterian kirk (church) could be re-established as a separate authority within the State. This, in turn, caused a rebellion in the Catholic Highlands.

In July 1689 'Bonny' (Viscount) Dundee led his barefoot Highlanders in a wild charge upon government troops in the pass of Killicrankie, four miles from Blair. The rebels won but Dundee was killed in the moment of victory. In the weeks which followed men of the Catholic Cameron, Maclean and Macdonald clans roamed central Perthshire, robbing and burning. Then, at Dunkeld, they were defeated by psalm-singing Covenanters. This ended the rebellion. Ragged survivors began the long, hard walk back to the hills; less lucky ones were caught and murdered. Catholic Scotland experienced an uneasy peace.

William's government decided to be merciful. Very few rebels were punished. Instead royal agents distributed £12,000 amongst the discontented clans in return for an oath of loyalty to be taken by 1 January 1692. By that date only Alexander Macdonald of Glencoe had failed to take the oath. Delayed by bad weather, he reached Fort William to find the government sheriff gone. The chief then walked across fifty miles of snow-covered country to take the oath at Inveraray on 6 January.

William was a Dutchman who knew nothing of clan feuds. When his Scottish adviser, Sir John Dalrymple, suggested punishing the entire Macdonald clan he did not know that Dalrymple and his Campbell friends were the traditional enemies of the Macdonalds. He permitted an attack providing that it could be proved Macdonald had not taken the oath. Behind the King's back, Dalrymple sent additional orders to 'extirpate (destroy) that sect of thieves in Glencoe'. In Edinburgh, another Campbell, saw to it that the written evidence of Macdonald's oath was destroyed.

Glencoe—scene of the massacre in 1692

In February 1692 Captain Campbell of Glenlyon and 100 soldiers went to Glencoe with instructions to kill 'the old fox and his sons'. At first the Campbell troops stayed in the Macdonald villages as guests. Then one night they rose and butchered thirty-three leading Macdonald clansmen, and four women and children. Only a handful escaped across the snowy mountains.

It was not the first or last Highland massacre. In this case, however, it could be used by William's enemies to stir up hatred against his rule. In the years which followed the story of the Massacre of Glencoe was repeated many times, helping to keep alive old feuds.

Victory at the Boyne

For the Irish, James's flight was a disaster. Under his rule they had tasted religious freedom for the first time for centuries; by 1688 all Irish judges, sheriffs, army officers and town councillors were Catholic. Only the Protestant settlers in the North were dismayed by such changes. Even before the Revolution they had begun to fortify Londonderry and arm themselves in case the triumphant Catholics attacked them. Suddenly the position was reversed. Now it was Catholics, not Protestants, who feared for their rights and liberties. When James II himself landed at Kinsale with a French army (March 1689) they rose in rebellion against the Protestant William. Against such a fierce Catholic sea only two Protestant 'rocks' stood firm, Londonderry and Enniskillen. At Londonderry the citizens held off James's French-Irish army for 105 days. Food ran short and dogs and rats were eaten; horse blood was sold at fourpence a pint. Fewer than sixty were killed in battle, but 15,000, including most of the children, died of disease or starvation.

Throughout the siege an English fleet lay outside the harbour, unable to enter because of a boom (barrier). In July 1689 an English supply ship, the *Mountjoy* sailed at this barrier, bounced off and ran aground in shallow water. It was decided to fire all cannon on its landward side. As if jet-propelled, the ship floated away. Then her captain sent it at the boom again and broke it. Londonderry was saved and the Catholic armies marched away south. On the same day Protestant volunteers beat their enemies at Newton Butler and relieved Enniskillen.

William was more interested in a new European war with Louis XIV than Irish affairs. His English Parliament took a different view and demanded that he go in person to Ireland and save the Protestant settlers. At first the reluctant King sent an almost worthless army. Its supply general, secretly loyal to James, pocketed money intended for his soldiers. Its Treasurer drew pay and allowances for a 'regiment' which consisted of two clerks and a flag kept in his bedroom. The men who did exist were in no condition to fight. 'Not one in four', reported their Dutch commander, 'has the slightest idea how to fire or load a musket.' That winter 7,000 such troops died of disease in Dundalk.

With James ruling openly in Dublin, the English Parliament demanded firmer action. William was forced to take command and he

Protestant stronghold—the old fortifications of Londonderry, Northern Ireland

landed with a new army at Carrickfergus. The royal enemies faced each other for the first and last time on 1 July 1690. In a fierce action William's men crossed the river Boyne and drove the French and Irish away. This famous battle need not have finished the rebellion had not James fled as swiftly from Ireland as he had from England. Left without a leader, the Irish Catholics were finally defeated at Aughrim (1691). When Limerick surrendered soon afterwards the Protestant conquest of Ireland was complete.

Limerick's brave defenders were offered fair terms. The Articles of Limerick contained promises that all Catholic soldiers and 'all such as were under their protection' would keep their lands, liberties and religious freedom. They also allowed rebel Irish soldiers, 'Wild Geese' as they were called, to 'fly away' and join Louis XIV's armies.

England's Parliament was not in such a forgiving mood. It ignored the sentence concerning those 'under their protection' and allowed Catholic civilians to be punished. William replaced the words in his own handwriting but it was no use. As a result 4,000 Catholic landowners lost nearly 1,500,000 acres. Later, an almost entirely Protestant Parliament at Dublin stopped Catholics from buying land, or serving as soldiers, sailors, schoolmasters or town councillors. Not for nothing is Limerick still called the 'City of the Broken Treaty'.

The Old Lady of Threadneedle Street

The Dutch King's long wars against France were very expensive, costing on average £5 million a year. To raise such enormous sums it was necessary to reintroduce the Cromwellian land tax. Paid at a rate of four shillings in the pound, it made ownership of land less valuable than before. Socially and politically, the landowner was to remain 'king' of his district for centuries to come. But increasingly the man who invested his money was often better off financially.

Apart from an annual allowance from Parliament, William levied the usual customs and excise duties. He also devised several new taxes, including one on windows. The window tax was fixed at two shillings for houses with under ten windows, six shillings for those with nineteen or less, and ten shillings for dwellings with over nineteen. The idea was not popular, and indignant owners sometimes bricked up their windows. Equally unsuccessful was a tax on births and deaths, because it was found difficult to collect money from babies and corpses.

Of more lasting financial importance was the foundation of the Bank of England. It was a Scot, William Paterson, who first suggested a bank which would loan money to the government in return for regular interest payments guaranteed by Parliament. Thus the problem which arose in Charles II's reign when he could not pay back money he had borrowed would be avoided. The plan proved popular because William was more likely to pay his debts than Charles. When he asked for £1,200,000 and promised 8½ per cent interest and the right to form such a bank, the amount was raised in a few days by London's goldsmiths. This first National Debt became a

The old Bank of England
building

permanent part of government finances, proving that investors were
more interested in receiving regular interest than in a quick repay-
ment of their loan.

The Bank of England began its long life in Graces Hall, London.
Forty years after its foundation it was moved to Threadneedle Street
where the Old Lady' has remained ever since. Because people trusted
the Bank it was soon able to issue paper money, including cheques,
bills of exchange (written orders to pay a certain sum on a given date)
and promissory notes (written promises to pay). With 'liquid' money
of this sort available complicated trading deals could be arranged
without large sums of money being transported from place to place.
Modern business organisation became possible.

Two years after the creation of the Bank of England a new

coinage was introduced. Because most coins of those days were made of pure silver or gold, criminals made a living chipping or filing their edges. As a result many shopkeepers weighed coins to assess their true value. The new government decided to do away with this debased coinage. With ten furnaces melting the old money, new coins were issued at the rate of £100,000 worth a week. To prevent any more filing, the edges of large coins were stamped with the words *'Decus et tutamen'* (Ornament and safeguard) and small ones were marked with lines. In this way it was possible to see at a glance if a coin had been defaced.

The Grand Alliance

In May 1689 William persuaded Austria, Spain, Sweden, Bavaria, Holland and six smaller German states to form a Grand Alliance with England against France. Officially the allies were pledged to stop any border territories being 'reunited' with France. Secretly they promised to resist Louis XIV's claims to the Spanish throne when the childless Charles II died.

This was war more total than any previous conflict with Louis (see Chapter 26). It was fought in Belgium, Italy and Spain and at sea in the Channel and Mediterranean. Against the might of France, William proved to be a better statesman than soldier. Allied successes were few and French troops captured the great barrier fortresses protecting Holland. William's army was defeated in battles at Steenkirk and Landen (or Neerwinden). Only after the death of France's best general, Luxembourg, in 1695 did William manage to capture Namur in Belgium.

At sea affairs went no better. In June 1690, Tourville, the French admiral, defeated the English fleet off Beachy Head. This was one reason why France was able to keep James's army supplied in Ireland. Meanwhile French privateers captured or destroyed hundreds of Dutch and English merchant ships. Not until 1692 did an English sea victory at La Hogue regain control of the seas from France.

William's tax-payers did not like such an expensive and un-successful war. They wanted the sort of swift crushing victories common in Cromwell's day. By 1697 Louis, also, wished to rest his war machine ready for the coming fight over the succession to the Spanish throne. The Peace of Ryswick (1697) was an inconclusive end to an inconclusive war. France gave up all its conquests except Strasbourg. The Dutch were allowed to reoccupy some of the lost fortresses and Louis agreed to recognise William as King of England.

As expected Ryswick turned out to be a truce, not a lasting peace. In 1699 William and Louis agreed that when the Spanish Charles II died, Spain, the Netherlands and the South American colonies should go to the Habsburg Archduke Charles, and France would receive Spain's Italian territories (the Partition Treaty). Unfortunately, on his deathbed the dying Charles made a will leaving all his posses-sions to Louis XIV's grandson, Philip (1699). In this crisis the French King went too far. When news of the will reached him Louis decided to ignore his treaty with William.

Even this dishonesty might not have caused a war. In the weeks which followed England and Holland made it clear they would accept Philip as King of Spain. But Louis was still not satisfied. First he ordered his troops to seize the barrier fortresses in Holland. Second he declared the Catholic 'James III' King of England when his father, the deposed James II, died in 1701. Finally he formed French trading companies to compete with English commerce.

The English still regarded trade as the 'fairest mistress of all'. A Parliament filled with merchants declared war on France. This time Louis did not face his old enemy. As William rode in Hampton Court Park in March 1702 his horse stumbled on a molehill and he was thrown. The sick and weary king was carried to his palace where he died on the 19th. Whilst his enemies drank toasts to the 'little gentleman in black velvet' who had caused William's horse to fall, Anne became Queen. One of her first acts was to appoint John Churchill, created Duke of Marlborough later in the year, to command English forces in the Netherlands. After forty years of success, the armies of Louis XIV were about to face the greatest soldier of the age.

More about William III's reign
Books
G. Berry, *Discovering Coins* (Shire Publications)
D. Edwards-Rees, *Ireland's Story* (Longman: Young Books)
I. MacPhail, *Scotland* (Arnold), 2 vols
J. Prebble, *Glencoe: the story of the massacre* (Secker & Warburg; Penguin)
A. H. Quiggin, *The Story of Money* (Methuen: Outlines)
D. Thomas, *The Story of Newspapers* (Methuen: Outlines)

Visual aids
William and Mary (Visual Publications)
William and Mary *(film)* (Rank)

Visits
Bank of England, London
Glencoe, Scotland
Londonderry, Northern Ireland

To write and find out
1 Make a 'family tree' to show the descent of the present Queen from William and Mary. When did the Hanoverian monarchs cease to rule Hanover and why?
2 Write a song or poem telling the story of the Massacre of Glencoe.
3 Why are present day Protestant Irishmen sometimes called 'Orangemen'? Find out more about Irish history so that you can understand modern problems in Northern Ireland.
4 Find out what the National Debt amounts to today. What 'expenses' in recent years have made it so high?

26 The World of the Sun King
Europe 1660-1685

In 1689 two ladies were travelling to the court of King Louis XIV of France. 'We had scarcely reached the top of the hill from which we suddenly saw displayed below the magnificent palace whither we were bound,' wrote one. 'What do I see?' asked her companion, 'Is that what you name the little house of the greatest king on earth?'

'Yes,' came the reply, 'that is Versailles, Madame.'

Louis XIV (1638–1715) was King from the age of five. During his youth a seesaw struggle had raged in France between the forces of his mother, Anne of Austria, and her chief minister, Cardinal Mazarin, and those of various nobles and the French parliament. What started as a protest against war taxes and a fight for parliamentary rights soon descended into a murderous conflict between groups of ambitious men and women. At one time or another nearly all the leaders were defeated and imprisoned. But the anti-royalist *Frondeurs* (named after a child's sling, but meaning, in effect, one who grumbles) had no nationwide support such as the first English Roundheads had enjoyed nor a leader of the quality of Pym. After five years' civil war Mazarin restored order, destroying all hope of a strong French parliament.

Of the Fronde one rebel remarked later, 'We were all playing a comedy'. But it was no joke for the French people, who suffered terribly. The young prince, himself, 'beautiful as an angel', had seen a Parisian mob break into his palace. He hardly needed Mazarin to tell him that only a strong king could prevent such disorders. Taking charge in 1661 Louis ruled without interference for the next fifty years, justifying Mazarin's prediction that although 'a slow beginner, he will go further than any'.

Louis believed a king should display his power and wealth in various ways. His power could be shown by fighting successful wars; his wealth by erecting buildings to impress future generations. The most famous result of the second policy was the gradual enlargement of his father's hunting lodge at Versailles, near Paris. Throughout almost the entire reign one block of buildings after another was added until the palace became a miniature town and centre of French government. Here the 'Sun King', as he was called, lived surrounded by the 'planets' who were his nobles and courtiers.

Versailles is a memorial in stone to Louis's idea of himself as 'God on earth'. It is a temple of royalty so vast and imposing that, although copied by other European monarchs, it remains without equal. A complex of palaces was set amid spacious gardens, decorated with pools, fountains and fine trees. Inside are enormous apartments, elaborate plaster ceilings, splendid staircases and a hall of mirrors. Every painting, statue or design emphasises royal glory, and Louis's glory in particular. The King's seven rooms, for example, are named

Versailles, near Paris—
home of the Sun King

after the seven planets, whilst the staircase leading to them has ceiling decorations showing the four continents he claimed to rule.

Courtiers sometimes complained about Versailles. It was built on marshes in an unhealthy valley. The air was bad and for a long time there was no proper water supply. Almost to the end of Louis's long reign, it was disfigured by scaffolding and surrounded by debris. But the Sun King loved it, often taking visitors around personally and even writing a guide book to the gardens. It was here he went on view to the public each day, from the moment when he

was ceremonially dressed, through the conferences and merry-making until a duke was allowed to take away the royal candlestick as a sign that the King was going to bed.

The cost of Versailles helped to bankrupt France. Its grandeur was created by a man whose wars brought death and misery to millions. Of Louis's France it was said truly: 'It is a country in which the joys are visible but false, and the sorrows hidden but real.'

Louis XIV's bed-chamber in the Palace of Versailles

Nation-states

Of the nation-states which replaced the kingdoms and dukedoms of medieval Europe, seventeenth-century France was the most powerful. Surrounded by weaker neighbours, Spain, Holland and the German states, it was hardly surprising that the French should extend their territory by wars. In particular, the idea that France's 'natural' frontier was the river Rhine became popular with French statesmen. This policy made France a menace once Louis came to power, for it involved gobbling up chunks of land not previously thought of as French. In a world where war was regarded as a normal part of life, and where the Sun King spoke quite openly of 'chances to make war', it is not surprising that Europe experienced large-scale conflicts between 1667 and 1714.

The King chose good ministers to carry out his plans. Best of all was Jean Colbert (1619–83) who reorganised the country's finances and set about constructing a French navy. Sailors were conscripted, naval depots established, forests laid low so that more suitable ships' timber could be planted. By 1677 France had 116 fighting ships and the efficient dockyards at Toulon and Brest could assemble a new one in a week.

Similar military reforms increased the land power of France. Gone were the days of the private army, for experience in the Thirty Years War had shown that they could be untrustworthy and inefficient. Under Louis the national army became an essential part of the national state. From 1672 onwards about a quarter of a million men were kept permanently under arms in France. The soldiers that Louis and his enemies recruited were often foreigners; both the Scots and Swiss made a business out of supplying high quality fighting men at a price. But now such men fought for a country not a private individual or rebel lord.

Behind the nationalised army lay a country organised for war. A soldier-engineer, Sebastien Vauban (1633–1707) divided France's borders into sectors, providing each with a complicated web of trenches, fortifications and other strong points. In this way France was enveloped in a cocoon which protected it from its enemies, and gave it a safe base from which to carry out aggressive attacks.

During 1667–68 Louis's forces occupied the Spanish Netherlands (Belgium) because he claimed them after the death of his father-in-law, Philip IV of Spain. The loss of this buffer state between France and Holland alarmed the Dutch who went to war against France. After some fighting the French withdrew, leaving garrisons at strategic spots (Treaty of Aix-la-Chapelle, 1668). Those who thought these fortress towns were launching pads for more attacks were soon proved correct. In 1672 Louis sent 110,000 soldiers into Holland without warning.

Even warlike Europe was horrified by such 'armed burglary'. After all, the Dutch leaders, John and Cornelius de Witt, had tried hard to be friendly with France. But Louis was furious at the freedom allowed Dutch newspapers; one had shown a cartoon of his French 'Sun' obscured by a Dutch cheese! The more sensible Colbert resented the fact that French goods had to be carried in Dutch ships and French trading companies were far less successful than their Dutch rivals.

Louis expected a swift and easy victory against a people he called a 'nation of shopkeepers'. He was in for a shock. A Dutch mob lynched the peace-loving de Witts and chose as their leader a descendant of the family which had led them against the Spanish. William of Orange (later William III of England—see Chapter 25) was appointed *Stadholder* of the United Provinces, a position which made him virtually king. He at once set about a task which became his life's work—the defeat of Louis XIV's France. To deal with the immediate danger William ordered lowlying lands to be flooded. His troops then defended the high spots, as crops disappeared and cattle drowned. The mighty French army became bogged down in mud and water. It could burn villages and eat the food grown by starving peasants, but it could not win victories.

William realised that France was too powerful to be beaten by Holland alone. He decided to form alliances with other European powers against the French. This was not difficult because most of Louis's neighbours were worried by his behaviour. An alliance of Holland, Spain and the Holy Roman Empire soon turned a small war into a European conflict. After three years warfare Louis signed the Treaty of Nymegen (1679). By its terms he received Alsace, Artois and Franche-Comté (see map). The Sun King was very pleased. 'I rejoice in my clever conduct', he wrote, 'whereby I was able to extend the boundaries of my kingdom at the expense of my enemies.' Nymegen represented the high point of his career. For the next ten years France was the richest and most powerful state on earth.

'Bells for the Turk'

Seventeenth-century Europe had its own 'iron curtain'. The lands ruled by the Ottoman Turks stuck like a Muslim sword into the heart of Christian Europe, stretching over a thousand miles from the Adriatic to the Sea of Azov. Where the two civilisations met there was a no-man's-land of warfare, as Tartar (Turkish) and Christian raids devastated the countryside. Of all eastern European states, Austria and Poland were the most vulnerable because the two best routes into Central Europe were the Danube Valley and the Moldavian Plain (see map).

It was nearly twenty years since the last Turkish invasion had been stopped at St Gotthard, fifty miles from Vienna. It was two centuries since a Turkish army had possessed better weapons than its opponents. To Leopold, the Habsburg Emperor, Louis seemed more dangerous than the Sultan and he had joined in William's war against the French King. Consequently he was unprepared when Sultan Mehmet IV's grand vizier (chief minister) Kara Mustafa, began to plan 'Operation Red Apple', an attack on Vienna itself.

In fact there were plenty of signs of approaching danger. In 1681, for example, a peace treaty between Russia and Turkey left the Sultan free for other wars. Several Austrian ambassadors sent to Constantinople to negotiate a treaty mysteriously died. Turkish military

The Siege of Vienna, 1683

engineers began to repair the bridges across the rivers Maritsa and Morava so that troops could be moved into the Balkans. Then, in January 1683, horsetails were hung outside the Sultan's palace at Adrianople as a signal for an invasion of Austria. Over 140,000 men began to move west, driving flocks of sheep and herds of cattle before them for food.

Austrian peasants heard a sound many had forgotten, — the ringing of the Turkenglocken (Bells for the Turks) which summoned them to pray for deliverance. By mid-July Kara Mustafa was outside Vienna, demanding that it should surrender and accept the 'true faith' of Islam. Men, horses, camels and guns soon encircled the city. An elaborate camp was established for the Grand Vizier's use. Complicated trench systems appeared near the walls. The Siege of Vienna had begun.

'God conquered'

Fortunately the Emperor had as an ally the monarch most likely to treat the attack as a crusading matter. John Sobieski, King of Poland, was a warrior whose grandfather and brother had been killed by the Turks. From the day when he saw his grandfather's blood-stained sword and cloak, there had never been any doubt of his future ambition. At school he learnt special Latin poems calling on him to take up arms against the Turks. As a young soldier he defeated them so often that in 1674 the Poles elected him king. Without waiting for Leopold's call for help, Sobieski began to assemble his troops. Good sense mingled with his religious feelings. Obviously it was better to defend Poland at Vienna than in his own country. Like a true soldier of the Cross, however, the Polish King prayed for God's help at his country's most sacred shrine before marching to the rescue.

Speed was essential if the Habsburg capital was to be saved. The situation in Vienna grew worse daily as disease killed its citizens and Turkish mines exploded under its walls. Throughout August the defenders held on grimly, with bombs, stones and arrows showering down and Turkish flags waving nearer and nearer the main forts. Two factors saved them from disaster. First, the Turkish artillery was not strong enough to destroy the defences. Second, Kara Mustafa, believing the relief force was far away, took his time.

This was his greatest mistake. It was true that by early September the capital seemed about to fall. But Sobieski's army, swelled by German troops, had made good time and was near; at night their rockets flew upwards to give hope to the defenders. On 9 September Kara Mustafa's generals warned him that the enemy would be over a mountain called the Wienerwald within hours. They wanted the army turned round so that it could fight in the plains between Wienerwald and Vienna. The Grand Vizier refused, possibly because he was convinced Vienna would soon fall. For this reason the Turkish forces were badly positioned when the Polish–German army came down the hillside, 'like black pitch destroying all in its path'.

The battle fought on 12 September 1683 took place amongst wooded hills dotted with vineyards. From dawn, masses of infantry marched backwards and forwards, firing volleys of musketry, blasting away with cannons, and closing in desperate hand to hand fighting. By midday well over 100,000 men were engaged. It was also clear that the Poles were crushing the Vizier's finest foot-soldiers.

In late afternoon Sobieski, dressed in blue and white 'as though for a wedding', led the Polish hussars (cavalry) in a final charge. Line after line of his men, gorgeous in their shining helmets, armour, tiger skins and eagle feathers, tore into the exhausted Turks, sending them flying in all directions. Within half an hour they were inside the Grand Vizier's encampment, 15,000 Turks lay dead, and the battle was won. 'We came, we saw, and God conquered,' exclaimed the triumphant Polish King as he sat surrounded by jewels, treasure, rich furnishings and Ottoman battle flags. The Turks had suffered their worst ever defeat in Europe. Vienna was saved.

The Sultan knew whom to blame for the disaster. On 25 December, whilst Christians celebrated, his messengers reached Kara Mustafa's headquarters at Belgrade. They brought bad news. The Grand Vizier must give up all the symbols of his high office, including the Seal of State and the Holy Banner. He obeyed and asked, 'Am I to die?'.

'Yes, it must be so,' they replied.

'As God pleases,' he murmured and knelt down to pray. An executioner stepped forward, placed a silk cord around his neck and strangled him.

His Most Christian Majesty

The Battle of Vienna was a turning point in European history. After 1683 the Austrian emperors realised that expansion to the east against the Turk was possible. Within thirteen years they had re-conquered Hungary, leaving Dutch William and his allies to hold back the advance of Louis XIV's armies in the west.

The Sun King had taken little part in fighting the enemies of Christianity. 'His Most Christian Majesty', as French Kings were styled, had contented himself with sending a fleet to crush Muslim pirates who were attacking his ships in the Mediterranean. Yet at home he became more intensely Catholic with every day that passed. Urged on by his religious advisers, he began to persecute the several million Huguenots who had been left alone in the early years of his reign. 'Protestants', remarked one minister, were to 'have no rest or quiet so long as they live in a religion which displeases his Majesty'.

During 1681 some local authorities sent soldiers to Huguenot villages as 'missionaries . . . to instruct the lost sheep'. Soon thousands were said to be turning willingly to the Catholic faith. The truth was far different. The soldiers used rough methods to obtain 'conversions'; in some cases they dragged people to Mass by their hair! Even the rumour that they were coming sometimes proved enough because they usually wrecked the villages where they stayed. Such Dragon-nades, as they were called, managed to produce about 38,000 new Catholics but the way it was done caused even Louis to stop them in one region.

Dragonnades were only part of the story. For many years life had been difficult for Protestants as spiteful officials took advantage of

Plan of the Siege of Vienna

German army

Polish army

WIENERWALD

Wiedlingsba

Hermannskogel

Weidlingbach

SOBIESKI CAVALRY

Dreimal

Grünberg

Schafberg

Heuberg

Galitzinberg

John III, Sobieski, the Saviour of Vienna

oldsberg

Grinzing

Nussdorf

ering

R. Danube

MAIN
TURKISH
LINES

VIENNA

R. Wien

Km. 3
Miles 3

loopholes in the Edict of Nantes (see Chapter 17). When Louis became King there were between six and seven hundred Huguenot churches in France. By 1685 over four hundred of these had been pulled down. At the same time fewer jobs were available to Protestants. For example, they could not be policemen, civil servants, doctors or farmers. It came as no surprise therefore, when Louis revoked (cancelled) the Edict of Nantes altogether (1685).

Whilst Louis's priests praised this act, thousands of Huguenot craftsmen and merchants prepared to emigrate. Silkworkers, papermakers, clockmakers, jewellers, shipwrights and textile workers went abroad; 65,000 reached Holland and 10,000 came to London. In every case the country which gave them shelter benefited. Huguenot clockmakers founded the Swiss clock industry which is still prosperous today.

Louis seemed unaware of the unhappiness he had caused or the mistakes he had made. 'My realm is being purged of bad and troublesome subjects,' he remarked. His foreign enemies knew better. Their propagandists were able to blacken the reputation of the French King and stir up war against him. Today, when many of his more bloody acts are forgotten, Louis is still condemned as the monarch who revoked the Edict of Nantes.

More about Louis XIV's France
Books
H. Judge, *Louis XIV* (Longman: Problems and Perspectives in History)
R. Lewis, *Everyday Life in Ottoman Turkey* (Batsford)
J. Levron, *Daily Life at Versailles* (Allen & Unwin)
D. Ogg, *Louis XIV* (Oxford University Press)
J. Stöye, *The Siege of Vienna* (Collins)
G. Ziegler, *The Court of Versailles* (Allen & Unwin)

Visual aids
Versailles (BBC Publications)

Visits
Versailles, near Paris, France
Spitalfields Museum, London (contains work of Huguenot weavers)

To write and find out
1 Try and find out more about other European palaces modelled on Versailles.
2 Compare the Turkish defeat at Vienna with their success two centuries earlier at Constantinople (see Chapter 1). Give reasons why they won the first and lost the second battle.
3 John Sobieski was the grandfather of a man who played a famous part in British history. Find out who he was.
4 Kara Mustafa was executed because he failed. Can you think of another nation whose soldiers believe they should die if defeated in battle?

In the fifteenth and sixteenth centuries the most powerful states had been in the West, England, Spain, France and the Empire. During the seventeenth century an eastern European country began to make its presence felt—Russia.

The earliest Russian civilisation was around the Volga and Dneiper rivers (see map). In the thirteenth century however, its chief city, Kiev, was captured by the Mongol armies of Temujin, usually known as Genghiz Khan (meaning 'the power of God on earth'). Those lucky enough to escape fled north and settled beside the Moskva river. A new capital, Moscow, arose amongst the forests and rich farm land of this area, defended by a central fortress known as the Kremlin. Before long the Grand Dukes of Muscovy, as it was called, began to conquer the peoples around them.

Ivan the Great (1462–1505) started with a state about the size of modern Switzerland. During his reign he trebled this area. He also defied the Mongol Khan and married a niece of the last Emperor of Constantinople. Through this connection Ivan claimed that 'All Russia', as he now styled Muscovy, was the successor to the Byzantine Empire. Calling himself 'Tsar', meaning Caesar, he took as his badge the double-headed eagle of Rome and Constantinople. This remained the emblem of Tsarist Russia until 1917.

Ivan was encouraged by his wife to adopt the elaborate ceremonial of the Byzantine Court. He became Head of the Church and gave landowners their estates in return for military service. These Pomeshchiki often ruled conquered provinces where the peasants had little freedom. Thus Ivan's reign saw the Russian people take a step nearer to becoming serfs (slaves).

Ivan the Terrible

Muscovy was a landlocked country with few 'natural' borders—seas, rivers or mountains. Its best means of trade with the outside world was via the sea, either to the north or south. Its best form of defence was to conquer surrounding areas and so enclose itself within subject territory. In any case early Russian monarchs had little choice. Threatened on all sides, they could only conquer or be conquered.

In 1533 Ivan IV, called 'Grozny' which means 'the dread' but is usually known as 'the Terrible', became Tsar at the age of three. During his childhood ambitious boyars (nobles) battled for power, imprisoning Ivan's nurse and killing his brother. Thirsting for revenge, the young monarch took charge of the government as soon as possible. A parliamentary-type council of richer citizens was formed to give him support against his nobles. The chief boyar, Andrew Shuisky,

The expansion of Russia, 1500–1725

Ivan the Terrible

was arrested and torn to pieces by hunting dogs. After that, nobody doubted who was ruler of Russia.

Ivan realised that armies with western equipment were necessary to defeat his enemies. He therefore encouraged foreign experts to come to Russia. In particular, he wanted 'cunning engineers' and 'architects who could construct fortresses, towers and palaces'. This was why the English Muscovy Company was granted trading privileges (see Chapter 9). In fact Queen Elizabeth I was more interested in trade than in the modernisation of Russia because she could not afford to annoy Russia's western enemies, Sweden and Poland, and so ruin England's Baltic trade.

Knowing that Sweden and Poland were too strong for Russia, Ivan tried to avoid war with them. As a result his main conquests were in the south. In 1552 Russian troops drove the Mongols from Kazan after dreadful fighting. It was a great victory, indicating that the Russians had taken revenge on their old conquerors. In Moscow the triumphant Tsar erected the Cathedral of St Basil, with its onion-shaped domes, to celebrate. Four years later his troops captured Astrakhan on the Lower Volga River. This reopened the water routes for trade to the east, which had been used by the old Kiev civilisation.

The last years of Ivan's reign were grim. As he grew older he became suspicious of everyone. On one occasion he left Moscow and threatened to abdicate. His simple, superstitious people begged him to carry on as their ruler, and allowed him to make his own conditions. Ivan returned and began slaughtering all 'suspects'. A special secret police, the Oprichniki, was formed. They carried brooms 'to sweep away' traitors and wore a dog's head badge to show their loyalty to the Tsar. Thousands of boyars lost their lives and land during these investigations. Later, 60,000 people were killed at Novgorod because Ivan believed the citizens were negotiating with his enemies, the Poles. It was during these dark years that the Tsar killed his son in a fit of temper.

Modern Soviet doctors examined Ivan's corpse in 1964. They found quantities of mercury in the body so it is possible he was poisoned. Certainly the Tsar who first made the Russians 'look west' was a hated man before he died in 1584.

The Raskolniki

Only slowly did the West learn about this strange and savage land. It was the seventeenth century before European travellers published descriptions of Russia. Of Moscow a Captain John Perry wrote: 'Whenever any traveller comes within a fair view of the city, the numerous churches, the monasteries, and noblemen's and gentlemen's houses, the steeples, cupolas, and crosses at the top of the churches, which are gilded and painted over, make the city look to be one of the most rich and beautiful cities in the world.' Giles Fletcher recorded that the Muscovites' houses were 'of wood without any lime or stone'. Even the roads were formed by laying tree trunks side by side.

SIBERIA

Muscovy (Russia) in 1462

Volga — Kazan
Moscow
Oka
KAZAN

ASTRAKHAN

Don — R.Volga

Astrakhan

TARTARS

CASPIAN SEA

Land gained by Ivan III 1462-1505

Land gained 1505-1589 (Death of Ivan IV)

Peters' Land

Russian in 1667

Another English visitor penned his descriptions in verse:
The cold is rare, the people rude, the princes so full of pride
The realm so stored with monks and nuns, and priests on every side
is a typical example.

The country 'so stored with monks and nuns' was deeply religious and against all change. When the chief Russian priest, Patriarch Nikon, suggested reforms to bring Russia in line with the Greek Orthodox Church there was uproar. The idea that the sign of the Cross should be made with three instead of two fingers, and that 'Jesus' should be spelt Iisus rather than Isus appalled the faithful. But Nikon was a determined man. Those who refused to obey, called Raskolniki (Old Believers), suffered hanging and torture. Many lost their tongues and hands. One was imprisoned underground for twenty-two years before being executed. In some areas entire congregations burned themselves to death rather than obey the new rule. Usually they assembled in a wooden church, set fire to the building and sang hymns as they died. At least 20,000 cremated themselves in this way in six years.

In spite of these troubles Russia continued to expand in most directions. The Pacific coast of Asia was reached in 1643 and the borders of China by 1689. Altogether five million square miles of Siberia were colonised by Russia in the seventeenth century. At the same time ordinary Russians grew less free. After 1649 peasants could be sold or exchanged by their employers and set to work in mines and factories as well as on farms. A Russian 'Robin Hood' named Stenka Razin, led a revolt to make the peasants free in 1670. He failed and was cut up alive. Russian social classes became as frozen and immovable as the ice on the winter streets of Moscow.

'A man of hot temper'

Russia's greatest Tsar was Peter, who ruled with his brother from 1682 and alone after 1696. While first his father and then his elder brother Feodor reigned he was given expensive toys, allowed to use a golden coach and waited on by loyal dwarfs. But when Feodor died his half-sister Sophia seized power and persecuted Peter's mother's family. During these upheavals, the Streltsi (palace guard) actually murdered several of Peter's relatives in front of him. Although the ten-year-old boy said nothing as he watched, these terrible events influenced his entire life. From that moment Peter hated both the Streltsi and Moscow, the city where he had suffered such awful experiences. Not surprisingly, Sophia was imprisoned when he became Tsar.

Peter grew up to be a giant, standing nearly seven feet tall and with sufficient strength to bend silver bars. He did not like reading, preferring instead practical work like carpentry and boat-building. One of his first acts as Tsar was to travel abroad to learn Western ways. He pretended to be an ordinary citizen but every government knew who he was. In Holland, for example, the Burgomaster (mayor) of Amsterdam gave a magnificent banquet to 'an eminent person, living here incognito' (unknown).

St Basil's Cathedral, Moscow. It was built to celebrate the Russian conquest of Kazan

The young Peter the Great

The young Tsar worked in the shipyards of the Dutch East India Company. He then travelled to England. It was his first sea trip and he loved it, asking many questions and climbing up the mast in bad weather. In London he continued to study the art of shipbuilding at Deptford, where he was allowed to live at Sayes Court, the home of John Evelyn. Unfortunately, the energetic Russian spent his spare time in heavy drinking. Before he left, Peter and his drunken friends smashed fifty chairs, broke three hundred window panes, tore up twenty-five pictures and ruined Evelyn's beautiful garden. Repairs cost £350 — a large sum for those days.

The Bishop of Salisbury described Peter as 'a man of very hot temper, soon influenced and very brutal in his passion'. Just how brutal he could be was shown when the he heard that the Streltsi had rebelled during his absence. Although one of his generals had crushed the revolt Peter began a thorough investigation. Soon his torturers were busy thrashing and burning those Streltsi who refused to confess. His wife Eudoxia was sent to a convent because he suspected her of a part in the plot. Altogether 800 men were hanged, beheaded or had their limbs broken on the wheel before being left to die. The imprisoned Sophia became a suspect so Peter had three dead Streltsi hung outside her cell window.

That winter mangled corpses littered Moscow's squares and streets, some still tied to wheels, others headless in frozen pools of blood. The boy who once saw his relatives killed had taken a grim revenge.

'A window to the West'

Peter was always in a hurry and under his rule Russia experienced whirlwind reforms. All the old government departments were swept away and replaced by provincial authorities each ruled by a Senate. The Tsar's government itself was remodelled in the Swedish style. Ten 'Colleges', or departments, were set up for Foreign Affairs, Commerce, Industry, Justice, War, Admiralty, State Revenue, State Expenditure and Finance. Peter also ordered the use of a simplified alphabet, had foreign books translated into Russian and founded an Academy of Science. Some of these plans remained on paper, or proved inefficient and wasteful. In many cases, however, they became the basis of Russia's government for the next two hundred years.

Above everything, Peter wanted a large port in the North; he called it his 'Window to the West'. In 1703 he ordered a new city to be founded on the foggy marshes beside the river Neva. Work began with a timber fortress set on an island in the river. Conditions were appalling. The unfortunate peasants had few tools and no wheelbarrows; earth was carried 'in the skirts of their clothes, and in bags made of rags and old mats'. Many died and the trenches were frequently flooded. This did not worry Peter, who ordered the construction of a large town around the fortress. Even flowers were planted in rough ground unsuitable for cabbages and turnips.

As St Petersburg (now Leningrad) developed, nobles were told to come and build their own houses in brick and stone. Meanwhile an Italian architect, Domenico Trezzini, designed magnificent palaces which rivalled Versailles. Nothing was allowed to slow down or spoil the work. Writing in 1706 from his own house in St Petersburg, Peter described it as a 'paradise' when inches of water were swirling around his feet due to serious floods! Few Russians agreed with their Tsar. His half sister wrote: 'Petersburg will not endure after us: let it be a desert.' In fact, Peter's 'window' became one of the world's great cities.

The Great Northern War

Building a port was not enough. Peter knew he would have to fight for a place in the north against the power of Sweden. The result was a twenty-one-year war.

At first Russia's armies did badly. Charles XII, the Swedish King, was an odd soldier who made a habit of winning battles against 'impossible' odds. At Narva in 1700 Charles marched his men through thick mud, attacked in a snowstorm and completely destroyed Peter's army. He then contemptuously turned his back upon Russia and spent seven years campaigning in Poland and Germany. Peter spent this valuable breathing space desperately reorganising and modernising his army and creating a new navy.

In 1708 Charles invaded Russia with 44,000 men. Peter's troops fell back, burning the crops as they did so. The Swedish King viewed the vast, empty wastes before him and decided to go south instead

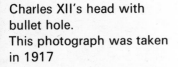

Charles XII's head with bullet hole.
This photograph was taken in 1917

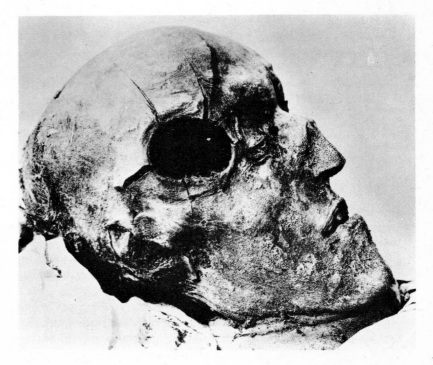

of striking at Moscow. His men endured one of the worst winters in Russian history, marched backwards and forwards by a crazy King who refused to let them rest in a comfortable base. By the spring only 18,000 men were fit enough to fight Peter. At Poltava the Swedish army was almost entirely destroyed (1709). Charles took temporary shelter in Turkish territory with about 1,000 men.

Peter knew this victory made it certain he would have his 'window' in the Baltic. On the evening of the battle he wrote: 'Now, with God's help, the last stone has been laid of the foundations of St Petersburg.' Long years of fighting still lay ahead. It was 1718 before his great rival Charles was mysteriously shot dead in front of a Norwegian fortress and 1721 before the two countries signed a peace treaty which gave Russia the northern provinces of Ingria, Karelia, Livonia and Estonia. But after the battle of Poltava few doubted Russia's power in the north.

The great Tsar was not popular. The Church hated his reforms; the peasants were crushed by heavy taxation. Many suffered at the hands of his spies and executioners, and the foreign ways of his nobles created an even greater gulf between themselves and the ordinary people. Yet Russia made more progress during Peter's reign than under any other Tsar. When he died in 1725 an Asiatic backwater had become a European power.

More about Russia
Books

P. Grey, *Ivan the Terrible* (Hodder & Stoughton)

J. Hasler, *The Making of Russia* (Longman)

R. M. Hatton, *Charles XII of Sweden* (Weidenfeld & Nicolson)

A. Johnson, *Peter the Great* (Hulton)

J. Laurence, *Russia* (Methuen: Outlines)

D. Sturley, *Short History of Russia* (Longman: The Study of History)

J. H. Sumner, *Peter the Great and the Emergence of Russia* (English Universities Press: Teach Yourself)

Visual aids

History of Russia to 1700 (Common Ground)

To write and find out

1 Charles XII failed in his attempt to conquer Russia. Since his time two more large scale invasions of Russia have taken place. Find out more about them.

2 Secret police activities have been a feature of Russian life for centuries. Find out about the police system in operation in Russia from 1917 until 1953.

3 Find out about Tsars Alexander I, Alexander II, Nicholas I and Nicholas II. Which two were murdered and why? Russia has also had several Tsarinas (empresses). Which one was known as 'the great'?

Anne, Protestant daughter of James II, was the last Stuart monarch. She had, wrote a friend, 'a person and appearance not at all ungraceful'. Her look was majestic but 'mixed with a sullen and constant frown'. If this was so it was not surprising. Throughout her life she was troubled by ill-health and all her seventeen children died either at birth or in their early years. When she did at last become Queen her reign was afflicted by war abroad and fierce political battles at home.

Anne was a timid, obstinate and not very intelligent woman who relied on strong-willed friends for advice. Fortunately for England, her closest companion was Sarah, Duchess of Marlborough. When alone together they forgot they were monarch and subject. Anne insisted upon being called 'Mrs Morley' and Sarah was 'Mrs Freeman'. It was natural therefore that Anne should appoint 'Mr Freeman' as Ambassador to Holland, and Captain-General of all her armed forces. It was a decision which altered European history.

Marlborough revolutionised the slow-moving warfare practised by Louis and William, replacing elaborate sieges and defensive marches with swift movement and crushing victory. Under his direction war became 'fluid' once more; while his opponents marched he preferred to fight. This was not because he was rash. The Duke prepared his campaigns most carefully, training and equipping his men well, planning every detail, even positioning each gun before a battle. But once in action he attacked boldly, taking advantage of any enemy mistake with charging cavalry and massed gunfire. At one time or another Marlborough broke most of the rules of eighteenth century warfare. Yet he died without ever losing a battle or failing to capture a town.

The march to the Rhine
Initially Marlborough's Dutch allies forced him to play the old game around the barrier fortresses. In 1704, however, Bavaria's alliance with France caused military operations to shift nearer the Habsburg lands (see map), as Louis decided on a combined Bavarian—French thrust at Vienna. In this way he hoped to knock the Empire out of the war and so cause the collapse of the Grand Alliance (England, Holland, the Empire and some German states).

Against William the plan might have succeeded, for the Dutch and English would probably have stayed in Flanders, leaving the Austrians to fight alone. But whereas the Dutch King would have looked on Louis's scheme as a problem, Marlborough saw it as an opportunity. Soon after the French had marched out of Strasbourg on their way east, he unexpectedly set off across Europe to join the

Queen Anne—last Stuart monarch and first queen of a United Kingdom of Great Britain

imperial (Austrian) army commanded by his friend, Prince Eugene (May 1704).

Bypassing several fortresses, Marlborough's men were soon storming the Schellenberg Hill, near Donauworth on the Rhine (June 1704). The surprised Bavarians fell back defensively and awaited the arrival of the French. Marshal Tallard, the French commander, eventually joined them at Augsburg after a leisurely march. He was not over-worried by Marlborough's move, for he still hoped to defeat the English and Austrians before they could unite.

By early August it seemed he might succeed. Eugene wrote anxiously to Marlborough: 'The enemy have marched. It is almost certain that the whole army is across the Danube. . . . The plain of Dilligen is crowded with troops. . . . I have held on all day here: but with 18 battalions I dare not risk staying the night.' He begged Marlborough to come quickly. The Duke's reaction was to perform a series of clever marches which brought him to Eugene's aid in six days.

Tallard now placed the Franco-Bavarian army in the angle formed by the river Danube and its tributary, the Nebel, near the village of Blenheim. It was a strong position. To the right he was protected by the Danube; to the left by the villages of Oberglau and Lutzingen. In front lay marshes. Between the French around Blenheim and the

The Duke of Marlborough

Route taken by Marlborough on his march to Blenheim

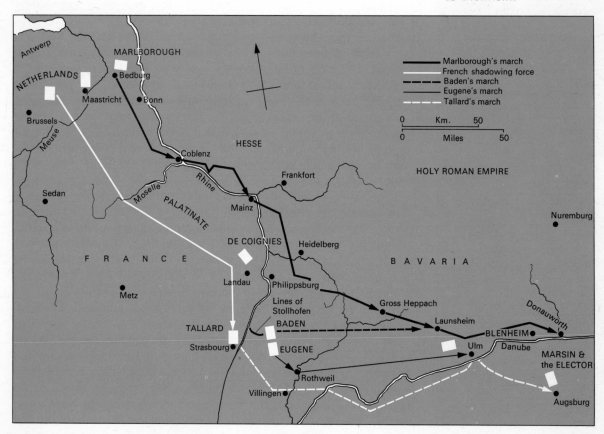

Bavarians on their left he placed only a thin thread of cavalry because any thrust across the marshes could be crushed in a nut-cracker way by attacks from the two villages.

It seemed a possible trap. But Marlborough must have known that if he successfully assaulted both Oberglau and Blenheim at once, the way would be open through the middle of the enemy army.

'A glorious victory'

Tallard did not expect Marlborough to attack the well entrenched French and Bavarians. To his surprise the Englishman decided to give battle. By early morning of 13 August 1704 the allied army in nine columns and the Franco-Bavarians in their battle positions were close enough to exchange trumpet calls and drum beats. Even so Marlborough delayed his assault for some hours. Only when Eugene was in position before Oberglau did he begin the battle.

At midday General Cutts led the English against Blenheim but his men were driven back after a fierce fight. The French commander in the village then made a blunder which probably cost his side the battle. Worried by the strength of these attacks, he brought large numbers of extra French troops into Blenheim. Soon the burning village was packed with soldiers. 'The men were so crowded in upon another that they couldn't even fire. . . . Not a single shot of the enemy

Blenheim

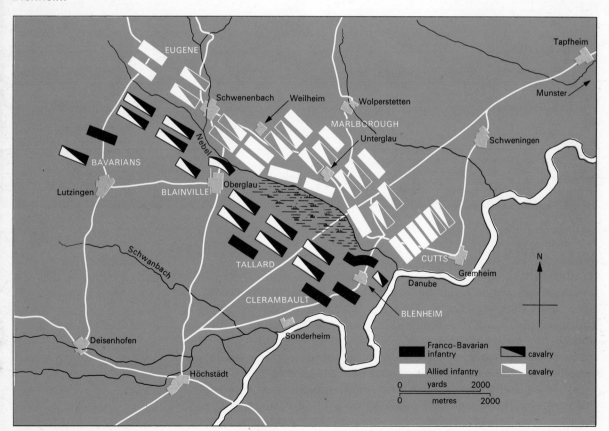

Marlborough at Blenheim, from a tapestry

missed its mark', recalled a French survivor.

Meanwhile, Eugene launched desperate assaults upon Oberglau which was stoutly defended by Irish 'Wild Geese' fighting for France. Soon both village garrisons were too heavily engaged to launch attacks of their own. The time had come for Marlborough to drive through the centre. Tallard saw what was happening but with so many of his men trapped in Blenheim he could only spare a few recruits to reinforce his threatened cavalry in the centre.

By early evening close range artillery and musket fire had wiped out the infantry in the French centre leaving only a few horse regiments. As line after line of Marlborough's cavalry charged home sheer

weight of numbers lifted up some horses and their riders, carrying them backwards in the crush. Thousands were killed. Of those who escaped some were drowned trying to swim the Danube. The Franco-Bavarian army was cut in two, and large numbers in Blenheim forced to surrender.

It had been a shattering defeat. About 34,000 men were killed, wounded or captured. Tallard himself was taken prisoner, Vienna was saved and Bavaria virtually knocked out of the war. That night Marlborough scribbled a message to Sarah on the back of an hotel receipt: 'I have not time to say more, but beg you will give my duty to the Queen, and let her know that her army has had a glorious victory.'

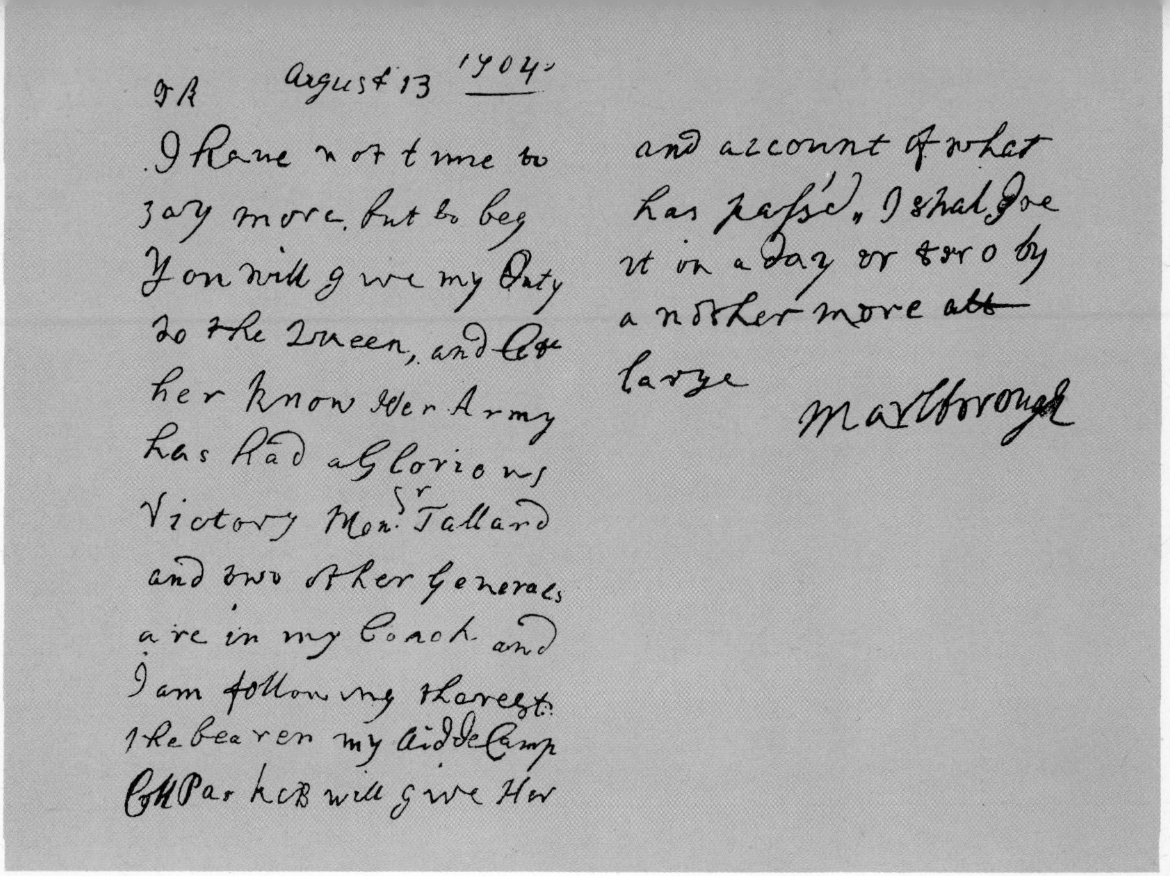

JR August 13 1704

I have not time to say more, but to beg you will give my Duty to the Queen, and let her know Her Army has had a Glorious Victory. Mons.r Tallard and two other Generals are in my Coach. and I am following therest. the bearer my Aid de Camp Coll Parke will give Her and account of what has pass'd, I shall give it in a day or two by a nother more att large

Marlborough

Marlborough's note to Sarah telling of his victory at Blenheim

In England there was great rejoicing. Bells were rung, bonfires lit and copies of the Duke's note printed. A grateful Parliament decided to build Marlborough a vast house at Woodstock, near Oxford. Today Blenheim Palace still stands in the quiet Oxfordshire countryside, a memorial to a fierce battle won far away and long ago.

Scotland and England

The war with France was unpopular in Scotland. In the same year as Blenheim, the Scot's parliament passed an Act of Security stating that they would not join in the war, nor accept the Hanoverian monarchs after Anne's death, unless their parliament, laws, religion and trade were left free of English interference. They followed this with preparations to conscript the entire male population 'if necessary'.

The causes of this hostility went back some years. Since 1603 England and Scotland had shared little except the same monarch. The Covenanters' Presbyterian religion had been persecuted; even the Bible had never been translated into Gaelic, the original Scots language. Cromwell had conquered Scotland by armed force and after the Restoration Charles II's government granted an independence which existed on paper only.

Another grievance was the English refusal to let Scotland benefit from their own growing empire. Where trade was concerned Scots merchants were treated as foreigners and forced to pay duties on goods entering England. It was not surprising that patriotic Scotsmen resented a situation which left their country, 'totally neglected, like a farm managed by servants and not under the eye of the master'.

Even worse was the English determination to stop the Scots developing their own empire. In 1695 a Scottish company was founded to trade with Asia, Africa and America. A colony was planted on the Isthmus of Darien, 150 miles from the site of the modern Panama Canal. When it failed because of Spanish attacks the Scots blamed the English parliament for withdrawing its promised loans of money.

Act of Union 1707

On the face of it there seemed little hope of a union between England and Scotland during Anne's reign. Most Scots hated the idea of joining England. As the Act of Security showed, they even talked of defying the Acts of Settlement and crowning a different monarch after Anne's death. English merchants, for their part, still refused to give Scotland commercial privileges, whilst English people generally despised the Scots as barbaric foreigners. Indeed, only Scotland's Protestantism stopped many Englishmen from giving the Scots the same treatment as the Catholic Irish.

But there was another side to the coin. In their saner moments Scots leaders knew that a war with England would bring military conquest or economic ruin. The English also had reason to seek Scottish friendship. Queen Anne's ministers were engaged in a life and death struggle with France. A peaceful, friendly Scotland seemed essential to prevent it becoming a 'backdoor' for the French as it had been in the sixteenth century. For these reasons representatives of both countries met during 1706 and after three month's debate produced a workable plan for political and economic union.

Even though they knew it was unavoidable the Scots resisted to the last. To obtain a favourable vote, large bribes were offered to Scots M.P.s. Even so, the voting was close—116 for and 83 against. By the terms of the Act of Union Scotland kept its Presbyterian system and own laws, including the Highland chieftains' courts. But the Scots parliament was abolished. In its place 45 Scots M.P.s out of a total of 512, took their seats in the English parliament and 16 Scots peers were forced upon an unwilling House of Lords. English money and English weights and measures were adopted in Scotland and free trade was allowed across the border.

On 1 May 1707 the United Kingdom of Great Britain was proclaimed and Queen Anne drove in procession to St Paul's Cathedral to give thanks to God. Few people at the time saw much reason for rejoicing. Scots trade reacted very slowly. In some cases it was ruined by English competition. Later generations have often taken a different view. Scottish education was one of the best in Europe in 1707. As a result an almost unnoticed flow of educated men and women took the road south, giving their talents and skill for the benefit of Britain. Britain's empire-builders also gained from the thousands of Scots who first helped to conquer and then people the new colonies.

Defeat of the Sun King

Blenheim was only the first of a number of defeats inflicted on the French by Marlborough. In 1706 he destroyed a second French army at Ramillies in the Netherlands, going on to capture Brussels (now capital of Belgium). Louis then offered peace but when the victorious allies demanded that his grandson Philip give up the Spanish throne he decided to fight on. Two years later Marlborough marched his men fifty miles in two days, encircled the French at Oudenarde and again defeated them, killing 15,000 men.

The old Sun King now proposed to give up Philip's claim to the Spanish throne. The Whig government in England foolishly demanded that he drive his own grandson out. Declaring, 'If I have to fight I will fight my enemies not my children', Louis called upon his people to defend their homeland against Marlborough. At Malplaquet in 1709 the great Duke won his last and most expensive battle against desperate resistance.

The Allies were nowhere else as successful. In 1702 an English–Dutch fleet failed to capture Cadiz. Two years later an allied squadron was returning from another unsuccessful expedition when its commander, Admiral Rooke, decided to attack the Spanish base at Gibraltar. Its garrison, which was not expecting trouble, surrendered after a heavy bombardment. The only allied losses occurred when a group of English sailors ran into a gunpowder magazine with lighted matches, and blew themselves up! The value of gaining Gibraltar and thus controlling the entrance to the Mediterranean was not realised by Englishmen at the time and it was twenty-five years before a dockyard was built to maintain fighting ships.

Gibraltar was the first part of Spain conquered for 'Charles III', the Habsburg candidate for the Spanish throne favoured by the Allies. Next year the Earl of Peterborough landed with an English army and tried to take Barcelona. There seemed little hope of success until Peterborough switched his attack to the citadel of Montjuich, high on a hill above the city. At first his men were repulsed. At this the Earl, we are told, fell 'into the horriblest passion that ever man was

Reward for the victor—
Blenheim Palace,
Oxfordshire

Unexpected conquest—
Gibraltar drawn in 1725

seen in'. Rallying a few soldiers he led them personally into one of the bastions and the fort was captured. Barcelona surrendered soon afterwards.

In later campaigns Peterborough overran the Spanish provinces of Catalonia and Valencia. For a short time 'Charles III' was installed as King at Madrid. But Peterborough's strange behaviour—he once gave two opposite orders about the same matter to his chief general and admiral respectively—led to his dismissal. Finally in 1707 an allied force was severely beaten at Almanza and Philip, Louis's grandson, became effective King of Spain.

Peace of Utrecht

By 1711 both sides were tired of war. The Dutch had never been keen on capturing the barrier fortresses for Charles. When he became Emperor on the sudden death of his elder brother (1711) they were even less enthusiastic. Now if they won the war a Habsburg would rule as much territory as Charles V had in the sixteenth century, that is, the Empire, Italy, Spain, the Netherlands and the Americas. Britain shared their misgivings. A new Tory Parliament, elected in October 1710, represented the landowners who were tired of paying taxes for a 'Whig' war. They stopped Marlborough's advance on Paris, deprived him of his command and unjustly accused him of dishonesty. It was 1714 before the great soldier could return safely to his own country.

Louis realised that his best chance of getting out of a disastrous war was to come to terms with Britain. The Peace Treaty of Utrecht (1713) was negotiated privately between Versailles and London. Its terms gave Britain most French North American colonies, including Nova Scotia, Newfoundland and the Hudson Bay Territory of Canada. It also allowed England's merchants the 'Asiento', a

thirty-three year monopoly to supply Negro slaves to Spanish America. Gibraltar remained under British control, giving her navy a commanding position in the Mediterranean. Philip became King of Spain on condition that France and Spain were never ruled by the same person. Austria made peace some months later and received Milan, Naples and Sardinia. Holland obtained the barrier fortresses and a fair commercial treaty with France.

The peace-makers of Utrecht said they wished to 'establish the peace and tranquility of Christendom by a just balance of power'. What really happened was far less noble. Ministers and monarchs played with the map of Europe like a jigsaw puzzle, grabbing a piece of land here, seizing an economic or military and political advantage where they could. Their 'balance of power' held within it the seeds of future wars.

Trade and colonies

What sort of England had helped defeat Louis XIV's France? In 1688 Gregory King, one of the first statisticians, published a survey of England and its population. Whether this one-man census is exact or not, it provides a rough guide to late seventeenth-century England.

According to King, England was inhabited by nearly 5,500,000 people, of whom three-quarters were labourers or paupers. Well over a million were farmers and their families living on £50–£100 a year. In addition there were 40,000 shopkeepers and tradesmen, 85,000 soldiers and sailors, 20,000 clergymen and lawyers, 2,000 rich merchants, 12,000 gentlemen and 160 lords. Top families could receive over £3,000 each year; but about 1,500,000 were living on less than £15 per year.

Social distinctions were not as rigid as on the continent. A man could begin as a tradesman and end as a lord. None of the old aristocracy which had dominated England at the time of Bosworth (1485) now existed. A Tudor executioner had wiped out the last medieval duke, Norfolk, in 1572. Stuart kings had sold titles to their favourites. As a result most dukes in 1700 were descendants of successful sixteenth- or seventeenth-century politicians, merchants or adventurers. As Daniel Defoe wrote:

But England, modern to the last degree,
Borrows or makes her own nobility.

England was still relatively empty with only a quarter of the population of France. Spread thinly throughout the land, something over half the number in present day London lived isolated lives. Poor roads, wild moorland, hills, marshes and fens restricted contact between one area and another. Counties were still called 'countries'. Each had its own dialect, habits and customs.

Farming remained England's chief occupation. To the east this was usually cornland; to the west pastureland for sheep and cattle. The enclosures of Tudor times had covered much of southern England with a 'string vest' of hedges. Elsewhere, particularly in the Midlands, the land was still farmed in open fields. Textile manufacture remained England's major industry and in 1700 one-third of the country's export trade was in cloth.

The real difference between the England of Henry VII and that of Queen Anne was in the extent of its trade and the fact that it possessed colonies. In 1485 England had been an insignificant island. By 1714 its position had changed dramatically. English ships roamed the seas, bringing timber from America, sugar and tea from the West Indies, furs from Canada, carpets, fine porcelain, cloves and other spices from the Far East. English traders could send their goods about the British Isles, free of the customs duties which made continental commodities expensive.

London was the capital of a new Great Britain and centre of its growing colonial empire. Its food demands alone caused vast changes in England's farming. Cattle from Scotland, cheese from the western counties, corn from Sussex or Hampshire travelled by sea, river or road to its merchants. Eggs and poultry from Bedfordshire and North-amptonshire, sheep from Gloucester, fruit, hops and vegetables from Kent, Essex and Suffolk, came to feed its rapidly growing population. Large, proud and semi-independent, it was a worthy capital for the new Imperial Britain as the Early Modern Age drew to its close.

More about Queen Anne's reign
Books
A. P. G. Macdonald and I. L. Macdougall, *British Battles*, vol 2
  (Macmillan)
Marlborough (Cape: Jackdaw)
G. M. Trevelyan, *England under Queen Anne* (Longman) 3 vols

Visual aids
Duke of Marlborough *(film)* (BBC TV)
Anne (Rank)
Seventeenth-century Occupations (Hulton)

Visit
Blenheim Palace, Oxfordshire

To write and find out
1 What famous modern political leader was related to the first Duke of Marlborough?
2 Find out more about Marlborough's three victories at Ramillies, Oudenarde and Malplaquet.
3 In what way has Britain's possession of Gibraltar caused trouble in recent years?
4 What other British general campaigned against the French in Spain nearly a hundred years after Lord Peterborough? How successful was he?
5 From details of the 1971 Census compare Gregory King's England with present-day Britain. What new trades and professions have come into existence since King's time?

Index